MANIA

MANIA

Tartan, turmoil and my life as a BAY CITY ROLLER

Stuart 'Woody' Wood
with Peter Stoneman

First published in the UK in 2025 by Blink Publishing
An imprint of Bonnier Books UK
5th Floor, HYLO, 105 Bunhill Row,
London, EC1Y 8LZ

A CIP catalogue record for this book is available from the British Library.

Hardback ISBN: 978-1-7851-2198-2
Trade paperback ISBN: 978-1-7851-2202-6
eBook ISBN: 978-1-7851-2199-9
Audio ISBN: 978-1-7851-2200-2

1 3 5 7 9 10 8 6 4 2

Design and Typeset by Envy Design Ltd
Printed and bound in Great Britain by Clays Ltd, Elcograf S.p.A.

The authorised representative in the EEA is
Bonnier Books UK (Ireland) Limited.
Registered office address: Floor 3, Block 3, Miesian Plaza,
Dublin 2, D02 Y754, Ireland
compliance@bonnierbooks.ie

www.bonnierbooks.co.uk

I would like to dedicate this book to my wife Denise and Elvis (my wee dug), also to all the Bay City Rollers past, present and future and not forgetting the fans

CONTENTS

AUTHOR'S NOTE

I met Tam when I was sixteen years old. He was intimidating and a bully, and all the disgusting things said about him are accurate. He was a predator. He abused me as he did others. It was a horrific and harrowing time. The drugs he plied us with were part of that control. The abuse eventually stopped; we never discussed it . . . any of us . . . it just happened. Because of recent and past pressure from media at certain points and social media 'experts', I felt like I was being forced to speak about it and to go into great detail, but that is not something that I will be doing.

I moved on a long time ago and don't want that beast to be any part of things concerning my life. I don't need therapy; I have coped in my own way and have no need to spill my emotions or go into any more detail. Unfortunately, abuse is something that many of us have had to deal with, and we all do so differently. I've been lucky to have people around me who care and understand and who I can talk to, as well as my own inner strength that has got me through this, as well as many other things in my life.

The band have always been dragged into Tam's vile ways. It seems that this is the only part of our story that a lot of people, especially the media, want to focus on. I find that an unfortunate flaw in human nature: 'Tell us the dirt, share everything. We want details . . .' I don't need to share. I am focusing on the future and he shall remain in the past. This book is my attempt to tell my story and to describe what it was like to be a part of the Bay City Rollers back in the '70s up to the present day.

FOREWORD

I first met the Rollers in the early '70s at *Top of the Pops*, I walked up to Woody and said, 'You lot have nicked my stage look!' (which at the time was as much tartan as was possibly human to wear, including underpants!).

Woody said 'Yeah, we know, Rod, sorry about that,' he then added, 'but we're Scottish, Rod!' At that point I admitted defeat and Woody and I have remained great friends ever since.

I've always loved the Rollers! They were honest blokes making hordes of teenagers happy with their music and I appreciated what a gift that was in itself. Unfortunately, the boys didn't receive their just rewards for all their hard work and effort due to unscrupulous music business types.

In my mind, the Rollers have earned their place in pop music history, and I don't think you'll ever see their likes again.

Woody is still flying the flag for the Rollers and, with a few new band mates, they're still lighting up people's lives with great, timeless songs and boundless energy. Go and see for yourself when they play a gig near you. In the meantime, enjoy Woody's book!

Sir Rod Stewart CBE

April 2025

Prologue

ON THE BORDER

Autumn, 1974

I'm seventeen now, and completely wet behind the ears. Somehow, though, almost by accident, I'm also a pop star! I've been a bona fide Roller a few months now, earning £10 a week for my trouble, and this is a standard club night for me.

Every night, I pinch myself, turn up someplace new, plug in and play, then run for cover. I'm barely home anymore, never seeing my mum and dad, because I'm on the job every day between now and Christmas. I'm not privy to the itinerary. That's kept locked tight in Tam's briefcase, rolling around with all the yellow bottles of pills and potions he has in there, uppers, downers and speed, rattling around like a set of maracas. All I know is, if the day has a Y in it, chances are we're playing a show somewhere, or there's a photoshoot, or a press call, or a

TV appearance. Sometimes – usually – it's all the above, all on the same day.

Only now we've taken the bandwagon across the water, to Northern Ireland of all places. We're doing midnight flits across the border between north and south, and this club is completely stowed. A few hundred Irish girls getting hot under their collars, a gaggle of mums and dads lining the bar at the back wall, watching the clock for last orders, knocking back the Guinness and Campari and soda, so everybody's happy, or they're on the road to getting there.

Me and the guys, we're feeling fine too. We're on good form, after a last-minute cancellation led to our first night off in a wee while. This was after we pulled up for last night's show to find the road outside was an actual bombsite. There was choking black smoke everywhere and the streets were barricaded off. Everywhere you looked, it was grubby-faced kids in V-neck jumpers and snorkel parkas stopped on the pavement gawping, mums with their hair in nets, arms folded, shaking their heads at the state of the world.

Outside the venue, a couple of paratroopers sidled up to our car, rifles at 45 degrees, and told the driver to roll the window down. Firebomb, they told us. We all craned to see down the street, and the two buildings burning to the ground in the middle distance. Yeah, right. A couple of British-owned businesses, now charcoal-crackling infernos, like on the TV news every night.

'You're not playing tonight lads,' a sergeant told us, thin moustache and thick Cockney accent. After a few minutes back and forth, we got an armoured car escort back to the B&B,

inconspicuous as you like. I took it in my stride. I dumped off my bags, bought a load of sweeties and juice – maybe a Marathon bar and a tin of Fanta – a couple of comics and I was right as rain watching the telly a while, flicking between the three channels. A couple of the guys broke out a pack of cards, while Les drew a bath, forgot the water was running, and left it to overflow. The landlady wasn't too happy with us when the water and Matey suds started pouring down into her neat, chintz sitting room below. She was there tutting and shaking her head at the foot of the stair, and Les was on the landing in his bathrobe acting the innocent.

I wandered out to see the commotion, shrugged, went back to the room and my comic books: Spider-Man caught up in a life-or-death tangle with Dr Octopus or some other three-colour nonsense. Wet soapy walls and fire bombings to one side, it was a good day, all told. Better than today, at least.

Under the hot nightclub lights tonight, I'm wearing my standard stage outfit: a white jersey with a red and blue collar, a three-quarter-length pair of Skinners trousers, half a yard up from my ankles, with red, white and blue socks and a pair of Dr Martens (for stomping). The press haven't reported on the phenomenon yet because it's all happening in the provinces, but I'm here to tell you it's going off all around us. God-honest hysteria wherever you care to look. From the stage, it's a joyous scene. Twenty rows back, until you can't see any further, it's a sea of shiny, smiling faces, and for a minute there, the cancelled show, the military escort and all that, is forgotten in the sheer delight of the moment. I won't try to be blasé here – tell you it's run of the mill, dull as dishwater – because that would be a fat lie. The truth is: nothing comes close to this feeling. I think for a minute I'm never coming down from this high, that you could inject this into my veins every day from now until the end of time and I'll be quite satisfied.

Then I change my mind, come freefalling back to Earth. I'm looking down into the audience and there's this guy, sticking out like a sore thumb. He's giving me the real stink eye, amid all the chaos, all the girls in their lippy and freckles, tears and snot streaking their mascara. He's standing stock-still, the eye of the storm, staring right at me, giving me absolute daggers. Ever the optimist, I flash him a wonky smile, but he doesn't smile back. Not even a flicker. He's glowering, eyes locked on me. Then, what's this? He's holding an imaginary gun to his head – finger guns, like you do in the playground – then taking aim at me, slow and deliberate. Bang! Then again. Bang! Only then does he smile, but there's no joy there. It's just this grim, mirthless grin and I don't know how to respond to this at all. Tam, our manager's always telling us to smile, wave and fuckin' smile, but I can feel that smile sliding off my face about now as I wonder *What's this guy's problem?*

I glance upstage, across the creaking boards, more used to bearing the weight of one of Norn Iron's showbands, panic starting to rise. Back on the mainland, the shows are so out of hand, Tam's hiring big lads from the local rugby clubs to act as security. Whole teams of hard men with cauliflower ears and busted conks, but out here, it seems like our safety is being left in the hands of Lady Luck. We've no one here to save our skins and no one else seems to have noticed this guy. Les is prancing about, getting the girls riled up, not that they need much riling at this point. Eric is jockeying for the limelight, edging toward the heart of the mayhem, making Les bristle that someone's got the nerve to try to share his kill. The other guys are just getting on with it, holding the line, getting us from here to the encore. Tam is at the side of the stage shouting, telling me to bloody well smile and wave at the crowd, like he tells me every night and I've got this guy down front looking at me like he's got my name on a kill list. For the whole show, a solid hour, he's rooted to the spot, staring me down, and I've no idea how I've wound up in his crosshairs. Then it dawns on me. It's the colours. The red, white and blue, I realise. I'm wearing fuckin' unionist socks. We're practically on the border between Northern Ireland and the Republic, the heart of what the newspapers are calling 'The Troubles', and fashion details like that are liable to get you in a jam, I guess.

We get in the car after the show and I'm still shaking. The guys are laughing, telling me it's nothing. 'Don't worry about it, Woods.' But I'm scanning the crowd of people spilling out into the night, looking out for the guy with the imaginary pistol, or anyone in a balaclava, frankly. Around me, the Rollers assemble and they're gassing among themselves and burning off the last traces of adrenaline from the show. None of them is in the least bit anxious, all caught up in a wee post-gig world of their own. Not me, though. I'm on high alert. Holding my breath, waiting for the car to start moving. Then, finally, the car peels away from the kerb, the promoter driving, and he's doing a fair Jackie

Stewart, up through the gears, taking us out of the town fast and into the countryside.

'Great show tonight, lads,' he's saying over his shoulder, but I'm not listening. I'm up in my seat, staring out the back window, clearing the condensation from the glass with my sleeve, trying to make out the headlights of whoever is behind us. Around us, the town melts into countryside, then dark, deep woodland and there's a car, 50 yards back, edging closer. I feel my throat dry up. My palms are hot and wet.

'There's a car following us,' I say, finally.

'Ach, they're just wantin' the money,' the promoter says, like there's a distinction between a terrorist in a balaclava wanting to kill you (bad news) and a common-or-garden bandit looking to have it away with the night's takings (just a wee bump in the road). He takes a leisurely pull on a Rothmans, like it's fine. Just the cost of doing business here in bandit country.

'I'm gonna put my foot down,' he says and we're tearing through the darkness, and I'm still looking out the back, as the following car keeps pace with us. After a couple of miles doing 60, 70, 80mph, finally, the other car slows up and I can feel my heart start up again, like it's been in my mouth the whole time like a giant gobstopper. Up ahead, at the side of the road, there are these red lanterns, an army checkpoint, and a British soldier steps into the road and flags us down. We're pulling up, and out back, I see the pursuing car's lights go out, a Ford Escort or Cortina performing an angry three-point turn in the darkness and heading back the way they came. Our car gets searched and we're given the once-over by a couple of squaddies, more

Cockneys acting like them being here is the most natural thing in the world, patting down a bunch of sweaty longhaired guys after a high-speed chase along this dark B-road in the dead of night.

'Okay, on your way lads. Stay safe.'

The promoter turns on the car radio, nonchalantly sparks up another ciggie and starts making chitchat again, and I'm shaking, laughing, but it's one of those nervous, this-isn't-funny kind of laughs, staring down at my red, white and blue socks as we make our way back to the B&B. Back to normal now. Derek wondering about getting some chips for our tea, everyone chiming in, the promoter telling us where there's a good local chippy, mentioning he's got to go back to the venue to sort a couple of things, that he'll be along to pick us up after breakfast. And breathe.

Next morning, we're breakfasted, packed, ready and waiting at the kerbside for the promoter to come back and take us on to the next town. Or maybe it's the previous town, the cancelled show. I don't know. I just turn up, tune up and get on stage, smile and wave, wherever I'm told. As the car pulls up, I'm half-asleep, opening the door, about to get in. Then I stop in my tracks. Behind me, Eric tells me to get in, practically puts his boot in my arse. But I'm standing there, door open, staring into the back of the car. There's red smeared all up the inside of the door and across the back seat, evidence of a hasty clean-up job. I look up, and the promoter catches my eye in the rear-view.

'Ah, don't worry. I found a guy at the side of the road after I dropped you lads off at your B&B.'

'Really?' we're all wondering. 'So, it's not ketchup?'

'Ach, no. Just some fella got himself kneecapped,' he says, still cheery as you like. 'Terrible business. Found the guy bleeding at the side of the road last night and dropped him at the hospital.'

I feel my jaw hanging open, feel myself about to double-take. He taps the face of his watch, telling us 'Come on, time is money.' The guys cram into the car, jockeying elbows for more space on the back seat, talking about what's for dinner and the next show. I'm not thinking about dinner or the next show, though. I'm looking at the red smear on the car door, thinking, *Maybe £10 a week isn't enough. Maybe I need danger money*. Also, it crosses my mind that I won't wear the red, white and blue socks tonight.

Chapter 1

IN THE STAIR

Edinburgh, 1957–71

We live in the stair, a few yards down a line of looming Edinburgh stone buildings on Marchmont Street – several tenements, laid out in a neat triangle configuration, with an arcing crescent. A five-minute walk, should you choose, takes you around the backside of the houses and to the shared gardens there. The backyards are an oasis. The morning wash flutters on washing lines across everyone's own wee garden, scruffy strips of lawn and concrete, clumsily divided by rows of fences or sometimes – where the iron fenceposts were taken away and melted down to support the war effort – by no boundary at all.

You can find me there, up three flights of stone stairs to the top floor, and across the threshold to our family nest. We share the stair with our neighbours below us and across the landing, families divvied out across the three storeys, two families at a time on each floor at the top of each flight. Whenever we pass, either up or down, our footsteps resound against the stone walls. My dad tells us the walk up and down helps to keep us all neat and trim, like butcher's dogs. I don't mind either way. It's worth the walk up, just to peer out the window sometimes. Beyond the foreground, the grey stone edge of the windowsills, there's so much sky, so much green to see that it will take your breath away if you think about it. There are views across Marchmont to the nearby links, the 36-hole pitch-and-putt golf course and down towards the Meadows and, if you narrow your eyes, out to Edinburgh Castle in the far-off distance.

It's a nice house to grow up in, although it's the only one I know, so I may be biased, but it seems to me we have a fine life here. We're not poor, by any stretch. Right in the middle of the middle class, I suppose. Three bedrooms, a living room, kitchen and bath. We even have a sitting room for entertaining guests, a room I'm never allowed in, except at Christmas maybe, or special occasions.

I don't know why you would, but if you ever tire of the view and the damp Scottish air up there, the walk down to the streets is worth it too, unless it's a school day and you're dragging your heels. If the weather's fine, sometimes I'll take a pal and a pair of clubs, and we'll stroll either up towards Bruntsfield and the putting green or down to the meadows 36-hole pitch and putt course. Perhaps I'll take the 7-iron and putter my father cut down to half-pint size for me and we can lose a couple of hours there easy. One of my best pals, a wee lad called Horace who lives around our way, he'll knock on my door, or I'll knock on his to go out to play. This is my life for a couple of years. It's a brilliant time, then one day I knock but his mum tells me Horace is poorly and can't come out today. Then the next day too. A couple of days later, I'm playing outside with my other pals. Someone's put up a wee tent and we can hear the Beatles song 'All You Need is Love' coming out of Horace's bedroom window across the street. The next day, we hear Horace has passed away from a kidney problem. He was here, but now he never will be again. When I hear that song now, it always reminds me of him.

Saturday morning, there being no school, is the only day we get out the bed with a spring in our steps, whatever the weather. There's no need to pretend I'm poorly and try to con my mum into giving me the day off. After breakfast, maybe we'll have a kickabout on the green. I play outside left, but maybe best left outside, as I like to kid. That or I'll head out somewhere looking for adventure. A half-hour walk across the Meadows to the Castle. Sometimes we'll try to shin up a lamppost and climb the castle rock, fail miserably, then double back on ourselves and walk through the front gate like every other tourist. There's a ten-inch gap at the top of the portcullis, and because I'm wee and skinny, I'll sneak up via the gatehouse room, shimmy past the heavy chains and across the top of the iron gate, 20 feet above the oblivious sightseers below and hawk a mouthful of phlegm onto the heads of the day trippers as they pass underneath. When we're out of gob, we walk the streets, past the statues of all the old Edinburgh ghosts – Robert the Bruce, William Wallace, Greyfriars Bobby – then maybe take a wander up to Arthur's

Seat. Climb to the top, have a look-see and come back down again, hungry for our tea.

In our house most days, there's me, my two brothers and my mum and dad. During the war, my mother's neighbourhood in Glasgow got bombed out by the Luftwaffe, so her family, seven or eight brothers and sisters in all, got cast to the four winds and she found herself here in Edinburgh. First off, she worked as a nurse, spending her working life attending the ailments of the people of Fife, then part-time at a nursing home for the elderly, prior to getting wed and the arrival of Gordon, my older brother. My dad was born and raised in these parts, a real Edinburgh native. Having started out as a telegram messenger, fresh out of school – flitting around the grey Edinburgh streets, carrying news of births and deaths to the people of the town on a black bicycle with a bell and a basket over the front wheel – he pulled himself up by his bootstraps to become a big cheese at the Edinburgh post office.

Gordon takes after my dad and is the clever one. When I arrive on the scene eighteen months later, I'm the designated naughty one. Or, tricky, as my mum always describes me. Ronald, my wee brother, is last on the scene and rounds off the family unit, just as I turn seven. His status in the pecking order, from smart to tricky, has yet to be defined. It's the nature of things that I take my older brother's hand-me-downs, which is fine, all things considered, but my wee brother has drawn the short straw and gets his sweaters and trousers third hand, and they hang loose around his tiny frame like he's been struck by a shrink-ray. Because there's a year and a half between us – although it might just as well be a century at our age – Gordon and me are together, but apart. The age gap is too big. Like the distance between one Christmas and the next, it's almost impossibly huge. He has his pals and I'm the annoying kid brother and never the twain shall meet – unless I get into a scrap with someone and say, 'I'll get my big brother on you' and then he's there at my side, punching fuck out of them and stomping heads on my behalf.

Other than that, we don't play together or hang out, unless we're with our mum and dad and we've got to be around each other. We're only together at the dinner table or shopping in town, or on our holiday once a year to Burntisland, an hour north on the train across the Forth Bridge, but another world: swimming with the jellyfish, portions of soggy chips on the way to the B&B, the funfair, the helter-skelter, arcades full of machines that gobble your pennies.

It's the same between me and my wee brother, only instead of a year or so, we're seven years adrift, a couple of lifetimes apart. Ronald has his little life and I have mine. See you at teatime, see you at breakfast and that's about it, except for all the giggling we did, especially at dinner time. I was usually sent to the kitchenette with my dinner so we could all finish eating without the nonsense. On Saturdays, or perhaps after school, we'll be taken on the northbound bus to visit our grandparents, five miles down the road to Leith. Huddled around the tiny black-and-white TV, roast dinner, jelly and ice cream, then home on the bus, Ronald dozing off against my mother or father in the pitch darkness. Every Sunday after church, Gordon and I help with the housework, polishing the skirting and the like, taking turns doing the dishes after our tea. One day I'll wash and he'll dry, and vice versa the next day.

Since Ronald came along, I've had my own private kingdom, this ten-foot-square box room at the end of the hall, my own room. After sharing a room and a bunk bed with my older brother for seven years, it feels like the lap of luxury suddenly. I sleep every night beneath a skylight and I'm always the first to know when it's been snowing, because the sun is blocked out by the grey snow gathered there on the glass above. At nights, the sound of the Scottish rain against the window sends me to my sleep, or the sound of *The Clitheroe Kid*, Jimmy Clitheroe's radio show, on my transistor radio beneath my pillow, while I think about maybe tidying up the place before usually deciding I like it fine the way it is. My clumsily painted Airfix model airplanes hang from the ceiling by cotton thread, Spitfires in eternal, plastic dogfights with German planes, played out against a backdrop of walls lined with colour posters of the latest pop singers. I don't have a particular favourite pop star; the wallpaper is just blotted out by whatever posters came free with last week's magazines – the Stones, the Beatles, Roy Wood, T.Rex and the like – and the magazine remnants are scattered across the carpet like gaudy-coloured tiles.

Over by the door, the room has a brass light switch, but it's a long haul from my bed to turn the light off. Because I'm a tricky bastard, I've fixed the room with a contraption: two lengths of string, running through metal hoops, one set along the skirting, the other down the side of my bed. One string to turn the light on, the other to turn the light off. I'm industrious like that – taking things apart, wanting to see how they work. When I want a bike, there's no talk of going into town to the cycle shop or my dad and mum having to pay for a sparkling new bike in weekly instalments. No, I salvage a frame from the local scrapyard and build my own from various bits and pieces I root out on various junkyards around the city. At first, it has no brakes, but I finally have a bike for my paper round. Then I pinch some brakes off some other poor sod's bike while out delivering papers one morning, so now I can stop without dragging my feet on the pavement when I have a sack full of newspapers or when I'm heading off to swimming practice after school.

We're a happy lot, for the most part, my family. Loving and caring, but not overbearing. Whether I'm tricky or good, I have a great relationship with my mum and my dad. They're strict, but not too strict. Not strict for this day and age, in any case. If I'm bad, my mum will roll her eyes, tell me I'm too tricky for my own good. If I'm very bad, maybe I'll get the belt. Not so bad. Certainly not as bad as at primary school – starting with Primary One – but then school was never my favourite place. My favourite thing about school is coming home, leaving the place behind me and finding a new route to get home. I make it an adventure every time, testing the boundaries of the world, climbing a wall, skipping across the gardens, helping myself to an apple or a pear from someone's tree.

I'm left-handed, so that has its drawbacks when you're seven years old and your teacher's a nun. It being a Catholic school, there's a few nuns teaching us. A couple have stayed with me.

They're like good cop, bad cop, only they pray more and are kind of married to Jesus. The bad nun tries to get me to write with my right hand as it's looked upon as evil – sinister, she says – to write left-handed. I think I believe her for a while and start to think my brain is wired differently to the other kids. One time in class, the bad nun comes up behind me, wrenches the ink pen out my left hand and sets about whacking the back of my hand with a wooden ruler, breaking the strip of wood in half with the sheer force of the blows. All the other kids, and even the nun herself, are stunned. She's staring at the splinters and back at my battered hand. She never does it again, but my left hand is red and sore, and for a time, the sting reminds me to use my right hand, though it didn't last.

Once I move into Primary Two, I graduate from getting thwacked with the ruler and I'm on to the belt (or strap). I see a lot of the belt, usually for laughing in class or talking to someone or not paying attention. It seems unfair, especially as there's nothing I can do about my attention span. My last name's Wood and I'm always at the back of the class alphabetically, always drifting away, never noticing what gets scrawled on the chalk board, just an eye out the window, thinking about break time or, as summer draws closer, dreaming about those seven long weeks away from school. Summer holidays, ya beauty! A lifetime of happiness, the most wonderful feeling, until the depressing crash of autumn and going back to class, the very worst. Sometimes I get so bored listening to the teacher droning on, I fall asleep, waiting for the school bell and wake up to a teacher's face, puce with rage, shouting the odds at me.

The difference between Primary One and Primary Two, I think, is that the teachers who hand out the beatings get more of a kick out of it than the nuns ever did, and the punishments are handed out for the slightest step over the line. Or sometimes, even if you go to a lot of trouble to not walk over the line. Our school is for boys and girls alike, and fraternisation is against the rules. At playtime, the sexes are kept apart by an eight-inch-thick painted yellow line across the playground which we're under strict instructions to never cross. One day, I get an idea that my pals and I can circumnavigate the school, climb a few walls and get into the girls' side of the playground in a bid to impress them, all without crossing the dividing line. We're not subtle, so we get caught in the girls' section celebrating our tiny win and are hauled in front of the headmistress. 'But we didnae cross the yellow line, miss,' we tell her. True enough, but we get the strap regardless. You hold your hand out – both hands if you're very bad – grit your teeth and gird yourself against the pain, but you see this glint in their eye, this look that says, *You're really gonna get it this time, boy*. When I'm eight, our headmistress drops dead, but she's given so many of us the strap by now, none of us mourn her passing.

We're Catholic, as you probably gathered when I mentioned nuns, but I don't really think about it until I turn nine or ten. A wee pal of mine – this kid called Quentin, although he goes by Paul – are inseparable for a while, going off on adventures, getting into scrapes, breaking into abandoned houses and the like, just being kids. He tells me he's a Protestant, and I tell him, 'Oh, I'm Catholic, I think', and a weird change comes over him for the rest of the day. Next time I knock at his door, he doesn't come out. And the time after that too. In fact, I never see him again, which is kind of sad, I suppose.

We're not exactly staunch Catholics, you know. We attend the weekly service, but I hate every minute. Not because I have the devil in me, but because I hate having to go somewhere just because I'm told to. Kneel. Stand up. Sit down. Wearing my Sunday best and getting itchy feet from standing while the priest delivers his blessings and damnations to his flock. When I turn 14, I'm allowed to go to church on my own, so most times I'll find a way to skive off. I walk around for an hour, skulk a while in the stair, and finally head home with a look on my face like butter wouldn't melt. Despite going to church, on and off, I'm not religious, I decide. Unlike that kid Quentin, I don't mind if people are Catholic or Protestant or whatever. I don't judge. People are just people. I believe there's something maybe. I believe in good and bad, but beyond that, I don't know.

Anyway, after church, or not going to church, the rest of Sunday is heaven. Actual heaven: a black-and-white film on the tiny telly in the living room while mum cooks our tea. I love the Marx Brothers, especially Harpo, but I must be a strange kid because my favourites are all from decades into the past – and usually something with a musical bent. I don't remember when that kind of thing first catches my attention, maybe I'm ten, possibly younger, but anything with Louis Armstrong, Jimmy Stewart in *The Glenn Miller Story*, Benny Goodman, and I'm sold. You know that Kirk Douglas film, *Young Man With the Horn*? The one where he plays the trumpeter, and there's a scene where he's looking down into this basement seeing all these black jazz players? I wanted to be that guy, looking into that basement. Or Jimmy Stewart finding '*that* sound' in the Glenn Miller movie. That stuff was manna from heaven to me. Find a Sunday-afternoon film that has a hint of old-timey jazz, and I'm transfixed for two hours. I won't move away from the television set for even a minute.

A friend of my mum and dad left the family an upright piano in their will. I'm curious about it, but it's become my brother's domain. Gordon, being the eldest, the boy most likely, is sent off to a piano teacher to learn scales and to advance through the grades. The halls chime with the sound of clunky Beethoven and Brahms, and I'm a wee bit jealous, I think. My folks must feel sorry for me, because my mum takes me to the local music shop and buys me a recorder, pays for a few lessons and a book to study. At school, I'm asked if I want to join the music class and I'm given a cornet – kind of a stunted trumpet – and lessons (and, later, the clarinet). The cornet is so loud that it drives my parents nuts, so I open the back window and play out into the garden and the tenements. The sound – the way it echoes and clatters off everyone's walls and back into our house – to me it sounds great. For the neighbours, though, probably not so much.

Occasionally I'll tinker on the piano at home and after tea – five o'clock every day without fail, when my dad gets home, usually something hearty, mince and tatties, or fish fingers, roast chicken on Sunday – maybe I'll play a wee piano duet with my dad. Normally I play a left-hand boogie while my dad covers the right-hand part, and as I get older, we switch places, and I can find my way around the keys with ease. After that, I want to play all the time, whatever the cost. There's a church opposite my primary school, the big old steeple type with a grand church organ right at the back by the altar, about 15 feet up in the gods with its own wee balcony. Sometimes my pals and I will sneak in and I'll play a tune for them. One time I'm up there playing 'In the Mood' by Glenn Miller, not realising a funeral procession just entered the church. It goes without saying that I got the belt that day.

After primary, Gordon follows in my dad's footsteps and goes to the Holy Cross Academy down the road, the place where all the bright kids go, but I don't follow suit. In the last term of school, you take a test, to sort the wheat from the chaff, and you have three possible destinations: Holy Cross for the clever ones, the wheat, the kids who are going to make something of their lives, or Saint Andrew's or Saint Anthony's for the rest, the chaff. After my brother, my parents have great expectations of me, but I'm too busy daydreaming. I fail the test with flying colours and go to Saint Andrew's.

Around this time, two of my neighbourhood pals, Stuart McFarlane and Rab Cuthbert, form a wee three-piece jazz band, with me on the cornet, Stuart on clarinet and Robert on trumpet. After a few rehearsals, we figure we sound brilliant – because everything's brilliant when you're 14 – and play our first shows around the tenements, playing Christmas songs in the stairwells. The echo is amazing and I think about that Kirk Douglas movie. In my mind's eye, we're real bona fide jazz players and the crowd is eating it up. The truth is, we make a little loose change from some of the kinder folk, but mostly we get people shouting at us to shut up and set a few mongrels barking, and some guy says he's going to call the police if we don't pack it in. The occasional boot gets thrown, but I won't let it put me off jazz. More than any pop records in the charts – although, truthfully, I'm not paying any attention to that – it's still the music that speaks to me. I have a few records by now, a copy of the Herb Alpert & the Tijuana Brass album my parents bought for me, but there's no Beatles or Stones.

I know the Beatles, of course. To fund my addiction to sweets and comic books, I do a paper round before school. My mum and dad don't want me lying in bed all day and want to instil the work ethic and all that. It gives me a little purpose, a reason to get out of my bed. One week, as a treat, the newsagent gives all us paperboys tickets to see the Beatles movie that's showing and I'm watching these four guys getting out the back of a limo and getting chased around all about the place by hordes of screaming teenage girls and I'm thinking, *What a strange sight to behold, people behaving like that.*

Chapter 2

FREEZIN' HEET

Fourteen going on fifteen now, as a chilly 1971 melts into 1972. It's school dinner time, an hour away from the misery of the blackboard. My secondary school pals and me – Bernie Gray, Robin Ross and Ronnie Blakey – are on our way to the chippy, skipping school dinners because they're plain horrible. If you tasted that shite, you'd skip it too. It's grim, grey muck and, because we're men of good taste, we've devised a workaround. It's a scheme built from the ground up and honed over a couple of years at secondary school, and by now it runs like clockwork, like a wee kids' version of a heist movie. At the start of the school week, my mum lands a goodbye peck on my cheek as I leave and gives me some money to buy dinner tickets for the week's school lunch. If you're a fool, one ticket can be exchanged for one lunch, a grey slop or some ugly meat and lumpy tatties, with semolina or rice pudding for afters. But I'm no fool, you see.

The scheme goes like this: I sell Monday's ticket to another kid, spend the money on something from the nearby shops instead – kids are allowed to go home for lunch or, in our case, to just wander the streets at lunchtime – then show the remaining four tickets to my mum after school. I'll leave the four tickets sticking out of my blazer pocket, just visible. I don't know why. I just figure if she sees them, I'm free to do what I want on Tuesday through to Friday maybe, but she never checks, because why would you?

On Tuesday, I take the four remaining tickets and sell them for 10p a throw to some other kid. Then, with my ill-gotten gains burning a hole in my pocket, I play pitch and toss with a few pals – maybe win a couple of pennies, maybe I'll lose tuppence – before heading down the road to the chippy for a 5p bag of chips and, if I'm feeling extravagant, maybe a bag of Dolly Mixtures from the sweet shop on the way back to the playground. On other days, if I can't be bothered to go to the chippy, I'll buy a gargantuan fruit cake dripping with icing sugar and currants from the Co-Op across the street, eat the whole thing in one sweet hit and I'm wired, bouncing of the classroom walls for the rest of the school day.

'We have a band,' Bernie tells me one day. He's got salt all over his lips and I can barely hear him over the sound of my own scoffing. 'You wanna be in it? Play guitar maybe?'

I think about that a minute. I'm still playing my cornet and my clarinet. I still want to be Louis Armstrong or Benny Goodman, but Bernie says we're going to learn a bunch of Beatles songs and make ourselves rich and famous. I don't know too many of their songs. The Beatles have passed me by; I'm too young. However, I've seen Slade on *Top of the Pops* playing 'Gudbuy T' Jane' and there's something there. I've never touched a guitar, but I tell him, 'Yeah, sure.' Just one problem. 'I don't have a guitar.'

'S'okay,' says Bernie. 'Borrow one of mine.'

Later, I go over to Bernie's and he hands me this scruffy acoustic guitar, strung for a right-handed player. I hold it upside down, left-handed, all the strings the wrong way up. I've no idea how to tune it or how to change the strings around, so Bernie has me turn it downside up and that's me playing right-handed now and that's how I play forever. Now I think about it, except for football, where I play outside left, everything I do is kind of left-handed adapted to right-handed. By default, and maybe because of the nuns, I've become a right-handed lefty. Even the golf clubs my father cut down to size for me are right-handed, but I adapt. The right-hand guitar is a struggle at first – it's counterintuitive – but I start to find my way up and down the fretboard and, in no time, can form a couple of chords.

So I have a band now with a couple of pals from school and I feel myself drifting away from jazz and movie musical stuff towards actual pop music like you hear on the radio and telly. We spend our lunch hours together talking about band stuff and what we're going to do when we're famous. At first, it's just a fun thing to do to take my mind off hating school, but it starts getting in my bloodstream. You see the reaction on the telly when someone plays a song and it's exciting to me, enticing. Just getting together for rehearsals and feeling the energy transferring between us when we work out something new is the most fun

I've ever had. Even a band meeting is more exciting than anything school has to offer.

We usually strategise on our way to and from the chippy and that's when Bernie or someone says, 'What'll we call ourselves?' We're half a mile from the chippy, walking through some greenery. I look up, then down and around.

'What about Grass? Let's call the band Grass.'

Everyone nods. That's fine. We're called Grass now. We walk another hundred yards down the road. Someone says, 'Hang on', and we all stop there on the pavement in our blazers and caps.

'Grass. That's drugs, isn't it? We cannae call it that.'

The band 'Grass' lasted all of a hundred yards. RIP. We walk another hundred yards and stop in our tracks.

'What about something, I dunno, something hot and cold,' someone says. 'Something like Freezin' Heat. But "heat" with two E's.'

Everyone agrees it's brilliant, and so we're not called Grass anymore, we're Freezin' Heet and we're off slathering salt, brown sauce and vinegar on our chips at the counter. We all agree we're gonna be massive. The same night, we get a big drum skin and paint Freezin' Heet on the front, so it's too late to turn back now.

School is so far by the wayside now that it's practically invisible, like a fly on the windscreen. I'm all in on this crazy scheme. Not the dinner ticket scheme, you understand. The pop group scheme. Freezin' Heet is my life now and every waking minute is devoted to the dream. We're lacking in money and equipment, but never short of ideas. I pack in the paper round and get a morning job at the local dairy shop, Trotter's, where I work for Mr Trotter, because everyone old enough to grow whiskers is Mr-something-or-other. Every morning I push a trolley up and down the streets of Edinburgh delivering pints of milk in glass bottles. I buy a couple of singles, Chicory Tip and the like, but mainly my £1 a week goes to fund my sweets and juice habit, maybe the odd comic book. It's hard graft delivering milk, especially when it's cold and your hands are getting frozen to the metal handles on the trolley, but I've found a way to peel back the silver foil bottle tops so I can take a cheeky swig of cream and replace the cap before I leave the bottle on whoever's doorstep I'm delivering to. After work, Mr Trotter tells me what a good lad I am and agrees that I can take home a couple of giant wooden bread boxes for a project I have going.

'What are these for?' he wonders, and I tell him 'You'll see' – all mysterious, like I'm this master carpenter or something. Then, back at Bernie's, we saw the bread boxes in half, build a three-foot-by-three-foot speaker cabinet to house the tiny 3-watt junk shop amplifier I got, spray the whole thing black and stretch a couple of yards of strawberry netting over the frame. It looks amazing, but it sounds pish. As for the drum set, it's all we could scavenge from round and about: basically, a hi-hat, a snare and a bass drum but no pedal, so the drummer's got to boot the bass drum with his foot to get anything out of it. We are undeterred, of course, because we're on a mission. In no time, we're rehearsing at Bernie's in his parents' living room for our first show. The big time – an afternoon set at an old folks' home in town, with two acoustic guitars, an electric guitar and a broken-down drum. We play a bunch of Beatles songs and the pensioners tap their hands in appreciation – or maybe impatience – on the arms of their chairs and clap along, waiting for the nurse to come back and put the telly back on. When we finish, one of the helpers arrives with a squeaking trolley of tea and biscuits – our payment – and we take a bow and soak up the applause, while the old folks soak their biscuits in their tea.

It's okay, but it's not perfect. We know that we need a proper drum kit fast, so we help the nuns at St Margaret's with the convent jumble sale to raise a couple of bob. While we're kicking about, loading stuff on shelves and whatnot for the nuns, a psychic reads my palm and tells me my name will be up in lights someday, and that raises a laugh. But we get £1 and that's enough for a shabby second-hand drum kit the nuns found in a cupboard somewhere. A drum set with a drum stool, a tom, and, at last, a bass drum pedal. Now, suitably equipped for stardom, we play our second show in a hall for Edinburgh's down-and-outs, basically a room filled with drunks and homeless guys. No tea or biscuits this time, but after the show, Bernie's dad drives us home in style, like we're the Beatles coming back from Shea Stadium, all our gear stashed on the roof rack of his car. As we head up a steep hill, we all do a double-take out the back window and watch the bass drum roll off the back of the car and down the road, sending cars and pedestrians scattering for safety.

Before you sit your O-levels, you take a test run – prelims, we call them – and it's like this bizarro-world 15th birthday treat for me. Just ugh. A couple of weeks sitting quiet and morose in the school gymnasium, teachers prowling the aisles to make sure you're not cheating, all to prove the point that I've not been paying attention to anything for the past ten years. Every exam I sit, I'm the first to finish up, raise my hand and ask to leave. Obviously I fail them all. Years of staring out the windows are coming back to haunt me. Practical things like metalwork and woodwork, I'm okay at. I can throw a decent pot in pottery class, I'm good at music and swimming, but English and maths, science, geography, anything where you need to think about it too hard, I'm pure shite and I know it. I'm just waiting to have it confirmed at this point.

I'm sitting in class, still with half an eye out the window at what's going on in the world outside, as our teacher tells us how well we've done and to keep up the good work. I'm looking at my disastrous results, wondering *What are my mum and dad going to say?* They know by now I'm not academic but, still, I can't help but visualise the scene when they see how I crashed and burned. I can see them in my mind's eye; my mum in tears, my dad pacing the floor, a look of disappointment on his face.

Then the classroom door opens and I'm told I must go see the rector. Everyone in the class starts a low murmuring kind of noise, speculating over whether I'm going to get the belt on one or both hands this time. Head down, I walk out the class, a stone's throw across the wet playground to the rector's office. I'm hoping if I walk slow enough, the world will come to a natural end before I get to the other side of the schoolyard. Disappointingly, the world doesn't end, so I walk in, take a seat in front of the rector and wait to take my medicine. He's smiling,

I'm not. I'm expecting a frown, or for him to go through my prelim results line by line and tell me what a disappointment I am and hand me my death papers. Instead, he tells me one of his pals is an electrician and is looking for an apprentice and asks if I'd be interested. He just threw me a lifeline, I realise. It takes me less than a second to agree and all my tension and inner turmoil falls away.

'When do I start?' I ask. The rector, still smiling, tells me it'll be a couple of weeks, so I chance my arm. 'Can I just leave now then?' I say, and he mulls that over for a minute. I'm just thinking that if he says yes, I'll be home by lunchtime and done with school forever. Actual forever. Finally, he says, 'I don't see why not.' Probably before the words have landed on my ear, I'm back at my desk, picking up my school bag. I walk out the school gate, as happy as a sandboy. See ya. When I get home, my dad is delighted too. He tells me for the thousandth time that it's good to have a trade behind you. His dad was an engineer at the *Edinburgh Evening News*, a job for life, fixing the printing press whenever it bollocksed up, so me walking into a trade as an electrician is a good thing – like I'm following a family tradition or something, rather than being the disappointing kid who wasn't interested in school.

I get two weeks of absolute bliss, watching my brothers leave for school every morning and pulling the covers back over my head. The afternoons are all about Freezin' Heet, obviously, and then I start work. A month ago, I was a kid, kicking about a school playground, and here I am today, a working man earning the princely sum of £5 per week. Until I get my first pay packet, my mum subs me my bus fare and sends me on my way on my first morning. Four miles south, half an hour on the bus, to a narrow, cobbled lane just off Dublin Street. There, a one-panel van sits out front of the building, bearing the name 'Arthur McKay & Co. Electricians'. I walk in off the cobbles, announce myself and I'm taken to meet Mr McKay himself, who talks me through the day-to-day. He tells me I'm working the counter in the electrician's shop, with the tools and this neat wall of tiny wooden drawers with every kind of screw or nail or fitting you can imagine. If one of the dozen or so electricians come by, I grab him a new screwdriver, a certain light fitting or a socket, or a box of bolts and nuts. If there's a crew that needs five metres of 2.5cm cable, I'm shown how to measure that out, using the length of my arm to my chest to make a yard, plus a little more to make it up to a metre, now we've gone over to the metric system.

After six months in the store, you get to work on site – out on the tools, we call it, working around the city with a couple of full-grown electricians and learning the ropes. I don't learn too much, though, because the two guys I'm with are lazy bastards. I rock up to the work site every day, and they're sitting around the howf, drinking tea, scoffing biscuits, talking about the Hearts game on the radio last night and doing nothing else besides. Sometimes, I just pull open a cupboard door, lean in against the shelves and treat myself to a 20-minute standing kip in the cupboard and don't come out until I hear my name called. Occasionally, I get to bang a nail into a wall, or maybe lay a yard of cable, but mostly I'm the gopher, getting handed a list of everyone's lunch requirements and sent off to the nearest chippy or sandwich shop.

Meanwhile, Bernie Gray's sister tells us the Odeon picture house is advertising for a band to play Saturday mornings between the cartoons, so we cart our gear across the Meadows – literally on a go-kart, one made from the same bread boxes as the speaker cabinet, with a pram wheel on each corner. We drag the gear down to the cinema, set up on stage and then the guy says, 'Let's see what you've got.' There are a couple of dozen eight-to-ten-year-olds, high on sugar and sweet drinks, filling out the front two rows, but the rest of the seats are empty. The air is thick with hotdog and popcorn stink, and the kids, who've all been abandoned by their mums and dads while they do a couple of hours shopping, are already borderline feral. We plug in, my pal Ronnie Blakey and me on guitars, Robin Ross on drums and Bernie Gray on bass, and rattle through the usual bunch of Beatles songs. Robin, who's in the marching pipe band, steps forward, hangs the drum around his neck and sings 'Yellow Submarine' and we all harmonise, and I reckon that's the clincher for us.

The Edinburgh journalist John Gibson gives us a wee mention in the paper, saying we passed the audition, so we come back the week after. Same routine as last time. Cartoons, then a half-hour set from Freezin' Heet, followed by a main feature, one of those Children's Film and Television Foundation affairs, with a bunch of wooden child actors solving a mystery in a cove or a haunted house or something. It's a cup of Kia-Ora and a bag of sweets each as payment and we head up to the balcony to watch the movie and scoff our wages. A couple of weeks later, it's not two rows anymore; it's three, then four. We're getting better, a little more confident. By the seventh week, the crowd is growing exponentially and getting a bit exuberant. The whole downstairs section is full to bursting and we're getting things thrown at us in all the excitement – sweets and fruit and such like. Kids being kids. I'm playing and singing along, and some kid throws a peach, and I'm thinking maybe I'd be doing the same if I were in the audience myself, although maybe I'd eat the peach and chuck something else.

On the eighth week, the cinema manager takes us to one side and says it's getting so popular that he's taking things up a notch and inviting some other bands to play with us. We're a sudden, Saturday-morning sensation. All the local bands – I mean, the proper bands – start playing on the same stage as us. We sit up in the balcony and watch them all. Bay City Rollers, that's one of the bands. I've seen their name around town, plastered on walls and bus stops. They had a top-ten hit, 'Keep on Dancing', not so long ago, so they're kind of local heroes around these parts. When they play, the place is mobbed and there's not a single peach thrown onto the stage. They have a decent singer, this guy Nobby Clark, and unlike us, they're in their twenties – actual grown men, proper professionals. They never dragged their gear down over the Meadows on a go-kart and got paid in bags of sweets. Oh no. They pulled up outside in cars, had a guy set up their equipment and – I'm only guessing here – probably got paid cash money for their performance.

I guess it's a few weeks later and we're playing again and there's a fella comes in, an older guy, suited and wearing an overcoat, so not your Saturday-morning dad who's had a barney with the wife and come to pick up the kids early. After we play, he tells us he's Jim Taylor and he's a manager. He's come expecting to see some other band and was set to offer to manage them, but saw us instead. We're all grinning ear-to-ear thinking it's our big break, obviously.

Jim takes me and Robin to one side and says, 'Guys, to be honest, you're pretty shite.' I can feel the smile kind of slipping from my face now. 'The two of youse are okay. You've got promise. But you've got tae get rid of these other two. They're dead weight. Build a new band and call it something different. Not Freezin' Heet, anyway. Or you can keep going, doing what you're doing. Maybe you'll stop being shite. It's up to you guys.'

Jim Taylor has been around the block a few times. He used to play with the guy Eric Faulkner from the Rollers in a group called Kip, so he must know what he's talking about, so we tell him 'Sure'. Suddenly, we're proper ruthless and jettison our two pals in the blink of an eye. I move over onto bass guitar and Jim drafts in this guy Colin Stewart from Newtongrange to play guitar and an Edinburgh singer called Vince Hughes. Before we know it, we're called Wot's Up and we take it up a notch or two.

On Jim's advice, over the course of the next three or four months, we move away from the Beatles-based set list. To set us apart from the other bands on the circuit that are knocking out the standard chart fare, we pick a bunch of songs we like – Marc Bolan, Bowie's 'Life on Mars' and 'Suffragette City', and the

Animals' 'House of the Rising Sun' – and we get the feeling we're making a bit of progress, actually starting to evolve organically, like a real street band. We rehearse constantly, honing our craft, and play a few shows – community centres around Edinburgh and further afield. To be honest, we still don't sound great, but because Jim has a bit of pedigree playing with bands around the scene, he knows a few tricks of the trade. Whenever we play a show now, we have a microphone set up behind the curtain and he chimes in with harmonies to make us sound less shite. Within a couple of months, Jim renames us again and we're called Kip, like his old band. Jim says to us, 'You know this guy Tam Paton? He wants to meet you.' We all know Paton. He's the manager of a couple of bands around – Bilbo Baggins and the Bay City Rollers.

Obviously, we all say, 'Aye, why not?'

Chapter 3

THE POTATO MAN

Thomas Dougal Paton, or 'Tam' as he's known to friends and enemies alike, is a local legend on the Edinburgh band scene. He's from Prestonpans, an old mining town, just east of the city. His parents have a potato business and he's spent half a life carrying huge sacks of spuds and loading them onto the backs of trucks. I see him sometimes at the Odeon when I'm playing with my band. He's not your regular music manager like you see in the films, pinstriped with a big cigar on the go. Far from it. He's a bit of a curious-looking guy, if I'm honest. He's in his mid-thirties, as old as the fuckin' hills from my perspective. He's got the nickname Tatty Tam, and it's well-earned. No matter what time of day it is, he always looks like he's just got up from his bed to answer the front door, forever in this denim shirt he wears, the fabric straining to hold in these telegraph-pole shoulders of his.

He's been doing the music thing a while now, I gather. A wee bell probably rang in the back of his head that there's more to life than spuds when he saw the Beatles on the telly making more money than British Leyland. He had an epiphany, so instead of humping great sacks of tatties for his mum and dad, he diversified his portfolio and tried his massive hand at band management. I've heard he once had an audience with the Beatles' manager, Brian Epstein. Epstein told him that if he wanted to be a successful manager, he needed to work real hard and focus on PR, get the look right, and that's his mantra now. After he was touched by the hand of Epstein, he's become this strange blend of two types of people when I meet him: he's a brick shithouse, massive, strong as the proverbial ox, but he's also this micro-managing fusspot, like a clucking mother hen of a man all at the same time.

I'm playing with Kip and, through Jim, we're getting some bigger shows. Bigger than the Odeon Saturday morning pictures, anyway. Certainly it's better now than during the final days of Freezin' Heet. Just a few months ago, pre-Jim, we were playing to servicemen at an airbase somewhere deep in the country. When we arrived we realised we had to play four hours. We'd only learned fifteen Beatles tunes at the time, so had to hope they didn't notice us recycling our hour-long set four times, just changing the running order, telling everyone we'd had a request to play 'Love Me Do' a third time. They all noticed of course, but after a couple of hours, they were too drunk to care. Over a couple of weeks of more shows, I notice Tam sizing us up from the audience. No, scratch that. He's sizing *me* up. He's either standing in the wings or he's half-watching us from the sea of tartrazine-fuelled kids in the Odeon pews. We all see him there and talk among ourselves and hear a few things on the grapevine. Not all the things are nice, but I'm still having stuff go in one ear and out the other, like I was at school. Some people will tell you he's a connected guy. Record companies, promoters, those kind of people, but others too, as it would turn out.

But I don't put much store in that kind of talk. I'm sixteen now and I'm just fixated on my band thing, learning chords and harmonies, and finding the energy to get through a week as an apprentice. I'm having these mad daydreams we're going to get better and better, and we're going to be famous, probably. Then, finally, after Tam's been eyeing us from a distance, Jim brings him to the dressing room. He looks me up and down, like a bear surveying its next meal.

'You wannae do a little work for me, Woody?' he says. His voice is like a high-pitched wheeze – half-comical, half-cartoon villain. 'Ah've this band, Bilbo Baggins, playing at the weekend. They'll be needing a roadie.'

I tell him, aye that'll be great, and the next weekend, I'm suddenly a roadie. No one mentions money, but I'd have done it for nothing, if I'm honest. Good thing too because it turns out there is no money, just experience. Tam calls the house again a week later and tells me he wants me to roadie for his other band, the Rollers. This time it's every weekend.

This guy Jake Duncan is the Rollers' head roadie – by that, I mean their *only* roadie – and Tam hooks me up with him and we hit it off right out of the gate. He's a brilliant person and a complete perfectionist. Over the course of a couple of months, he shows me everything that goes on in the background to get a show running smoothly. When I wasn't grabbing 40 winks in the cupboard at work, I picked up a few things from my apprenticeship, so I'm not a complete blank slate, but Jake knows every cable and where it leads, or is supposed to lead, and I pick it up quickly. It's hard work, a lot of graft, humping and carrying the gear and all that, but it's a laugh too. I'm out every weekend, learning the ropes from Jake, figuring out how to set up drums, amps and, importantly, the correct way to carry gear without knackering your spine. Some other things – well, you learn those through experience. A lot of the old bingo halls have a revolving stage. When there are two bands playing, the second band will be ready to go as the first band finishes up, then the stage starts turning, the emcee announces the second band, and they finish the first band's final song before starting their own set. Usually it goes like clockwork, though this one night the mic stands haven't been put on the stage and are left stranded on the part that doesn't rotate. Cables are going everywhere, like mad spaghetti, mic stands are tumbling over, and the Rollers are just standing there glowering at me from the wings.

In clubland, the Mecca circuit is a big draw. Since the 1960s, Mecca has been at the epicentre of entertainment with dozens of old theatres and cinemas bought out, gutted and turned into nightclubs throughout the major towns and cities of the UK. You see them on the telly most weeks on *Come Dancing* and sometimes *Miss World*. It's the housewife's first and only choice for a night on the town. There's one in every industrial town and although they're all different, they're also the same wherever you go. Without fail, there's always a couple of heavies on the door, ex-squaddies with dickie-bows, scrunched-up noses and cauliflower ears, growling you through. The carpet is usually sticky from the previous night's revels, spilt beer and Cinzano, and it kind of squelches under your feet as you walk backward into the venue, with Jake telling me 'Back a bit, left a bit' as we ease the gear in from the kerb, like Laurel and Hardy. Jake is patient enough with me, as I walk about the place gawping, reminding me what to unpack and which cable goes where.

Then the band heads off in one direction towards the dressing room, and Tam breaks away, stepping into the manager's office with a bunch of slick-haired old bastards in camel coats who look like gangsters off *Get Carter*, wily fucks who'd smack you as soon as look at you. Five minutes later, Tam emerges, cigar smoke wafting out the open door behind him. He's grinning, patting the place where his heart should be, a manila envelope containing the night's money. Meanwhile, the Rollers are in the dressing room, slapping on a little make-up and donning their stage outfits – a load of primary-coloured jerseys and slacks – and those teetering platforms that are all the go on *Top of the Pops* every Thursday. I never saw the like. Edinburgh in 1973 is kind of brimming with machismo – lots of gangs and fighting wherever you go. There's always a guy on most streets wanting to beat the shit out of you if you look at him the wrong way, or even in the right way in some cases. It seems like the streets are flowing on testosterone and dark bitter, but I'm seeing these big lads here, sitting in front of those mirrors, lined with 50-watt bulbs, popping on the mascara and foundation so they don't look all washed out and pale under the stage lights. One of the guys sees me looking in and tells me 'It's not what you think, Woody', like he's not like that Bowie fella or Marc Bolan. He's wearing a bit of slap, the same way Gordon Honeycombe does when he's reading the nightly news.

Once Jake and I have broken out the gear, laid the cables, testing-one-two-three and the audience has funnelled in from the cold, dark streets of whatever border town we're in, everything falls under a fug of cigarette smoke and Avon perfume. The guys stand at the back with a pint of mild, a bag of nuts gripped tight in their teeth, and hand a glass of Babycham or something with a glacé cherry skewered on a wee plastic sword to the wife. The place is stowed out with women. They all have their hair done nice, have their lippy and their sparkle, and they wave their hands and scream when the band move around on stage. It's a club, so they're not teenyboppers exactly, though there's a few – 16-, 17-, 18-year-old girls, out with their nanas and aunties, elbowing their way to the lip of the stage. The compere – usually a guy with a moustache and a crushed-velvet suit, mutton chops, big hairy chest and a medallion dangling, and pure stinking of Brut 33 – hits the stage, whipping up the crowd.

'Are ye ready for the Rollers?!' he says over the hubbub, and I'm watching it all from the side of the stage, partly daydreaming, and feeling the excitement in the air, thinking about Kirk Douglas looking in on the jazz band in that old black-and-white film I watched in the stair. I want to be on that stage.

The band seem to be good lads. There's the brothers, Derek and Alan Longmuir, drums and bass; Eric Faulkner on guitar; John Devine, also on guitar; and Nobby Clark, the singer. They're a bit older than me, all of them, but I can't help but notice that when Tam clicks his fingers, they all pay attention, the same as I do. If Tam tells me to jump, I say, 'Aye, how high?' Still, for the kid who's never even crossed the border before, it's amazing. Seeing different towns. Meeting new people. Trundling around the Highlands in a big Merc van. Drive to a gig, set the gear up, break it down and get back home at 2 or 3 in the morning like a proper stop-out, having picked up some warm white bread rolls from an all-night bakery and taken them home for my mum.

The Rollers are two years out from their last hit record by now. All the follow-up singles have fallen on deaf ears, but they can still fill out a club night in most towns in the north of England. North of the border, it's standing room only, girls screaming and the like. In Scotland, they're a hot ticket and feted wherever we travel. Being famous in Scotland is one thing though, and I think there's some jitters from some of the guys. I'm still a kid, literally just a kid, so my perspective is different, but I guess maybe the run of flops is getting disheartening and cracks are starting to form. A few months after I start working with Jake, Nobby decides that three flop singles is enough. He's been with the guys since they were the Saxons in the mid-'60s and I think waiting for fame to find him – years driving up and down the country and playing shows, arguing the toss with Tam every night, sometimes proper heated confrontations – is starting to take its toll. I don't get a chance to know him particularly, but he always seems like a nice guy and a good singer. Maybe he's just disillusioned by now, a little withdrawn, thinking there's more to life than this.

As if to underscore the point, Nobby walks out in November 1973 and Tam drafts in this new singer, Les McKeown. Les only has a couple of years on me, but he has a few years under his belt on the circuit. He was in this band, Threshold, and he joins the Rollers kind of reluctantly, making sure everyone knows he's the bee's knees and they're lucky to have him. The first story I hear about the guy is the one about him getting expelled from school for doing a shit in one of the lifts, which seems a strange origin story to my ears, because he's walking around now like his shite doesn't stink. The first thing I notice, and you probably realise I'm not one for noticing things, is he never says 'we' or 'us'. Everything is 'me' and 'I'. Whenever we pass each other, there's all this male peacocking going on. Deliberately walking into your path, shouldering you out the way. Kind of low-key bullying. I just roll my eyes. I'm not here to be in a pissing contest, I think.

As Nobby exits stage left, Tam starts preparing for the next departure, moving the pieces around the board, and asks me if I want to try out for the band. I tell him, aye, and he says I'm to carry on working with Jake for now, but to learn the songs in the meantime. A couple of weeks later, he says it's time. John's almost definitely on the way out, he says. So that's me, taking the bus out to Eric's house for a secret audition. Eric Faulkner's the music guy in the band, so he's the one you need to impress. Tam's more interested in how you look and whether you can be trained to smile and wave on command, so he leaves the music decisions to Eric for now. Over a can of cola each, Eric and I go through the Rollers setlist with a pair of acoustic guitars in his bedroom, Eric telling me the chord changes, what the harmonies are. I'm not a great guitarist, but I can play a bunch of chords now and I know enough from watching the band from the wings. It's not so hard.

'You got anything else?' Eric asks, so I show him a bit on the keyboard and mention I can play the cornet and clarinet. Eric gazes off into the distance, mulling it over. 'I'll tell Tam yer in,' he says, and that's that. It's a strange feeling. I've got the seal of approval, but I'm waiting in the wings for the next shoe to drop. I carry on working with Jake a couple of weeks, wondering when or if I'm going to be called in off the bench.

In the meantime, the new single 'Remember (Sha-La-La-La)' is in the shops and on the radio, and starting to creep up the hit parade. It's pretty bad timing for Nobby, walking out right on the cusp of the world starting to take notice. In contrast to Nobby, a good singer, Les is a real showman, a proper, energetic frontman. I think Les's shaking-up of things up has also energised Eric and it's suddenly like a new band every night they take to the stage. Jake and I are setting up gear at the shows and there's this sudden, newfound excitement around the Rollers. Some of these girls are so swept up, a kind of low-key mania, that they even try cracking on to Jake and me, like we're attractive by association somehow. If I walk on stage to adjust a cable or fiddle about with the drums, I'm getting screamed at and pawed; it makes you laugh and cringe at the same time. I could be anybody, just some wee scrawny kid in a leather jacket and jeans, but there's this madness around me even now. All the while, the single's edging slowly up the charts, now with Les's vocal replacing Nobby's. The band are on the radio and in the papers, and girls are rushing the stage. Their boyfriends, all standing at the back, leaning on the bar, pretty pissed off, and kicking off that their women are so interested, so there's these proper brawls kicking off all over the place and angry, pissed-up blokes storming the stage. There's no security, but Tam is well-built. He's a tough bastard when it comes down to it, so he's always ready to kick the crap out of someone if required.

Meanwhile, it finally looks as though the Rollers' guitarist, John Devine, is going. He's a quiet guy, keeping himself to himself. When he says he's had enough, Tam shrugs, tells me it's time and I'm sent home to my parents to seek their permission. I already know my answer, but as a minor, I need their approval. My dad doesn't want it to happen. Stay with the apprenticeship, he tells me, learn a useful trade, the kind of thing dads say. My mum is easier to sweet-talk and she gives her blessing right away – and, over the course of the evening, she sways my dad.

Next morning, I'm off to work to hand in my notice. When I leave, Arthur McKay gives me a letter telling me if things don't work out with the Rollers, I have a job waiting for me and that makes my dad a little less jittery. They meet with Tam and are instantly charmed by him. It's fair to say my mum and dad have no understanding of the music business – why would they? – but Tam is filled with enthusiasm for the Rollers and the year ahead, and he's got a real twinkle in his eye, so I think they trust him. They have no reason not to. Independent of one another, both my parents assess Tam as a loveable rogue. Whenever he's in their company, he comes across as a kind of amusing uncle, full of stories and completely harmless, and they seem reassured I'm in safe hands. As I'm still not eighteen – too young to sign a contract – they grant Tam power of attorney to handle my affairs while we're working. He can't switch off my life support, if I wind up in intensive care, but it means he can sign deals and arrange travel and insurance on my behalf.

I feel a bit shitty for stepping into the breach for John just as it's all about to kick off. I know I haven't paid my dues, but I was never going to say no, so the guilty feeling doesn't linger. I have my first day of rehearsals the following day. I take a bus down to Prestonpans, walk past the coal miners' cottages where Tam lives with his parents and down the muddy track to the massive potato shed there. It's a working potato merchants still, dirty as you like, the air thick with diesel. Trucks and tractors are coming and going, mud spattered everywhere, but the back room of the shed, maybe ten feet square, has been converted into a rehearsal studio. As I unpack my guitar – two quid from a junk shop in Fountainbridge, the old stomping ground of Sean Connery – I'm watching my breath in front of my face, like it's as cold inside as it is out there. I've not been paid yet, but I've had assurances. Derek oversees the money for Tam, all our wages and whatnot, and I'm told I'll get £10 a week, twice the money I was getting out on the tools, so I'm beside myself. I'm also nervy, though, after Tam tells me I'll be gone in the blink of an eye if I'm not up to snuff. 'You are replaceable,' he says, giving me the pep talk.

The potato shed isn't exactly Abbey Road. It's all a bit make-shift, but Nobby had a day job as a joiner and Alan's a plumber – in fact, all the guys are skilled working men with trades to fall back on – so they've made the best of things. To my eyes, the kid who made a speaker cabinet out of a bread crate not so long ago, it seems like a wondrous place. There's a drum kit set up in one corner, a bunch of amps and speakers to plug into and a wee booth with a mixing desk for demoing tunes. They've made some effort to soundproof the place, with great bags of sand stacked up against the walls, but as you work, you still hear people shouting the odds and unloading sacks of spuds, and tractors pulling up. Whenever it rains, which seems to be every minute of every day I'm here, the rain floods in and soaks the sand. It gets so damp that the walls are sopping and you can feel the spores landing in your nose and throat. I get hayfever, and Derek is asthmatic, so we suffer the most. Meantime, the new Rollers single is in the charts now and we're here in a potato shed, this room that pure reeks of soil. But if anyone thinks it's weird, no one says a word.

After everyone settles in, we run through a couple of numbers. Tam wheezes by and calls us up to his parents' house, where he lives, for a conflab. *Top of the Pops* is coming up, he says, and I'm paying attention but also kind of not, probably because the house smells of chip fat and it's distracting me. It's a curious meeting, held in Tam's bedroom-come-office, a real '70s mish-mash, including a massive stereo system and record collection to match. Tam jabs the air with his finger, telling everyone who's boss, just in case we forgot. Then, like someone's done a brain transplant on him, he's all sweetness and light as we file out. Mrs Paton fusses around us and asks if we'd like some chips for our dinner, and Tam's saying, 'Yes, that's fine. You go ahead.' We all nod and say, 'Yes please, Mrs Paton' and say hi to Tam's dad, the retired coal miner, as he sits in his armchair. After he says hello, he hawks a humongous black ball of phlegm into the spittoon that sits by the hearth.

The rehearsals go okay. I try to fit in, do what's expected of me. I've just turned 17, in the company of grown-ups. At 18, Les is the nearest to me in age (but still 100 years older and more assured), Eric is 20, Derek coming up on 23 and Al is the old man of the band at an inconceivably ancient 25. I can feel my shyness has me in its paws, but the guys make me welcome. Occasionally, they'll laugh and joke, but it's not exactly Morecambe and Wise in there. If someone drops something, misses a note or comes in late, they just start up again, straight-faced. I'm jumping in with the chord changes I picked up from watching in the wings.

Les, the other 'new boy', doesn't get involved so much. He skulks in the corner, not paying attention, reading the paper, making a show of being disinterested. I first met him in the dressing room a couple of weeks ago. My first impression was that he was a bit obnoxious, a little bit full of himself, but when he got on stage, I understood the appeal immediately. He was great. It was like he flipped a switch and became this great showman, so maybe he doesn't feel the pressure the way I do, I'm thinking. Then Mrs Paton calls everyone to the house for their chips and I stay behind a while to figure out one of the guitar parts, because I don't want to be seen to be doing it wrong. Also, I've been designated as the new Rollers keyboard player, so I'm fiddling around on this electric piano, learning those parts too.

I get the bus down to the tatty shed every day for two weeks. It's seven hours a day, working much harder than I ever did at school or during my apprenticeship. It's like Rollers bootcamp. Al drops a note, Eric throws him a look like, *Come on man*, and then a string snaps and it's the same. Eric is the most accomplished musician here by a mile and he's also the most serious-minded. He's got a proper artistic temperament to boot – the soul of a poet and all that. He's the guiding hand behind everything. Derek and Alan are well-drilled and they follow his cues. A couple of days of drilling though and we're suddenly in tune with each other. Eric isn't giving out so many disappointed looks and you can sense we're onto something. We're working hard on the harmonies – Eric, Al and me – and our voices are blending nicely with Les. Even Tam comes down from his office bedroom from time to time, and kind of grunts that it might be okay, or not too bad at least. Musically speaking, I don't think Tam gives a shit. The music side of things doesn't interest him, but he's got a sharp eye. The music could be dreadful and his only comment would be about your trousers not being tight enough.

On the final day, we play the Rollers live set, start to finish, and it's genuinely brilliant. Not brilliant like we thought we were in Freezin' Heet, but actual brilliant. I reckon now I should be fine for the next show in Doncaster, my debut performance with an actual top 40 band. Before that, though, there's the small matter of a little TV appearance to get out the way.

Chapter 4

TOP OF THE POPS

I was still staring out of classroom windows when it happened, but after 'Keep on Dancing' was a hit for the guys in 1971, it looked like the Rollers were going to go from strength to strength. I was not tuned in to pop music particularly, but even I was aware of them at the time. You couldn't listen to Radio Luxembourg without hearing something by the Rollers, but a couple of follow-up singles – 'We Can Make Music', 'Mañana' and 'Saturday Night', a proper foot-stomper of a tune – all stalled outside the UK chart, so this new single is probably going to be make or break for the band. And now for me too. The single, 'Remember (Sha-La-La-La)', is written by the Rollers' songwriting team, Bill Martin and Phil Coulter, the guys behind a handful of proper smash-hit Eurovision songs ('Congratulations' and 'Puppet on a String'), and the song is about to turn the band's fortunes around.

There are copies out there with Nobby's original vocal, but after he walked the plank, the new Les vocal was added and now it's selling hand over fist, motoring towards the top ten. People are hearing you on the radio, getting it trapped in their brains like a mind virus, then getting on buses, walking into town, going into Woolworths or their local record shop and handing over their hard-earned cash for a copy, getting the bus home, running upstairs and putting it on their wee Dansette. It's a commitment right there. Thirty thousand or so people must have done that already, just to get the record knocking on the door of the hit parade, and they're still doing it, driving the record up the chart. While we're rehearsing, news filters through to the potato shed that we're travelling to London for *Top of the Pops* to put on a wee show for the ten million or so people who'll be watching BBC1 on Thursday. Aye, we all say. Sounds good.

In the coming days, Tam calls our house maybe a dozen times, clucking mother hen that he is. He speaks with my mum and it's all on the pretext of seeing that I'm okay. The guys tell me to get used to that. Really, he doesn't want to know you're okay at all. He only calls because he can't see you and he wants to know you're not off down the pub or getting into mischief. I'm too young for the pub and am not the least bit interested in drinking. I got leathered at a New Year's party when I was fifteen and spent the following week thinking I was going to die of alcohol poisoning, so I'm hardly likely to start drinking now, but Tam talks to us all like he just caught us filling a trolley at the off-licence. Frankly, the calls are bemusing. These little volleys of high-pitched anxiety, seeing if he can flex his power from across town. I finish scraping the potato mud from my shoes, take the phone from my mum and she stands back. Tam tells me to be ready tomorrow when the van comes for me and I go back to my room, lie on my bed with a couple of comics, staring up at the skylight.

Next morning, crack of dawn, I'm waiting by the kerb patiently, with my life packed into my wee bag. The van pulls up, Tam rolls down his window and tells me to hurry it up. I'm the last pick-up, so it's heaving in there. Eric and Alan up front with Tam, Les and me in the back, and Derek sprawled out on this sofa chair with its legs lopped off the corners. There's a pile of coats and the like, and Les is across those, cigarette in hand, so it's literally standing room only. There's some gear and everyone's bags all over the floor, so I'm standing to attention, hanging on to the sides of the van for dear life as we pull away. Despite our time rehearsing, me coming out of my shell a little, I'm too new, too shy to ask anyone to budge up and make room. Truth to tell, I'm a little bit in awe and don't know where I am in the pecking order, so I figure I'll stand for hours on end, working on this crick in my neck that's gonna throb for the whole next day rather than create a fuss.

When we stop at a greasy spoon a couple of hours later, we get 20 minutes to stretch and yawn. We eat something nasty, wipe the ketchup from our lips and, as we file back into the van, I wedge myself back into the same uncomfortable position as before. The guys are all looking at each other. There's a hush, then Derek says, 'Hey Woody. Are you not gonna sit down?' Everyone laughs and I feel myself flush red. I shift a couple of things, make a wee seat for myself and the next six hours isn't so bad, thank God, following the A-roads down to the M6 and then, finally, the M1 to take us down to London.

First stop is Bell Records' offices in west London to meet the label boss, Dick Leahy. Bell is the home of the Rollers, and a host of pop acts, all troubling the charts: Showaddywaddy, the Glitter Band, the Partridge Family and their boy-next-door pop sensation, David Cassidy. We're shepherded around the place, meeting the head of A&R, the publicity people. It's overwhelming, gladhanding people, knowing I'm never going to remember anyone's name or face. Alan tells me we're on 5 per cent, or thereabouts, and I understand that. It means every time someone spends a pound on a Rollers record, we get 5 pence. But then Derek tells me it's not like that, and suddenly it becomes dead confusing. It's 5 pence, but also it's not 5 pence, because there's a line of people from here to the coast who take a cut from our 5 pence before it makes its way to us and then gets divvied up six ways, one-sixth for each of us, and one for Tam. We're up in this wood-panelled boardroom, getting our hair ruffled and our cheeks squeezed, and I'm spying all these gold discs on the wall and cut-glass decanters of scotch, gin and brandy, and wooden boxes of Montecristo cigars they bought with the other 95 pence from every pound.

Then we're whisked out onto the steps for our press photograph, the first with Les and me in the line-up. Tam says, 'You want to be Stuart or Woody?' I mull it over for a minute. There's a lot of guys called Stuart in the world. Not so many are called Woody – there's just me and Woody Woodpecker – so it's an easy decision. 'Woody,' I tell him, and he scribbles that down on the back of his hand. I look fuckin' terrible in the photo, by the way.

Late afternoon, we draw up to our digs near Paddington station. Not a nice hotel. One of those places that's named after a pack of ciggies. Something like, the Embassy, maybe. Clean, but unfussy. Narrow wallpapered corridors and stairways. Lopsided signs on the wall telling you no guests after 4pm, no smoking in your bed, breakfast from 7 'til 9. Snooze you lose. We all creak past the landlady with our bags. Tam's standing in the hallway, telling us who's bunking with who. Everyone has a shared room. He's worried about what he calls 'hanky-panky'. He talks about it all the time, like it's an obsession. Probably half the journey down is Tam telling us what Brian Epstein taught him, and the other half is him explaining that if you get a girlfriend, it'll ruin you. 'You'll be like snow off a dyke,' he says, meaning you'll be gone before you even know it. We've been in London maybe three hours, and he's been in constant fear of one of us finding a girl somewhere, somehow, and sneaking her upstairs past the landlady. As a result, none of us gets a room of our own. Alan whispers something to me, putting me in the picture. We always double up in hotels, he tells me. Different roommate every night, he says, so there's no 'palsy walsy' going on. I don't know what that's about. Maybe it means he doesn't want us getting too friendly with each other. He doesn't want any alliances forming. If we get too attached to each other, that means we're less inclined to listen to him, maybe, but I don't know. I have a better understanding of the inner workings of Spider-Man's life than I do Tam Paton's.

As we ascend the stairs, we're told to stay in our rooms until our tea, but Les and me make a break for it and run down to Paddington Underground station. It's like being in a film. I'm walking down the steps into the station, eyes wide, never seen the like before. We're mad giggling, desperate to explore this new world. Like, should we? Ach, why not? Between us, we scramble together a few coins, get a ticket from a machine, and just go round and round on the Circle Line for a while, seeing the names of all these places we never saw before: Hammersmith, Shepherds Bush, High Street Kensington, Ladbroke Grove and imagining what's up there, wondering what kind of folk live there. We don't get off the train until it arrives back at Paddington. You see, we're tricky, but we're not delinquents. Even so, it's like a whole new world. Just being in London, it feels like a mad adventure. We manage to get back without Tam noticing our absence.

When he knocks for us later, we're standing by our beds like good soldiers, and we walk out and find a place to eat. Just around the first corner, we shuffle into a restaurant and I'm sitting at the table, smelling all these strange aromas drifting out from the kitchen, wondering what the chips are like. Someone points something out on the menu and I'm scrunching my nose up, looking at all this foreign food, wondering if it'll kill me. It's not beef stew or mince and tatties, it's not chips or fish fingers, but after the excitement of the Circle Line and in the spirit of trying something new, I decide to give this new thing a go. Apparently it's called pizza, and I highly recommend it.

Next day is the *Top of the Pops* recording. Already I have butterflies just thinking about it. Only a month ago, I'd have been watching *Top of the Pops* at home with my family, so you'll understand when I say I can hardly contain my excitement. We need to jump through a few hoops first, though. There are these old rules at play at the BBC. It's all tied up with the Musicians' Union, making sure everyone who plays on the record gets their due. It's a complex business, but the long and the short of it is, you can't play along to your own record on *Top of the Pops*. You still mime, but it's got to be a different version. It's all bureaucracy, so way beyond my ken, but we're escorted to a studio and given three hours to re-record 'Remember' for broadcast, with every note and every harmony overseen by a delegate from the union. He's up in the control booth with the engineer, not paying attention, just smoking ciggies, and we're down on the studio floor wondering what's the point, but we get through the three hours and are taken back to the dressing room with a star on the door. We're all bantering, thinking this is all dead exciting. Tam's fidgeting nervously, telling us not to misbehave, like we ever would.

There are occasional knocks on the door. First, an old dear arrives with a trolley, a tea urn and some drab BBC biscuits. Now and again, a 30-year-old guy from the Home Counties with a plum in his mouth will stick his nose around the door to tell us it's time for the first run-through. We head down to the studio in our civvies and that's 20 minutes while they sort out all the camera angles, and then we're walked back to the dressing room. The tea lady comes back with some sandwiches. Tam checks his watch. We all get changed into our stage outfits – numbered red baseball jerseys, bebop shoes and white trousers, plus stripey socks from Chelsea Girl, because it appears to be a rule that you can't get anything other than grey, black or brown socks in any men's clothes shops.

There's another knock at the door. Dress rehearsals now. Same thing as before, but now we're looking the part. Then it's back to pacing the dressing room. It's been hours, but then suddenly it's showtime and you've no idea where the time went. We're ushered along these corridors, passing all these dressing rooms – Queen, Gilbert O'Sullivan, the Hollies, none of whom bother to look out as we pass. All the BBC folk are smoking pipes, these tweedy guys, wearing arran sweaters or cardigans with leather patches sewn on the elbows, pens behind their ears and clipboards held to their hearts. They all report to some ex-RAF colonel who came up through the Gang Show and found himself in the west London suburbs, overseeing this bright, brash explosion of youth on the telly once a week. It's a strange place to find yourself when you're 17. Looking on from your sofa at home, you think it's a big party, but it's this regimented thing instead, like you wandered into the cardigan section of your mum's Freemans catalogue.

Just as we're walking up to the stage, Tam's keeping pace with us, giving us his notes. Smile. Wave. Move about for god's sake. Look out for the red light. Follow the cameras. We're all nodding, saying, 'Yes, Tam.' The audience is being herded from one part of the studio over to our corner and we're on. Tonight's host, the DJ Emperor Rosko, says, 'Here's the Bay City Rollers . . .' and you can hear the backing track start up and suddenly it's happening. A week out from the tatty shed and I'm on the telly. The butterflies in my belly are doing somersaults now. I'm miming the keyboards and thanking God for that. If I were playing, genuinely playing, I think the nerves would have got the better of me. I mean, I can play the keyboard okay. I can certainly do what I need to get by, but I'm not a keyboard player by any stretch. Thankfully, I understand immediately this isn't the same thing as playing live. You can't play any bum notes. No one's gonna hear you if you get the words wrong. It's as if there's no real pressure, so no nerves. You'd think that, anyway. The truth is, when you see the red light, you can't help thinking there's ten million people looking at you.

I don't read the papers, I don't watch the news, but even I know it's a grim time out there. All that optimism from the 1960s, the screaming girls and joy of it all, was getting swept away under a grey tide. Strikes and terrorism, rubbish piling up. The world's a miserable place suddenly. The streets are violent, bloody places and, sure, you can put on a great coat and listen to Deep Purple and Led Zeppelin if you like, but maybe the world's plenty dark already. Suddenly, there are these five fresh-faced guys, a splash of colour and I don't know exactly, but maybe we're bringing a bit of joy to the world, something pure. When I think about that, I don't want this moment to end. Simultaneously, if you think about those ten million people too closely, suddenly you're a mess of insecurities, wondering if you look like an idiot, and you're just hoping for the experience to be over. Then it's finally finished. The cameras peel away, the girls in the audience turn toward the next stage and you're standing there thinking, *Was that it?* The guy with the cardy and the clipboard comes back to take us away. Back to the dressing room and the last of the biscuits. We're just another band. This is just another Thursday. To him, anyway. We're smiling, patting ourselves on the back, chuffed as fuck. But the truth is, none of us has any idea what's about to happen.

Chapter 5

MECCA

A couple of days after my first *Top of the Pops*, we're bombing down south in a Ford Granada, Tam Paton at the wheel. The rest of us are crammed in, legs and arms entwined, like one of those monkey puzzles. These guys have been doing this for seven years now, so they're all old hands, blasé about the whole thing, but I'm still feeling my way. The chat is low key, not exactly Alan Bennett. What was on the telly last night, this and that. Then they go quiet for a couple of miles. If our car passes a pretty girl, maybe someone will point her out and say, 'Check her out!' Up front, Tam will bristle and tell us to behave ourselves, but we'll all crane our necks to catch a look.

A short rest stop, pulling over at a shop to get some crisps and a comic. The guys are sporadically chatting (we ran out of telly talk as we passed into England), passing the morning paper to each other, and I'm studying the new issue of *Spider-Man* – Peter

Parker getting into all kinds of scrapes. I'm sitting in the back with Alan, elbow to elbow. I warmed to him immediately when I was working as a roadie, so I'm stuck to him like glue now. I realise already you can tell Alan your worst joke and he'll still find it funny. He's laid back, warm and gentle. Always well mannered, minding his p's and q's. He's a restful presence, brings your blood pressure down just by being there.

A lot of miles still to travel, feeling a bit icky from the motion of the car and one too many chocolate bars probably. I don't think I'm getting first-night nerves, but I'm getting antsy, squirming in my seat, wondering when we're going to stop for a pee, but I don't want to draw too much attention to myself, so I wait. 'Stops every two hours,' says Tam, so I cross my legs and hold it in. Then we stop for our dinner at the Whirly services – that's what we call it, this *Star Trek*-looking flying saucer building on the M6.*

Everyone creaks out of the car, stretches their legs a while and we order some food, a bunch of longhairs milling about with an army of hefty truckers and van drivers. The guys have got no airs and graces. They hoover up their dinner in seconds, mouths open, meat and veg hanging out the sides of their gobs as they prepare the next giant forkful of grub. There's Derek lining up his last row of peas on his knife and pouring them down his throat, standing up and patting his belly, and I've barely taken my first bite. I wonder what's the hurry, then look up and Tam's tapping the face of his watch getting me to hurry things up. Tam's in charge, always. He says go; we go.

* Forton Services, now known as Lancaster Services.

The final stretch and the guys are getting bored now, yawning, the chatter is at an end, but I'm still gawping out the window like a tourist. It's not Route 66 exactly, but there's a weird glamour to it all. I only ever heard of Doncaster when they were reading the names of the teams on the classified football results on the wireless and I'm checking the pools coupon for my dad. Same with Leeds. All these exotic new places that existed down south. Just driving past the signposts on the A74 saying Carlisle or Lancaster or wherever, and these towns, in my mind at least, shine like stars in their own firmament. It might just be a single night south of the border, back in the car when we're done and in Edinburgh by 2 or 3 in the morning, but I feel like I'm embarking on this grand tour. Seventeen and I'm off to see the world, kind of thing. Then, as afternoon drifts into twilight, we pull into Doncaster and find ourselves around the back of the venue, climbing out, creaking bones, and wandering through the back door to the dressing room, choking back the taste of last night's cigarette smoke. It's so dark, so dead here. It only comes alive when the people pay their money and come in. I see in the corner that one of the cleaners is smacking a mop into a drift of last night's puke, sending the stink of disinfectant around the whole room, and I can feel the sting in the back of my throat.

We all shout hi to Jake, seeing as he's nearly done setting up the gear and he looks up from his noodling spiral of wires to grin. Just a few cables to find. Hurry up and wait, we're told, so we're back in the dressing room, kicking our heels while they test the PA is working okay. Under flickering strip fluorescents, we dump our bags in front of the dressing table, help ourselves to a pack of crisps and a Coke from the meagre rider and grab a pew. Les and Eric spark up a ciggie, fill the room with blue-grey smoke, and that blots out the smell of the Dettol and last night's stale beer for a time. Someone calls by with some tea and says to me they love the accent after I say thank you. I never thought about it before. I'm thinking, 'What accent?' I didn't know I had one.

Then, finally, we're called out to soundcheck. Line checking: drums, then bass, guitars, keyboards and, finally, the microphones. One-two-three-four. Testing. This-is-mic-number-one. Isn't this a lot of fun? Then back to the dressing room. Chomp on a few more crisps. Sip the flat Coke. Listen out for the sound of the doors opening and the people coming in. A couple at first, and you can hear their voices through the walls. Then louder. A few dozen people now, and the voices are noisier, but less distinct, and then it's hundreds, and the noise is just a constant loud hum, like the sound of an airliner engine ticking over. You can't see it, but you can tell somehow, like it's a primal sense, and you just know the place is heaving with bodies on the other side of the wall. The only way I can describe it is to talk about the exact opposite feeling – the sensation of being outdoors, in acres of space, no one around you. The feeling is the opposite of that. A little intimidating maybe, claustrophobic even, but none of the band's feathers are getting ruffled. It's like water off the proverbial duck's back to these guys, so I follow their lead and feign nonchalance, my ear cocked to the wall.

The disc jockey, this guy Dave Eager, is getting the crowd hyped up, spinning something from the charts on the wheels of steel, and suddenly, there's a change in temperature almost, like someone dialled up the thermostat. Beyond this wall, it's a nightclub now, fizzing and alive, and I can feel something in the pit of my stomach. I'm strumming on a battle-hardened Fender Telecaster, checking I'm in tune, holding it up to my ear. Alan doing the same with his bass, holding it to my ear, then Eric's, and depending on the vibration, we decide whether he's good to go or not. The Fender used to be John Devine's but, somehow, it's mine now and I'm feeling the part suddenly.

A minute ago, we were five Edinburgh guys, playing cards and smoking, knocking back bottles of cola, and now, we're the Bay City Rollers, riding high in the charts and coming to a Mecca Ballroom near you. I can hear the DJ beyond the wall, between songs. 'Are ye ready for the Rollers?', and there's a wave of girls cheering, a few proper screams, a chorus of 'We want the Rollers!'. My guts do a wee cartwheel inside of me and I can feel a sort of electric tingling sensation pass through me – proper bona fide excitement. There are slight nerves, but they're offset by the adrenaline of the moment, and the music dies down, and the low hum starts getting louder. There's genuine delight out there as we shuffle out of the fluorescent light of the dressing room to the side of the stage. I'm holding the Fender up to my chest, finding a vantage point where I can see the crowd, getting a waft of their perfume, but they can't see me. And then, after what feels like a month, my mouth turning dry as a bone, Dave Eager announces, 'Ladeeez and gentlemen, the Bay . . . City . . . Rollers' and then it's pure bedlam.

It's 9pm now and here I am suddenly, standing in front of a glittery backdrop, like a tinsel waterfall, and under a couple of blinding spotlights, catching these tiny rays in my eyes as they bounce off the mirror ball. There's an ultraviolet light and I can see everyone's teeth, the clean ones anyway, and their white collars and blouses stand out against the blackness. Then, as I shift focus, Les shouts a throaty 'Hello', stomps around the stage like a precocious toddler and the band strikes up. I'm looking beyond the front rows of girls now because, as Tam says, you always play to the back of the room. Then I feel the earth move, or maybe the dancefloor creaking. Anxious, excited faces look up in the darkness and it's suddenly a million miles from the Odeon and the sugar-high 10-year-old kids chucking their sweets at us.

Les is running all over the stage, covering a lot of acres. He's kind of milking it, but knows what he's doing, and the audience is right there in the palm of his hand. Eric, you can see, he's not having that entirely, and he's doing his best to keep some of the spotlight for himself. Derek and Alan, like me, are just happy to be there. We don't need to be centre stage. It's fine here on the fringes and we burn through the 60-minute set in the time it takes me to stop and take another breath. 'Remember', the new single, a raft of covers, 'CC Rider', 'Shout' (the old Lulu song), '(Sittin' On) The Dock of the Bay', a couple of 12-bar tunes, the instrumental theme from *A Clockwork Orange* to give Les's tonsils a break, then an encore of 'Keep On Dancing' and it's thank you and good night. The curtain falls. The place goes mad and we're sneaking out the back door as the disco starts up again. It feels like it was a good show. We're all grinning, but I couldn't tell you if we were bad or good, because of the noise from the crowd and from the stage. Whatever the case, it felt immense. My heart is racing. My brain is overwhelmed with emotion – relief that it's over, but also a feeling I could get back out there right now and do it all over again.

I'm pouring with sweat and the adrenaline pumps through my system for two hours after. In the dressing room and in the car heading back north, I'm totally wired, ecstatic from doing the show, feeling that excitement pass from us to the crowd and then back again, like a neat electrical circuit. Tam does his best to bring us down, to deflate us. He doesn't tell us what a great show that was. 'Les, you were great. Woody, you did a good job there.' Nothing like that. I've no idea if he thinks he's doing us a service here, bringing us back to reality, or if he just likes to piss us off. We're not exactly celebrating, but we're happy, a job well done, but I guess he doesn't want us too happy. As the miles tick by, he's going from one of us to the other, breaking down the performance into these wee poisonous soundbites.

'Woody. You're standing there like a statue. Move about. Fuckin' wave. Fuckin' smile.'

I can feel my energy starting to wane, like air being squeezed out of a balloon. He does the same to all of us and we just sit there and take it. By the time we reach the outskirts of Edinburgh, I'm completely drained, cold from sitting in my own sweat for the past hour, climbing the stair, off to my bed. A pop star now – delighted but also dead miserable somehow. I pull the string contraption along the skirting, turn the light off and settle down for a joyless night's sleep.

Chapter 6

RISE

Spring 1974

Couldn't sleep last night. First time on a plane today. Rocking up to Edinburgh's Turnhouse airport for a flight down to London for another *Top of the Pops*. I get sharp elbows going down the aisle, making sure of a window seat for myself. Alan tells me to check to make sure the window's closed and I laugh at the thought of getting sucked out of the plane at 20,000 feet. I'm staring out this tiny wee porthole, imagining the world getting smaller and smaller when we take off, wondering if I'll be able to see my house from up there. Certainly, it's better than coming down to the smoke in a van, standing half the way because I'm too shy to cause a fuss.

Across the aisle, Tam is rambling on about something or other. No girls, he says, for the millionth time. 'You're untouchable,' he tells us. He means it literally. No girlfriends in the band. According to Tam's logic, if we dated, we'd seem less available to our fans who all dreamed that we could be their boyfriends. That's the story, the thing Tam says all the time, but the truth is, he doesn't want anyone getting close, getting in our ears. I think it's controlling at first, and it is, but it's insecurity too. He doesn't want some sharp-suited London shark, some Denmark Street spiv, coming into our world and dazzling us with ideas of the wider world because that'll take us away from him and then he's in control of nothing and no one. He's a strange fucker, all told. Half of what he says is pure poison, dripping in your ear like warm olive oil, but I'm looking at him now, grinning like a fuckin' pools winner.

Then the pilot comes over the intercom, giving us our flight time. We're just about to take off. The stewardess walks up and down the aisle, handing out bags of peanuts and checking we're strapped in. In his seat, Tam starts flapping his arms like a fat turkey, like he's pretending he's flying, getting us off the ground just through the sheer force of his will, pulling these strained faces like he's on the outside of the plane. I'll be honest, it's funny. This first time and maybe the time after that. He does the same when we go for a meal in a restaurant, grabbing a folded cotton napkin, putting it on his head and declaring, 'It's just like a party!' Sometimes you get the idea he's loving it as much as we are. Whatever you want to say about the guy, the Bay City Rollers are as much his passion as ours. Every time someone tells him it's not gonna happen, he's more determined and digs his heels in further. He sold his car to keep things going once. The thing was probably a wreck, but he did do that.

Landing at Heathrow, Bill, our chauffeur, picks us up in a stately black limousine, talks Cockney to us a while, and we try to decipher what he's saying while we're whisked to Broadcasting House to talk shite with the drive-time DJ before retiring to the hotel. Not some pokey dive in the back streets of west London this time. A new thing from the States, a cracker of a hotel. It's called a Holiday Inn and it's a notch or three up from Mrs Whatever-her-name-is and her grim Paddington bed and breakfast. We're down the M4 in Slough, pronouncing the word as Sluff, just for fun. There's none of that *Smashing Time* kind of vibe from before – Les and me jumping on the Circle Line and getting our bearings, giving Tam palpitations if he can't find us. Mainly because there's nowhere to go. There are no landmarks here, save for cows mooning about in fields, but it's fine by me. We lay out on the bed and light our own farts. We watch cine films on a projector because we're landlocked here and going out is just going to cause a fuss. We still share rooms, but no one knows we're here. There are no girls, just an army of businessmen, doing whatever it is that businessmen do. I take a dip in the pool and sprawl out on a big bed. There's not a big selection on the room service menu, but I check that they have sirloin steak and chips and a can of Coke or Fanta. I make sure to speak clearly when ordering, as last time out, the room service guy brought me up a plate of steak and CHOPS, blaming my accent for the error. I didn't realise until now that Scots were the only people who had one.

Routine now. Not quite famous, but we're here in the foothills, gazing up at the mountain. If I'm honest, I don't think I even want to be famous. I'm a daydreamer, sure, but my daydreams are the same as they were before. I'm a character in a film about this band, the Bay City Rollers. I don't need the trappings. I want to play, to be on stage, to experience everything, but it's like being a coal miner. You're going to get dirty, whether you like it or not – and I'm going to be famous. I've just got to get my head around it because every day it's something. I'm rarely at home anymore, as drear winter bleeds into spring. If I am, I'm either sleeping or answering the phone, eyelids getting heavy, telling Tam, 'Yes, yes, I am here. Nothing to worry about. No girls here.' Or I'm standing at the kerb, waiting for the car, the long drive – usually – south. With shows now every night, we're suddenly the toast of clubland. Every night in the provinces is packed to the rafters. Probably we could be playing theatres, big shows in every town and city, but these dates have been in the diary since last year and disentangling ourselves from those cast-iron contracts would be a nightmare.

The thing that's happening around me is something like hysteria, but not full-on. But even here in the foothills, everyone's wanting a piece of me – newspapers, magazines, radio. I'm knackered and could sleep for a week, but am somehow still happy to give them what they want because I'm seeing the results all around me. If I'm not home in my bed, I'm London-bound, staying in the same digs, falling into bed, dog-tired. Maybe I get a minute to call home and tell my mum I'm in the paper, but most times, I'm too tired even for that. I close my eyes, ears still ringing from that night's show, and a minute later there's the wake-up call for breakfast. We're trudging downstairs, eyes half-closed, carrying our bags, dressed up in our stage gear from reveille until bedtime tonight. At the foot of the stair, there's Tam standing in reception, checking the time, frowning. We don't wear regular clothes anymore. We've each got two or three outfits, alternating every other day because it's stage gear all the time now – and often it's carrying the last traces of last night's sweat. There's more salt in my jersey than you get in a pack of Golden Wonder. Usually, I'll give it a wee sniff test and hope it will be okay until I get home, when my mum can put it in the wash.

In the weeks following that first appearance on *Top of the Pops*, it's like the heat's been turned up and we skipped 'simmer' and went straight to 'boiling'. The single, 'Remember', has climbed to number six in the charts and we're asked back again. Radio 1 DJ Greg Edwards is hosting this time, but it's the same guys with cardigans and clipboards guiding us through the corridors. There are stars on the dressing room door. We're miming again, but we're old hands now. Tam's there, fretting, keeping us on lockdown in the dressing room, handing out his usual instructions across the paper plates of sandwiches: smile, wave, eye on the red light. Follow the camera, he says, so we do. But after he sees us all leaning forward, like drunk sailors in a stiff breeze, trying to maintain eye contact with the ten million people sitting at home, one of the cameramen tells us maybe we don't need to follow the camera so closely.

This time, we're on with Olivia Newton-John and Alvin Stardust, and there's Pan's People dancing along to the latest David Bowie record. In the meantime, we're back and forth. Gigs everywhere, but you're never heading in a straight line now. It's deceptive. We stop off at a red phone box, Tam piles in a pocketful of change and gets the latest update from the record company, or he's checking in with his mum in Prestonpans to see if there's been any calls. We set out for one place, and every time there's a detour along the way you knew nothing about. We don't know what's happening from one minute to the next. I'm like a dog getting taken to the beach in your dad's car – completely clueless about the logistics of getting from point A to point B, I'm just happy to arrive and to run about in the salt air a while. We just know Tam's got his itinerary, and it's covered in scribbled biro with these new additions to the schedule. There's no point asking if we're nearly there yet because we're forever being diverted to a local radio station and shoved into a studio, chatting a bit with the presenter for a minute or two as he plays the record, or even the next one, or plugs that night's show.

Six months ago, probably no one was interested in my opinion on anything, but you're speaking to the guy at Radio Clyde or Piccadilly or whatever and he wants to know what you think about something and it's a curious feeling. Once he's given the whole, 'Thanks guys . . . that's the Bay City Rollers there . . .', the DJ takes a wee bite of donut, wipes away the crumbs and rounds up last night's sports action, starts checking his notes for the rest of the show and the producer gives us the nod that the red light is off. I take off my headphones and, over the sound of the jingles, we file out, nod our thanks to the DJ (name and face forgotten, literally the second I exit the studio) and we're back on our feet, running through reception. Les and Eric might give a wee glance back at the girl at the desk, but then it's back in the car or the van and finally on to the venue. It's mad and exciting, but at the same time, it's like a full day's work before you even get to the stage. Pulling up in a northern town, under smoking chimney stacks, in through the back door, soundcheck, back to the hotel, Tam telling us who we're bunking with tonight, maybe a bite to eat, play the show, back to the hotel. Rinse and repeat as necessary.

Meantime, the record company is preparing to put out a new single, 'Shang-A-Lang', and there's the small matter of an album, to capitalise on the success of 'Remember'. When I arrive on the scene, there are five tracks already in the can. Much as we'd done with Les re-recording the vocal for 'Remember', I go into Mayfair Studios in London with our producers, Bill Martin and Phil Coulter, to record new harmonies and whatnot on a few songs – 'Summer Love Sensation', 'Remember', 'Shang-A-Lang', etc.

It's my first time in the studio, but there's not a lot of time for me to stop and smell the roses. There's a show later – because there's always a show later – and time is money apparently. We're driven up to the studio, Tam in our ear, his words hanging in the air like shitty cologne, whisked past the kid on reception and rushed down to the studio floor and I'm introduced to Bill and Phil. I'm still as green as you can get, so despite their legendary status, I don't know them from Adam. I just arrived at this new place and got told this is where I'm meant to be today, and I'm just there wagging my tail. I don't know if it's down to their reputation though, or if it's just because I'm generationally disposed to respecting my elders, but I get the idea they know what they're doing and I'd be best served by listening to them. Anyone over the age of 25 seems dead old to me, so I always give them credit for knowing better than me. It's the same when I'm at a TV studio, or in some other unfamiliar environment. I'm still learning the ropes, so I figure I'll follow their lead and hopefully I won't go far wrong.

Phil Coulter is this laid-back Irishman, a slight twinkle in his eye. He's more the music guy, and quite animated, full of enthusiasm. He's dressed casual but authoritative. Blue jeans, three-button cardigan, like the fellas at Television Centre, with a flary-collared-shirt and tie underneath. Bill is more business-like, a suited-and-booted Glaswegian fella with a shirt and tie under a fisherman's jumper. He's the man with his eye on the money side of things, the nuts, the bolts. His eye is on the clock, always alert to how many feet of tape is getting used. Once we get started, it's clear Phil's got his way of doing things. He likes the shuffle sound. Maybe throw a high voice in the mix. It's over all our records just now, like it's his trademark sound. He and Bill are up in the glass control booth, hands on hips, drinking coffee out of polystyrene cups, while this bearded engineer – Frank Zappa T-shirt, never seen a comb in years – takes their instructions and hits 'record' every few minutes.

Aside from a quick hello, there's no meeting, no run-through. We're scattered to the four corners of the studio: Derek's drums are miked up, Alan and Eric are placed in another corner, and Les roams about the place, laying down a guide vocal. I'm stuck in my corner with an acoustic guitar and the engineer tells us to go for take one. I'm keyed up, determined to get it right. We're not multitracking here. The point, Phil explains, is to capture the energy of the band playing together. We can always overdub later – lay down a finished vocal and harmonies, maybe spruce things up a bit where required. Two minutes later, the engineer shakes his head. Phil and Bill are pacing the booth, saying something, looking unhappy. Then the intercom crackles to life. Nope, sorry guys. Someone missed something. Bum note or something. Take two. Same again. Take three. Find focus, Woody, I'm telling myself. I'm extra careful and hit every note bang on. I hit the last downbeat – *Da-Dannng!* – and it's done and I'm beside myself. Derek hits the final note on the cymbal and it's still ringing out. I'm looking around at the guys, beaming with pride, and I let out a shout, 'Ach, that was brilliant!', like I just scored a goal at the World Cup. I look up, still grinning, wondering why no one else is celebrating and everyone in the control booth has their head in their hands. Over the intercom, Phil patiently explains that I ruined the take with my outburst.

'Woody. You're meant to wait,' he says. 'Now do it again and keep your mouth shut this time.'

My first lesson learned there: always wait for the engineer to tell you that's a take. After that mishap, I'm the perfect student. I listen intently to what Phil and the engineer tell me and, in the same way I've adapted to appearing on telly, playing these packed-out shows or grinning for some photoshoot, I think I've got this now. We record a bunch of harmonies and I'm even called into action to record the lead vocal on one of our own songs, 'Just a Little Love'. I can harmonise with the best of them but, truly, I'm no singer. Still, the engineer gives me the thumbs-up and I'm straight on the phone to my mum telling her about it. 'I'm gonna be singing on the record, Mum!'

After the session, we're up in the booth. Phil and Bill are nodding along to the playback. First up on the big studio speakers, everything sounding loud and brash, full of colour and you can hear every note you played, every nuance of your harmonies. I'm fascinated by the process, watching every move, part of me wondering why it takes so long, but at the same time, completely involved. They're going up and down on the faders and it's like an episode of *Doctor Who* and they're steering the fuckin' Tardis. Then the engineer scratches together a makeshift mono mix, basically bouncing the track down through a single channel, and playing it through a tiny speaker that's been ripped out of a car stereo, so you can hear exactly what it's going to sound like when it's coming out of their television sets. When he clicks play on 'Shang-A-Lang', it sounds like a smash hit record. Really, I could stay here forever, I think, listening back, revelling in the joy of it all. I'm about to say something to that effect and there's a tap on my shoulder. The car's outside. Time to head off for tonight's show. Rinse and repeat.

If we're not playing a show – there are 300 in the diary for 1974, I hear – there's always something on the schedule. A meet-and-greet, a signing or maybe we're having dinner with the record company to celebrate our newfound glory. That's not my thing at all. I'm seventeen and there's a million things I'd rather do than put on a shirt and sit with a bunch of adult strangers in a corner of a restaurant somewhere in west London. The chat is so tedious, I could literally die. Plates of chips arrive at the table on silver salvers and they're talking about markets and territories and making a big push on the album. Two tellies this week, radio up the wazoo and half-a-dozen photoshoots with the girl magazines. My eyelids are drooping, like I'm at the back of the classroom again. I hear the first five or six words of every exchange, then start to drift away, hoping someone else will pick up the slack. I open my eyes again. No one noticed. Just a wee catnap for Woody. A small win. Alan's looking across the table at me, a smile on his lips. 'What do you think, Woods?' he asks, catching me on the hop. I can't help but laugh.

Alan is fast becoming my anchor here. He's the easiest company, like a ready-made pal, built to specification. Further along the table sits brother Derek, moving some food around his plate with the end of his fork, getting his ear soaked in spit by a marketing guy who's telling him he's going to be bigger than Ringo probably. I can see him trying and failing to not roll his eyes. Derek is quieter, less demonstrative, but he's friendly, unruffled. The two brothers treat me like family, making the transition from skinny kid to popstar seem more natural. Eric – mouthful of chips, ketchup on his lip – is deep in convo with the label head, Dick Leahy. Eric is harder to define in a snappy sentence. He's quietly forceful, especially now Les has joined the band. He's always on the ball and answers every question concisely, sometimes throwing a question back, like a cat among the conversational pigeons. Les, on the other hand, has no airs and graces. When the waitress comes by with a tray of colas, he's eyeing her every move and would have his head up her skirt if Tam wasn't beside him, resplendent in double denim, quietly fuming.

Alan and Derek's mum has been sick for a while now and the anxiety is written all over their faces. Whenever they paint on a smile for a camera, while the photographer reloads, you can see the worry is etched there, immovable – the same as it is here now, pressing the flesh, making the best of a bad job. They're like old-school brothers though, characters out of a dark film. They don't speak to each other at all, like they've a lifetime of shared toys and bickering behind them, a metric ton of brotherly bullshit to unravel, so they never say a word to each other. They're the only two of us who never share a room, the only two that Tam never worries about getting too 'palsy'. Derek hands out our wages every week and Alan will barely look up from the game of cards he's playing to acknowledge the wee brown envelope. It's not a blood feud. They don't hate each other, but there's a kind of baked-in resentment. Good old-fashioned sibling rivalry, but with a dose of mute Scots stoicism thrown in for good measure. I guess they've just spent so long together they've nothing more to say. I'm naïve, though, barely picking up on any of it: their dying mum, or the endless silence between them.

I'm watching this new record climb the charts, thinking this is my life from now until the day I collect my pension. We've a *Top of the Pops* booked for this week – my fourth appearance, so I'm fast becoming an old hand – and that's right at the front of my brain. We're back up the charts and down to London and then we get the news that the brothers' mum has passed. I hear them sobbing in their rooms at the hotel and I'm thinking maybe all bets are off now. A death in the family, even in my adolescent brain, means we'll have to change our plans, right? Well, no. We record our appearance on *Top of the Pops* – bumping shoulders with Roy Wood and Wizzard, Alvin Stardust and, fresh from winning Eurovision, this boy/girl Swedish group called Abba – Agnetha, the group's blonde singer tells me she's quite nervous; I'm quite the seasoned pro by now, so I tell her, 'Don't worry about it, you'll be fine'; little did we know they would soon be one of the biggest bands around – before flying directly back to Edinburgh for the funeral the next day. We're sitting in the limo with Alan and Derek, still crumpled from the flight, and I'm looking across at the brothers, trying their best to keep it together and wondering, *Is this normal?* I'm thinking, *We've a show tonight. We're going to postpone that, aren't we?* The car sweeps through the Edinburgh streets, kids crying on every corner, holding up their banners – 'Rollers Forever', 'We Love You Alan', that kind of thing – and it's like I'm waiting for someone to say, 'Don't worry, there's a contingency plan.'

Standing at the graveside at Saughton Cemetery – the casket being lowered into the grave and the brothers tossing flowers onto the coffin – I'm still waiting for that someone to step in and take over. *Take a week to lick your wounds guys. We've got this.* But no one's got this and it's pure grim. We're back in the limo, on to the next thing. No chance to go to the wake. No opportunity to commiserate with their relatives. It's just, *Get in the car now.* It's the saddest thing I think I've ever seen.

Chapter 7

FIRE IN THE PROVINCES

Chased into the venue, like the last men standing in a zombie movie, wondering how this became normal. When did society suddenly crumble around our ears? We're out the back of the van; it's brand-new but looks like a scuffed modernist work of art after two months on the road. The paintwork's been scrawled with 'I love Eric', 'Les Forever', 'Woody's a Dream', and Alan's this or that, and we're on the tarmac, breaking the lines of fans just to get into the venue. A couple of hefty guys in black suits and dickie bows, men who wouldn't look out of place on the Saturday-morning wrestling, start scything a path through the weeping teenage army and suddenly, breathlessly, we're scooped up into their arms and ushered to safety. Once the door is slammed behind us though, it's like someone's turned down the volume on a telly. You can hear the muted screams through the doors. You walk through the golden foyer, down a half-dozen steps into the darkness, here's the stage, wave hi to Jake, and on to the dressing room, cracking open a tin of cola, and the madness is forgotten. We examine the wreckage of our clothes, compare who's had their jacket torn and then we're in Roller mode. Out for a quick soundcheck and back to the dressing room, listening to the sound of the doors opening, the disc jockey playing the hits of the day and the swell rising like the North Sea around a rusted oil rig.

It's the same thing in Ireland, darting across the border, shows in the north and the south, place names you hear once and forget as soon as the last syllable landed on your ear. An endless run of farmers' balls, youth clubs and whatever the equivalent of a Mecca is here. Everyone's happy to see you because no one comes here. You can kind of see why. There's paramilitaries and all kinds of turmoil. A couple of hundred years of pent-up hatred and we're in the heart of it, waving and smiling. Some of us, mentioning no names, wearing ill-advised red, white and blue socks. I've my provisional driving licence now and Jake lets me drive the graffitied van around the hotel grounds a while, flooring it, spraying the sides with mud and shite, while he sits beside me, turning white, then green.

I'm summoned to Tam's room straight after. I saw his fuckin' curtain twitching and him peering out at the scene. I'm there getting the dressing-down. Half of me is thinking maybe I just stick my hand out and he'll give me the strap, like the teachers in primary, but instead he's wheezing like a space hopper that's sprung a leak, giving it the whole 'I can replace you in ten seconds flat' spiel he trots out at least once a week. Okay, I get it,

Tam. I'm expendable. We're all expendable. He gives Jake a bollocking, turns to me and says, 'You'll be like snow off a dyke. Out of here. I got a hundred guys who can replace you.'

Back on the mainland, there's a fire starting to burn in the provinces. The big cities are taking a little longer to catch light, but this thing – we don't have a word for it yet – is happening and I can feel it whenever we drive into a new city. There's something happening and the signs are everywhere, it seems. Well, not quite everywhere *all* the time, because I'm at a show and fast realising it's not for me. It's not an off day – we're giving it plenty. It's just that we're a bad fit for this place. It's Sheffield University, if you want to paint a picture in your head. Not quite dreaming spires here, but close enough. Grey, smoke-filled skies and students drifting in and out of the refectory, Pink Floyd albums under their army coats, and masters running around in polyester suits and National Health specs rather than Dracula capes and mortar boards. Everyone's chugging thick brown pints of student-union cask ale and getting biscuit crumbs in their Che Guevara beards. It's not my natural environment, put it that way. Put me in front of a Mecca audience and I know what to do, but this is a cool student crowd and they're sitting cross-legged, looking like they'd cheerfully storm the stage if they could be bothered to get up off their arses. If this was the colosseum, they'd have their thumbs turned down, urging the gladiator to deliver the coup de grace.

When they're not giving us daggers, they're fixated on this girl, the only person in the audience having a good time. If looks could kill, there's a few hundred students who'd get a life stretch right now. This girl doesn't care, though. She's in a world of her own and only has eyes for one person. Unfortunately, that person is me. She's screaming, 'Woody! I love you!' and I'm pure dying inside. Not that I mind people expressing their love for me, it's just that she's the only one making a sound. There are no polite ripples of applause; they're not even booing. There's just her, punctuating our set with her loud declarations of love. It's maybe the longest hour of my life: me wishing it would all be over, the guys pissing themselves laughing, and me thinking, *If Tam tells me to wave or smile, I won't be responsible for my actions*. Then Les says, 'Thank you Sheffield!' and we head back to the car and on to the Hallam Towers Hotel.

The girl's screams are still resounding in my ears the next day at breakfast. We bump into the Bee Gees in reception and have a good wee blether. They roll their eyes when I tell them about the lone screamer, like they've been there seen it done it themselves. I don't know if the breakfast has disagreed with me, but when we get back in the car to leave, I spew up all over Tam. A full-on, steaming technicolour broth drips off his denim suit as he hits the indicator and pulls the car over to the kerb. 'Fuck's sake, Woody,' he fumes. He shakes his hands dry, sending spatters of puke all up the inside of the Granada. It looks like a Jackson Pollock.

It's not been mentioned in the papers yet, but university campuses aside, there's something happening around us. There are screaming girls, practically everywhere I turn. There are girls all around the car whenever we arrive somewhere or when we leave, so now we walk straight off stage, leave our gear in the dressing room and we're straight into the car. It's been happening a while now, so it isn't exactly a new development for us and we're getting acclimatised, slowly. It's not like everyone just woke up one morning and decided to turn feral simply because the Rollers arrived. The world's changing around me – people feel freer, society's changing – but you scroll back through the decades and there are plenty of examples of the same hysteria. The Beatles, Elvis, all those guys, right back to Sinatra and the bobby-soxers, all swooning away. Still, it's new to me and it's a weird situation to get my head around. It was happening before in my roadie days. Not as big and it's grown since, but it was there. Jake and me would be setting up the stage and having some girl furiously tugging at the hem of my jeans while I fixed a cable or messed about with a lopsided cymbal.

Now it's every time and I'm not a roadie anymore. It's at the shows and in the streets too. When I come home after a show, I'm dropped off in a different street, finding a way through the tenements and clambering through back gardens like a fugitive. I don't know how they know where I am or where I'm going to be – maybe it's smoke signals or the jungle drums – but wherever I am, there's a band of girls waiting on me whenever I stick my head above the parapet. I think about this as I approach the back door, simultaneously untangling myself from the neighbour's washing line. There stands my dad, waiting patiently at the bottom of the stair, shushing me with a finger held to his lips. He's got his ear cocked, listening to the murmurs of the crowd of girls on the street outside. We wait a second, he gives me the 'all-clear' signal and we run up the stair, closing the door behind us, dad at the window, checking the street outside, like a spy in a Cold War film.

Our third hit of the year, 'Summerlove Sensation', is number three in the hit parade and it's a strange time. People were getting screamed at in the 1960s, but it's different now. It's still 16- and 17-year-old kids, but younger too, and we're like five guys arriving at a party and hanging our coats by the door just as there's this weird cultural explosion of girl's magazines, stoking the flames of the past few months, turning a few embers into a raging fire. *Jackie* or *Diane* or *Mates* or *Sixteen* or *Blue Jeans* or whatever, all these strange magazines the young girls read on the bus to school all need an airbrushed blue-eyed boy to put on the cover so your daughter will cough up 20p of her pocket money. David Cassidy is there. Donny Osmond too. Good-looking, clean-cut, non-threatening guys who had their own fair share of being plastered on the front page of every teeny-bop magazines.

Now there's the five of us, scrubbed clean and ready to go, and we go everywhere they want us, larking around in front of a camera for a couple of hours for a spread. It's all about the look, Tam's specialty, but maybe a dozen questions get thrown out, like scraps from a table. Nothing that's going to exert the grey matter too much. I don't know why they bother to talk to us, because when you see it printed up a month or six weeks later, it's all made-up. They slap Vaseline on the lens and plant us in these photo-love stories and write a story around the pictures with speech bubbles saying this and that and you're scratching your head wondering *What the fuck?* They know there are thousands of girls who love the Rollers, so they don't want to lose them. They splash us on the cover, knowing the fans will have to buy the latest issue. Every line of text is just an excuse to run a big colour photograph of one of us gazing dreamily into the camera. Maybe it's a kind of shellshock, but no one remembers doing any interviews. It's just 'likes' and 'dislikes', like on a questionnaire. It was probably filled out by someone at the record company, I'm thinking, because I didn't say half those things. It's all, Woody's favourite food, Alan's favourite drink, Eric's favourite colour, so it's not exactly *Parkinson*. Someone prints a story saying that I'm so afraid of the dark that I sleep with a teddy bear. Whenever we read a story, we're all laughing, ribbing each other. 'Les, I had nae idea you liked this or that' and he's snatching the magazine away saying, 'What the fuck?' I say one time that I like milk – and I do, I can drink it by the gallon – but everywhere we go now, there's someone handing us a pint with a little wink. Or if it's a press conference, there might be five jars of milk lined up in front of us like we're working for the Milk Marketing Board or fuckin' Unigate.

These are serious times, but we're pop, and we know it. It never crosses our mind to try to be anything else, so we play along with all the hullabaloo. We could insist on doing something heavy, something dead serious, but that's not what we are. No one's getting high-minded, thinking they're the big 'I am'. Most of us anyway. Maybe one or two are starting to think about where they sit in the grand scheme of things. It's just a slight sense of some folk jockeying for position, like someone with sharp elbows at a buffet with an eye on that last pork pie.

None of us is suggesting a stark black-and-white photograph, perhaps me in a smoking jacket, looking all serious – for the front of the next album. We're the boys next door. When we do a photoshoot, we're not rocking up with our guitars and leathers. We're getting dressed up as schoolkids, or we're sprawled about on rugs with cuddly toys – sexless wee boy angels who you could take home and introduce to your mum. The editor wants to photograph us on horses, looking all sweet, like a teenage girl's dream, and we just say, 'Aye, which way do we sit? Facing its arse or its head?' We're making it up as we go, learning the rules as we write them. We're puzzled but fine. It's the same as when we start getting namechecked in the agony aunt columns, and there's some kid in Cleethorpes or Guildford saying they love you and their heart is aching and you're racking your brains wondering what's happening.

That first time you see yourself gawping back from the cover of a magazine is an unsettling experience. The second time, too. Then there's a gear change and it's like anything where you get too much. That first sweet out of the bag is divine, but by the time you're halfway through them, your guts are doing cartwheels and you wish you'd stopped a while back. It's the same with newspapers. *Oh, I'm in the paper*. Then it's *Ugh, I'm in the paper*. The strange thing about the press is they don't need it to be true for them to print a story, but they're not the same benign white lies they tell in the teen mags about you liking puppies or something. The music papers will send a serious frowning bastard down from their Carnaby Street offices to review the show, and next week you open the *NME* (aka the Enemy) or *Melody Maker* and read that it was pure shite and no one had a good time. You were there. You saw the reaction from the crowd. It's bollocks but it's also kind of depressing.

You start the year full of optimism, just happy to be there. You'll answer every asinine question, pose for a million photographs and, without realising, you've started putting up these guards against the world, suspicious of everything. We do an interview in the Enemy, just the nicest chat. We're laughing and joking together and getting along like old friends. Next Wednesday, Eric passes me the new edition, shaking his head. We're there in the centre spread and it's full of absolute vitriol. These edgy bastards, I'm thinking. Failed musicians, every single fuckin' one of them.

After that, you don't pick up a paper again because you know no one's got a nice word to say about you. Or even a true one. You only need to look at the photos from the shows. We've the same fans as T.Rex, Slade, even Bowie, but it's as if they want to convince themselves we're this teenybopper band, with an army of nine-year-old kids who've fallen under our wicked spell or something. The first time I saw myself in the paper, I was so excited that I called my mum straight away. She started collecting all the cuttings. Every magazine, every newspaper. Just the slightest mention of me and the guys and she kept it. On the rare occasions I'm home, I leaf through them, but after a time, I can't bear to read another word. Even Tam tells us not to read that shite. Tomorrow's fish and chip wrapping, you know, that old cliché.

Now it's growing, we head down to Tam's parents sometimes and we're in Tam's room, all of us, with this big sack of fan mail.

Tam's there, almost using it as market research. He's learning as he goes, but he's a shrewd bastard too, realising that it's not just the Rollers, it's the five individuals too. In the first letter I read from someone I never met before – and likely I never will – she's telling me, in a very chaste way, she loves me madly. It's a peculiar sensation. It's not like I'm going to be able to pick up the phone and ask her out on a date sometime, but it's a thrill nonetheless. I'm holding the letter in my hand saying, 'Eric, there's a bird fancies me, ya beauty!' What's not to like? You read the second, and it's the same. Then the next and it doesn't stop feeling great. You know it's not real, but it's like balm for the heart and the ego at the same time. On the bus home, I'm on cloud nine, practically flying. But when I arrive home, there's a message, inevitably from Tam. Only this time, he's not checking up on me. I ask my mum what he's after now and she says she's no idea. Only I've got to pack a bag.

Chapter 8

ROLLIN'

I arrive at Heathrow, already narky, and there's still a solid ten hours' travel yawning in front of me. Tam's waiting at the departures desk, bending the ear of the girl at the desk. He's grinning from ear to ear, dressed in his holiday finery – basically the same as every other day – and more denim than you'll see at a Status Quo concert, but sandals instead of shoes, his knackered yellow toenails hanging over the edge of the leather. I can see the girl at the desk rolling her eyes and I feel her tired boredom coming at me in waves. In front of her, he's waving plane tickets around like he's had a good day at the track, sidling over to me and asking, 'Hope you packed your trunks?' I feel my blood running cold. Derek is there too, grinning, looking a little embarrassed. I'm looking around to see if I can see the others. As if reading my thoughts, Tam explains the situation. 'Al is off with his dad. Les and Eric have other plans.' I'm thinking, *Yeah right. They're just older and smarter than me. Had the presence of mind to tell the great Tam Paton they didn't want to go to Jamaica on an all-expenses holiday with him acting as their constant chaperone, covering their eyes whenever someone saunters by in a two-piece.*

Still, I manage to stifle the groan that's stirring in me. Tickets to Jamaica, I think. It'll be fine. Don't act ungrateful, don't mention the fact you're secretly disappointed you won't be taking the annual trip to Burntisland with the rest of the family. More than anything, with all the excitement and responsibility of being a Roller, it's the first feeling I get of adulthood coming knocking at my door, having to say goodbye to childish things.

As the plane leaves the tarmac, Tam does his usual flying turkey schtick, flapping his arms, then pretending he's trapped outside and hanging on to a wing. I guess it's still kind of amusing, but my heart's not really in it. I'm thinking about how I'll survive two weeks of Tam malarkey? Then I see Montego Bay and it's not so bad. Crystal-blue water, tiny wee hummingbirds flying an arm's length from where you're sitting, evening meals illuminated by fireflies, white sands like I never saw before. Within five minutes of arriving at the hotel, I'm swimming in the sea and step on a sea urchin in the shallows. A local nurse comes out and spends an hour, maybe longer, applying melted candle wax to the wounds, gently pulling the spines out of my tender flesh. I spend the following day lying in my spartan room, watching the hours tick by. I'm advised to not spend more than 20 minutes in the sun, but obviously I wind up sunburnt. There are worse places to be, I know that, but it's not the same without Al and Eric, and I start counting the days until we're home. On the eighth day, Tam tells me over breakfast it's time to pack up and go. We're leaving early, he says. Need to fly home for *Top of the Pops* or some such nonsense. Part of me is sad to be leaving, another part is keen to be getting on with my life. It's like I've been in a holding pattern for a week or so, waiting for a landing slot. Truth to tell, as mad as it's been getting, I've missed the thrill of it all. I want to play. Make more music.

The first song I ever wrote was on the Wood family piano back on Marchmont Street. I've still got the melody in my head – a jumble of C and E minor chords, no lyrics, more of a piece than a song, really. I called the song 'Lonely'. It was a cool feeling, bringing something new into the world. I'd no idea about structure or melody, but I got caught up in those 12 notes a while and lost days of my life, leaning into the keys, coming up with something that wasn't there before. I mention this because now, just a couple of years down the line, the first Bay City Rollers album, *Rollin'*, is in the shops. A number-one record, if you can imagine that. It had hundreds of thousands of pre-orders and fans lined the streets outside their local record stores, desperate to get a copy on the first day of release. It's a smash right across the UK and, suddenly, we're making baby-step inroads in various places around the world: Europe, Australia, Canada, even Rhodesia,* for some reason I'll never know. We're probably on

* Now Zimbabwe.

the cusp of something, but I'm still like that dog in the car, getting to one place like, *Oh, here we are. What's happening today?*

One year back, I knew maybe five or six chords. I was out on the tools in Edinburgh, collecting lunchtime sandwiches for a couple of lazy sparks and, now, here's me smiling back at you, top of the charts, above *Tubular Bells*, John Lennon, the Carpenters and Rod Stewart. Granted, I'm not a millionaire, like all those chart mainstays – I'm still on a wage, doubled now to £20[†] a week – but I feel blessed to be in such exalted company. Martin and Coulter's sticky fingerprints are all over the album, of course, but I've got my name on three songs written with Eric: 'Angel Angel', 'Just a Little Love' and 'There Goes My Baby'. Eric's more adept at the craft than me, but I loved the idea of learning the ropes. It feels like I've come a long way in these past months and I'm desperate to get back to creating, building something from the basement up.

For someone who was always averse to school, it's nice to be interested in something, to learn a craft. Eric already has loads of songs and ideas written and I'll chime in. It's like if you were baking a cake. You can't just have a tin full of flour and hope it's going to come out okay. You need to meddle with the ingredients. Change this. Throw in a middle eight or a bridge. What about a counter melody here? Eric looking across at me, suggesting we chuck in an 'ooh-be-doo' here or an extra harmony there and there's something cool about

[†] Approximately £250 in today's money.

that. Eric's the main guy and, just by osmosis, seeing how he works, I'm picking up a lot. He's constantly jotting down lyric ideas or working the chords and taking on the suggestions I throw his way. It's like assembling a model kit and I'm taken with the process. Hearing the songs back, even the songs that aren't exactly Lennon/McCartney standard, it feels kind of supernatural. I realise I'm late to the party. Half the album was pretty much in the can by late 1973 before Tam roped me in, but even so, I get this swell of pride thinking about what we've done. Nothing can ruin this feeling, I think. Except maybe one thing. I've told my mum and everyone I'm singing on one of the songs – 'Just a Little Love' – and after returning from Jamaica and getting the record home, I call my parents in to listen. The world of pop music is entirely alien to them, like they're watching a movie about their son, and it's not real, but they're swept along by my enthusiasm – and reassured that Tam Paton is steering the ship prudently. I'm standing by the stereo, my heart in my mouth, and I realise they've replaced my vocal with one by Les. It wasn't good enough, I know that, but it's still a horrible feeling, finding out like that. I tell everyone it's fine. They told me they were going to do that, I say, but that's just me trying to save face. Truth is, I'm depressed for a full week.

Chapter 9

SOMETHING MANIA

Christmas 1974

Coming up on Christmas, the business end of 1974. I should be tired now. Not just a little tuckered out but getting into narcolepsy territory here, falling face first into a bowl of soup at dinner. But I'm not. Everything is slightly out of kilter, but I'm 17, got the constitution of an ox, and everything is exciting. The world wakes up in the morning and works from 9 to 5, but I'm having to adjust my body clock, playing five shows a week, with everything being upside down, back to front. Long hours on the road means adrenaline builds up at the wrong end of the day and I'm high as a kite between 10 and midnight and then crashing in the early hours. We've played 300 shows in 1974 and, like I said, I should be tired, but somehow I'm not. My main concern is, usually, is the hotel going to be okay? Is there a spare minute for me to pick up a chocolate bar somewhere? Will there be a hairdryer so I can blow-dry my hair before we leave for the show? And now suddenly the year is grinding to a halt. There's maybe 100,000 copies of our record nestling under Christmas trees from here to Cornwall and, aside from some light telly and phone interviews, we're done for now. In a month, the first issue of *Bay City Rollers Monthly* – from the publishers of *The Beatles Monthly* – will find its way to the stores, marking our ascent from 'kind of famous' to 'staring back at you from every newsagent shelf across the land' ubiquity. Actual fame, if not fortune.

Down in Prestonpans, back at Tam's parents, we're sifting through the fan mail, sending out Christmas cards, sorting out housekeeping stuff before the festive *Top of the Pops*. I've written a card for Paul McCartney, and the prime minister, whoever that is; I sneak a card to Robin Ross, my pal from Freezin' Heet, into the outgoing mail pile and his wee sister takes it into school. I've no idea why it's an issue, but Tam gets wind somehow and gives me a load of shit about getting too familiar with people and how it affects the band's image. Familiarity breeds contempt, he says. He tells me I'm easily replaceable, kind of flexing, trying to show me who's boss here, at the same time as he's clutching his heart, telling me he's getting palpitations, cracking open his briefcase to take out one of his dubious pills. It doesn't cross my mind to tell him to get tae fuck. I'm conditioned to behave a certain way or I'll get shown the door. I'm all 'Yes Tam, no Tam, whatever Tam', but I think about that telling-off for the whole day. Then I don't think about it again until I write it down here.

There are a couple of fans working through the sacks – volunteers maybe, they're probably not on the payroll – and they go all quiet and shy as we pass them, like you're walking through a bubble of embarrassed silence and blushes. I'm not jaded, not even close, so I'm still getting a buzz every time a girl writes her felt-tip letters of love and secondary-school poetry. It feels like I've got a responsibility to not let them down. I like smiling at the fans, or waving to them, trying to make sure they enjoy themselves at our shows. I'm always touched by the little gestures. The way they embroider our names on their clothes or wait for hours just to see us. I don't know if that's a display of character from me, or if it's down to Tam getting in our heads, telling us not to fuck things up with the fans, but the result's the same here reading the fan letters.

I'm leafing through the hearts and flowers when, suddenly . . . what's this? It's hate mail. Actual hate mail. A bag of it. One of the girls' magazines ran a photoshoot and there's a young female model in the frame with us. Two minutes of our time two months ago and long forgotten, but Tam's here with a sack full of bile from the girls in the Home Counties and beyond – a bunch of girls called Mary and Penny and whatever, totally fucked off with us for having the cheek to smile down the camera while in the proximity of some model. She's probably going to have to go into hiding, get plastic surgery or go into witness protection, poor girl.

Then, in the blink of an eye, we're back at BBC Television Centre for our festive *Top of the Pops* appearance. Don't ask me how we got here. I barely had my cornflakes before being thrust into a limo, through the grey streets of London, past a wall of fans and onto a stage. Another day at the office. We play our tune and bump into a couple of other bemused stars backstage. Nothing to report. Only, there's panic in the eyes of the clipboard guy. The plummy chap in the sweater and National Health Service specs has gone white. There are 50 teenage girls running amok here in the studios, he says. They've caught our scent on the breeze and they're after, well, I don't know what they're after. Presumably, they're like wee pups chasing cars, with no idea what they'll do if they ever catch hold of it. It's not something that's happened before, but the times are changing all around us. This is a new phenomenon and a couple of silver-haired ex-services guys in security hats and silver-studded epaulettes aren't going to cut the mustard anymore. They're running around the place, red-faced and puffed-out, like hapless cops in a Harold Lloyd movie. It would probably be easier for them if the pack of girls only had one quarry, but today we're sharing a bill with David Cassidy, the blue-eyed pop singer out of the Partridge Family, so there's two scents catching the wind. So, as the aged security go from room to room, there are dozens of hormonal teenagers ransacking the offices, turning over the desks and scouring every inch of W12 hoping to find us or Cassidy.

Owing to the rising tide of insanity that tracks our every move, we have security now – a couple of big fuckers you wouldn't want to mess with, Fat Fred and Paddy the Plank. They sound like characters from a *Carry On* movie, but they're super-professional, easy-going and cool. This couple of Londoners, blessed with impenetrable cockney accents, are minding the store today. I don't know if they're ex-military or what, but they're hired out of a company Tam's started using and they've both done a few tours of duty with the Osmonds. They've seen some sights, but it's more of a sedate kind of insanity that surrounds our Mormon cousins from across the pond. Everyone loves Donny, probably Jimmy and Alan too, but it's less crazy than what's starting to bubble up around the Rollers. As the names suggest, Fred is *Mr Men*-round and Paddy is tall and wiry. They never have eyes on us; they're always looking at the crowd, like secret service working a presidential motorcade. They're an oasis of calm pragmatism in a sea of confusion. They're also deep into their thirties, so whenever they speak, we all take heed. They give us the nod, tell us we need to get out of here and usher us out of a back door, past the panicking clipboard guy. 'Come on, go,' they urge, like we're doing a parachute jump. 'Go. Go. Go!' and we're running down these hallowed corridors, past the dressing rooms for *Blue Peter* and the like, half-laughing, keeping pace with them. We duck through one door, out of one studio, out the other side, into another labyrinth of corridors. You can hear the pandemonium.

These girls. I don't know where they find the energy to run and scream their lungs out, but it gives us a good idea which direction to not run in. The sound is growing faint and we're in our full stage gear, baseball jackets and these half-mast trousers, hidden away in a studio. We're skulking against a wall, trying to catch our breath while Paddy checks the exit is safe. You can hear the screams start to rise again, the sound edging closer. It's bedlam, like the sacking of Rome transposed to the west London suburbs. Then it's suddenly quiet. We're looking down the line, seeing if we're all still present and correct. Les, Alan, Derek, Eric. We're all accounted for. Maybe the coast is clear, I'm thinking, but someone mentions it's because the studio is soundproofed, so there's no way of knowing without peeking outside. Gingerly, Paddy opens the door, and you can almost feel the vacuum, the air getting sucked out of the room, and the sound of screaming and the squeak of plimsolls on the waxed floor outside is right on top of you. Paddy shuts the door quick smart and behind us, on the other side of the abandoned studio, another door swings open and a grey security guard bundles in, his chest heaving. He's practically dragging a limp David Cassidy from the corridor. He shuts the door behind them, leans against it, like he's a Looney Tunes cat and there's a giant fuckin' bulldog pounding on the other side. We run back the way he came in, passing each other in slow motion, double taking and having a kind of unspoken exchange: 'Alright, David?' 'Oh, hey, how are you guys? I see your fans are pure mental too.' We run out the door he came in and he runs out the door we came in. We should probably have followed him, because then we're right in the heart of it. Paddy and Fat Fred somehow keep us afloat on a sea of teenage hormones.

'Was that David Cassidy?' Eric's bent over double, trying to breathe, like he just ran for a bus.

'Oh aye, I think it was,' Alan laughs. We're all laughing, because this is our life now.

Chapter 10

THE COUP

January 1975

The first Rollers album sold a bunch of records. A dizzying number of copies. Bell Records line us up in front of a photographer, like we're the Beatles, and present us all with tidy gold discs as if to prove it wasn't all some weird fever dream. We're top of the heap suddenly – and maybe this is going to make you roll your eyes – but we're not entirely happy. After a handful of smash-hit singles and a chart-topping LP, you'd think we were fine, but not everything in the garden is rosy about now.

Among other things – Tam's psychological manipulation and Les's growing egomania (maybe his ego has inflated 30 or 40 per cent these past six months) – there's some beef developing over the song selections. It doesn't take a musical genius to work out the songs all have the same beat and follow the same format.

We may be disposable pop stars, but we're musicians too and we know what we want to do. Probably no one sees us as the kind of people who sit around strategising, but we start to think, *If we're going to make a go of this, we need to break out of this mould.* Meantime, we're writing songs between us, but we can't even get our tunes on the B-sides. There's hushed talk in the back of cars and vans, and I'm hearing that you get the same amount for writing the B as the A-side, a 50/50 split, but it's like a Martin/Coulter closed shop. We don't have a free minute to spend it, save for sweets and crisps at service stations, but I understand from Tam we're making good money. Every time a record is sold or one of our songs is played on the radio or telly, there's mechanical royalties coming our way – the money you get for playing or singing on a record – but we don't make the king's ransom that Martin and Coulter get from writing the hit records.

Also, they're cagey as fuck about even letting us play on our own records; they want to rely on their session guys, regardless of what we say. So, we're stuck on the same melody, the same shuffle beat every time, just with different lyrics and they're not gonna throw a single crumb down from the table. On our last session with those guys, I'm down on the studio floor, guitar in hand, waiting, and I look up to the control room and see Eric and Les getting into it with Martin and Coulter. It's a proper shouting match. They're waving their hands in exasperation. Phil Coulter, stands there red-faced, hands on his hips, as Les and Eric storm out of the booth.

In truth, we're all getting frustrated that the whole enterprise is being steered by Martin and Coulter. No offence to them, but we don't want to be part of that cookie-cutter thing they've got going on anymore, so after the single 'All of Me Loves All of You', basically the same single as the last one and the one before that, we stage a wee coup and they're politely shown the door. They say a couple of shitty things about us not playing on the records, but I don't know. Maybe it's not an unfair swipe. We weren't exactly in the studio 24/7. I hear this is the norm for some bands. Record companies have a pool of favoured session guys they like to use while the artists are on the road promoting the songs. There was always a car waiting, just ticking over outside, like we were robbing a jeweller's rather than making a record. Still, whatever's been said, we've a lot to thank Martin and Coulter for. We're just tired of doing the same song over and over. The same verse pattern, same bloody chorus. Playing them live, you could easily fall into the chorus of any one of them, just with the words rearranged and those two guys laughing all the way to the bank. We eventually realise you can transpose the words from one to the other and start to treat the Martin/Coulter songs as a medley when we play a show.

With Martin and Coulter out, it feels like we've a little more clout, but it's a hollow victory really. Eric tells me it doesn't matter how much control we have. Even if it were 99 per cent, the men in suits would still have that 1 per cent and could pull the brakes any time they want. In theory, we can record what we like, make a prog rock masterpiece if we want obviously we *don't* want – but when we deliver a new record, there's no saying whether they'll accept it or not, so you're over a barrel whatever way you look at it.

Still, despite the hollowness of the victory, we still want to change it up: record our own songs, or at least *pick* our own songs. With that in mind, we've got 12 songs, including a few with my name on them. Plus, there's the small matter of 'Bye Bye Baby', this old Four Seasons song which wasn't a big hit over here. It's the first song we pick for ourselves. We make it our own, I reckon. I hear that when the Four Seasons play it now, people say, 'Oh, you're covering a Bay City Rollers song',* which is kind of funny. I'm not looking too closely, but having my name on half a dozen songs means I'm starting to hear talk about publishing. I don't think about it in those terms though. It's just we need more songs for the album and I enjoy the process of working with Eric, bouncing ideas around and coming up with something new. Making a few extra pounds from songwriting doesn't cross my mind, but it's the first time I start hearing talk about the business side of things. Tam tells us not to worry. There's a new shell company getting set up every week: Stuart Wood Limited, Eric Faulkner Limited, etcetera. If I'm honest, I haven't a clue what he's talking about. Probably we should be paying closer attention, looking after the pennies and letting the pounds take care of themselves, but the truth is, we don't have much time. Maybe there's a once-in-a-while meeting with our accountant in London. Money comes down from the record company or from Tam, everyone above us in the pecking order, like accountants and lawyers, take a cut,

* In the US, this was never the case. People would be saying, why are you covering a Four Seasons song?

then the remainder gets filtered down into a group account and then siphoned into everyone's individual account. These are all adults sorting this out, so none of us pay it much attention – why would you? I've no concept of money. I don't check my bank balance. I just know there's cash there if I need it. I'm like royalty these days. I don't carry money. I don't need to because I'm on the road the whole time. Who even has time to think about spending it?

When the dust settles, we set about recording a new LP in Chipping Norton, an old manor house that's been converted into a residential studio. Tam sees himself as a promotions man and doesn't feel the need to shadow us in the studio, so it's just the five of us – and Jake, to keep the wheels from coming off our wagon. Three weeks cut off from society, and Tam, and it's perfect. No phones. No one telling us to be somewhere at a certain time under pain of death. I could get used to it, frankly. Phil Wainman, the guy who sprinkled a bit of glitter over a few records by Mud and the Sweet, is on board to produce the LP. Phil's a lovely guy with a reputation for delivering big pop hits. We were only in the studio for four days for the last album, and the producer kind of assembled the record in our absence, so Phil's remit this time out is to record the band. You know, the Bay City Rollers. Because it's our name above the door. And being as we're at a residential studio, we're not being hustled out of the place so we can make our stage time or having to do a photoshoot somewhere or talk nonsense over the airwaves on some provincial radio station while they line up the traffic bulletin. Consequently, we're all a lot more relaxed.

It's a little like a holiday – sauntering down to breakfast in the morning, talking shite a while before drifting into the studio. We work all day, then have some dinner and head off to our beds. Phil and the engineer are up in the control booth, speaking to us over the intercom, telling us to go again. There's none of that shirt-and-tie nonsense. He's T-shirt and jeans, like the rest of us. A little bit rock and roll, in a well-brought-up west London kind of way. He's authoritative, but not like a school master, or – God forbid – Tam, barking orders and pulling everything apart. I don't need my shortcomings pointed out for me; I can see them myself. I'm thinking maybe we've got a bit sloppy over the past few months because we're screwing up a fair amount at first. When you play live, you can get away with a few slip-ups because of the energy in the room and because hardly anyone's listening that closely, but here in the studio, every fuck-up is exposed. One of our new songs, 'La Belle Jeane', has a complex accordion part that Alan can't get straight. He's miked up, but every time he makes a pass, he's out of time, can't get his fingers up and down the keys in time, so we wind up perching the accordion on a stool, me on one side, Eric on the other, pushing it open and closed, like PG Tips monkeys getting a piano up the stairs, while Alan's going up and down the white keys and Les pushes the bottom-end black buttons.

Phil's over the talkback constantly; watch the tempo, keep eyes on each other, okay, try it this way instead. He brings the best out of us and I'm learning so much. I'm still keeping an eye on Eric most of the time, obviously. He's really alert to what's happening and, as the music guy, he's the one who picks up on things most quickly when we start a take and he's the one with the most creative ideas. But between us all, we're getting things done. Derek's over in the drum booth and the rest of us, scattered around the studio floor, are isolated from one another, but we can still see what we're all doing and create a bit of atmosphere and energy on the basic track.

Recording the album is probably the happiest I've been in the band. I love the shows, the excitement, the energy, but I realise I like being able to hear myself think. I feel an instant connection. You know, like when I put together my bike or built an amp cabinet from bread boxes. I'm fascinated by how you go about creating something out of thin air. After the basic track, we have a listen to the playback, point out the things that work and the things that are shite, then we're down to overdubbing, building the songs from the ground floor up while Les lays down a guide vocal. After that, we harmonise. We're working with the musical director, Colin Frechter, and I'm watching him like a hawk, soaking everything up like a sponge. He has us lined up around the piano working through all the harmonies – couple of oohs here and a few shoo-wops there – and I find I've got a good ear for this. I can spot it straight away when someone strays off key. So we go through it over and over until the harmonies are so sharp they could cut glass. No one else likes doing the high notes, so it's usually me that gets that job. Take 1, take 2, then maybe Phil coming over the intercom talkback saying, 'That's it guys. You've got it' or 'I think you've got one more in you'. Listening to a playback in the control room is a revelation: we're all up there, nodding along, seeing how these jigsaw pieces land in place. Les – who's been getting twitchy this whole time, floating in and out of the studio, expecting the studio staff to scatter rose petals wherever he walks, while we lay down guitar parts and whatnot – does a final vocal and the engineer fiddles around with the tape a while, and you've got one track in the bag. Repeat that process a dozen times and you've got yourself a second Bay City Rollers album – *Once Upon a Star* – coming to a record shop or branch of Woolworths near you soon.

Chapter 11

SHANG-A-LANG

Early-morning drizzle across the windscreen, sweeping into Manchester, the grey north. Spring hasn't quite sprung yet. It's as if the winter is hanging on for as long as it possibly can, and the world outside is cold and dismal. Driving out from the countryside, it's like the guy from Radio Rentals has taken away the colour TV set suddenly and replaced it with a black-and-white one. I look up ahead, fine-tuning the colour settings in my brain, seeing Tam's giant ham fists on the wheel as he grumbles on and off about the Lancashire rain, his screeching vowels blotting out the sound of the car radio – Noel Edmonds doing a wacky phone call and cueing up the new single by Slade. I'm not listening to a word, either to Tam or Edmonds. I'm here in the box seat, looking out over this new city, and my eyes are on stalks – the streets, lines of grey tumbledown dwellings, slate roofs, swathed in choking, thick air that tastes like burned rubber. Crack the window an inch and it's like the city's been smoking Capstan full-strengths for a lifetime. Looking at the rows of houses, I thought the brick was red, but as we pass closer, I can see the brickwork is scarred black from a million people's coal fires. You could scratch it away with your thumbnail, write your name in the fuckin' soot that's gathered there since the Industrial Revolution, and it would be black again tomorrow. I squint a couple of times as the city draws into focus and realise we're driving through the title sequence of *Coronation Street*, half-expecting one of the cast to step out onto the cobbles.

I elbow Al in the ribs, getting him to peer up from the morning paper as we pull up to Granada Studios. There's already a congregation of girls out front and some weeping at the sight of us. Tam immediately slides into his whiny sergeant-major persona and starts ordering us out of the car and up through reception like a bunch of longhaired conscripts. Not that we need to be pressganged. We're mustard-keen, excited that we've somehow landed our own TV series. *Shang-A-Lang*, it's called, coming to a teatime TV slot soon.

We've been on this caper a few weeks, since the album was in the can. You'd imagine that once the record was being mixed and pressed and all that other stuff that I haven't got an eye on, we'd be on for a wee break to rest our weary bones, but no such luck. The last note we played in the studio is still ringing in my ears when I'm told we're now making a TV show. To all intents and purposes, it's like a half-hour advertisement for the band, running for 20 weeks and we're getting paid for the privilege – not that I've any idea how much we're getting paid, or even have the nerve to ask, because it doesn't seem like it's my business. The BBC is a slow-moving oil tanker that takes years to turn, but ITV, the UK's commercial TV channel, have seen the tide turning, had their antenna up for the next big thing and they somehow landed on us. It's a little bewildering.

I'm a year in, feet under the table, and I've played more times on *Top of the Pops* than I care to remember, but I don't know that I've got the chops to carry a TV show. In truth, none of us have, but it's like, here's the next thing. 'Get intae it,' Tam says, so we all get to it. It's not the BBC, so there's none of that Home Counties ex-military atmosphere at play. This is more of a socialist polytechnic utopian vibe, right in the heart of this Dickensian sprawl. It being Manchester, it's different, but also the same, maybe with a little less military precision – hair and make-up, sitting around waiting while cameras are wheeled around the studio, and wondering how we got here exactly.

We've inherited the Tuesday teatime *Lift Off With Ayshea* slot, a show we've played a bunch of times, beamed into a few million homes up and down the country while the nation sits down for its tea. The format of *Shang-A-Lang* is set in stone and we don't have much input, aside from a quick word from Mike Mansfield, one of the directors, or Muriel Young, the show's producer, before we're pushed out onto the soundstage, right in at the deep end. Every week we play a couple of songs, but in truth, I think we just record a dozen mimed performances in one long hit, quick-changing from one lot of tartan and into another between numbers. That's right in our wheelhouse; we know what we're doing by now, although less so with the other material. We're fish out of water, all of us, and haven't a clue what we're doing half the time. So we have the Rollers getting thrown into performing a couple of skits, then it's cut to Eric and me in the studio, while a beardy folk guy runs through the scales on his guitar and educates the great unwashed in blues guitar or whatever. Probably because I'm the kid, the last one to join before we became this 'thing', I'm not the butt of the joke, but there's a running thread of 'Ach, Woody got it wrong again' in some of the links. I play up to it and, when I see it back, it seems obvious that we're not a manufactured band. There's been no media training here. Every line delivery is half-arsed, but we're grinning, giving it the best boy-next-door attitude before we cut to a bit of pre-recorded outside broadcast footage.

Watch the tape and maybe you can see it in my eyes, but I'm miserable. We roll up to this Lancashire farm in a big limo, and one of the crew is running through the itinerary, shouting orders through what looks like a rolled-up magazine. First things first: drive around on a tractor a while, laughing and joking. Don't let them see how cold and unhappy you're feeling. Then it's down to the banks of a wee creek on the farm. Launch yourself across the water on a rope swing, legs akimbo, dangling there like a numpty. Keep smiling. 'This looks great, guys.' Then back to the farmyard. Pose for some stock footage a while, holding a baby cow or whatever, something wholesome, while the farmer brings around five horses and it's 'Cut! Okay, guys. Get on a horse and we'll get some shots of you all riding around the farm.'

I've barely seen a horse before, let alone ridden one, but I figure I'll just do what's required and get the hell out of this muddy hellscape as quick as I can. The rest of the guys are clicking their heels ahead of me, getting their horse to do whatever they want like they're all John Wayne, and I'm swinging a leg trying to mount the bastard. I get down, give him a look, he gives me a look straight back and I can see he has the devil in him, like we've taken an instant dislike to each other. At the fourth attempt, once my arse is in the saddle, my devil horse senses my anxiety and immediately bolts. I'm hanging on for dear life, barely clinging to the tartan scarf I tied around his neck, which I realise probably pissed him off, watching Les piss himself laughing as I sweep past at a full gallop with two of the stable boys running after me through the icy mud. As the light starts to fade, I'm bruised and battered, feeling cold in my bones, all for two minutes runtime and a couple of cutaways to a crowd of fans, all waving their DIY tartan scarves over their heads.

The tartan is a happy accident in some ways. We already have an identity, what you might call a brand; clean-cut boys next door, obviously, like you see every week in *Jackie* magazine. We've been wearing a kind of uniform this past year. Our stage gear is a hotchpotch of styles, like a gang of droogs from *A Clockwork Orange*: these Skinners, half-mast trousers, US football shirts, Crombie coats and Dr Martens boots. Eric flirted with a plaid shirt in a couple of photoshoots, but it's not until we're sifting through one of the sacks of fan mail that we see a picture from one of the fans, a felt-tip blueprint of the future: shirt and trousers, with stripes up and down the seam, and Eric has the idea we could fill the stripes with tartan. We don't have a stylist, but once Eric's persuaded us that it's a nifty concept, he scribbles a design on a piece of paper and it's sent to our designer and arch-seamstress, Bambi Ballard. From that moment, it's tartan everywhere. We each have our own ideas – our own little takes, stabs of individualism – and it's this sudden, accessible DIY aesthetic. Throw in a couple of pairs of monkey boots, a pair of Converse or, if you're feeling like defying gravity a while, a teetering pair of platform boots and suddenly you have a uniform. Probably within a week of us wearing the stuff for the first time, the fans are all waving tartan scarves, adding plaid strips and skirting to shirts and jackets, and the image is locked in. There's a standing army of Roller fans from this moment forward.

Everything on *Shang-A-Lang* is rough around the edges. There are no second or third takes – it's just 1–2–3 Go! You plough on when you've fluffed your lines and just hope someone will fix it in the edit, or that there's enough primary colour and noise that no one will notice. One week you're interviewing Lieutenant Pigeon – who is neither a lieutenant nor a pigeon – and the next, someone in the production staff just hands you a washboard and a couple of tin thimbles and you're doing a piece to camera about skiffle music and interviewing Lonnie Donegan. Half the guests we never meet, but it's like a roll-call of the top 30: Cliff Richard, Marc Bolan, Lynsey de Paul, David Cassidy, Linda Lewis, Olivia Newton-John, Slade, Sparks, Alvin Stardust, Showaddywaddy, the Rubettes, Alan Price and Gilbert O'Sullivan. They're recorded while we're away on the grand tour that's happening at the same time and we just provide the links, a bit of banter – Eric teasing Les about his new car, his pride and joy, a new Ford Mustang that he's been tearing around Edinburgh in; telling the viewers we have tae go because Woody's getting hungry for his pizza pie about now.

The day Cliff plays, there's dozens of girls outside screaming for him. Fair play, he's Cliff Richard. Been famous since the arse-end of the 1950s, so it's only to be expected. He tells us, 'Uh guys . . . uh . . . so lovely to meet you' and we're made up. The actual Cliff Richard on our show. Thank you for your service, sir! We watch him walk out on stage and play, proper professional, then we're steered onto the stage for a burst of 'Shang-A-Lang' and we're done here. Just need to wait a while for the Cliff fans outside the building to move on and we're out of here, on to tonight's delights in some industrial town somewhere. Cliff is bundled into the back of a Transit and off to wherever it is Cliff goes, to his regeneration chamber or something, because he's the Peter Pan of Pop™. It's only when the van disappears that we realise the fans have stayed put. There's a kerfuffle outside and we see some people are weeping. Finally, word makes it through to us that one of the police officers on security just died of a heart attack and, God, how do you even process something like that? I mean, it's just a fuckin' TV show and some poor guy's dead, leaving a big dad-shaped hole in someone's family.

It's a curious situation to find yourself in, if I'm honest. Probably in another life, I'd be sitting at home watching, waiting for my mum to finish making my tea, wondering how this amateur shite got on my telly, but somehow I'm here, an unlikely TV star. Like everything else, there's no real thought process at play here. We're just getting away with it, rushing through the takes – a bit of this episode, a bit of the next – because the car is idling out front and we've got a stage time in, I don't know, fuckin' Norwich or wherever that same day. Three hours on a motorway, sitting in your sweat from the morning, waiting for two hours to tick by for the next comfort break so you can get out and have a piss and a walk around, shake some of that deep vein thrombosis out of your legs, play a show, escape the fans by the skin of your teeth and it's back up the road to Granada Studios the next morning to start again. Because why wouldn't you?

Chapter 12

WITH AN R – O – *DOUBLE L* – E – R – S, BAY CITY ROLLERS ARE THE BEST!

The Rollers' first bona fide theatre tour is off to a flyer. There's a week of pre-production in Dundee, getting everything just so. Even if it looks that way, nothing is happening by accident. There's a ton of new gear and we're having to learn how to use the bigger stages. There's more space to cover and more spots in the crowd we need to wave and smile at. No more tiny, provincial PA systems now: the required amplification is on a par with a hard-rock band. It's maybe louder, because we've got the noise of two or three thousand fans screaming to contend with. We've been shackled by the Mecca circuit to some extent, I think – a few hundred souls, shoehorned into a nightclub, standing room only. It was fun while it lasted, but it started to feel unsafe, hence the shift up to bigger venues. Also, money. You make more money this way and probably that's the motivation. Three thousand fans' pocket money is better than 400, so maybe no one's thinking about health and safety. One thing is that encores have gone out the window for fear of us fanning the flames. There's police and local councillors saying, 'This is the curfew. Play for an hour if you can, but don't come back out because there'll be riots.' It's all debris from the Rollers explosion, that phenomenon I couldn't put a name to last year. It's here now.

With the press interest reaching fever pitch, there are some negative stories doing the rounds. Not about us – we're all spotless, shiny white and virtuous, except maybe Les, who is never far from the headlines. He's like a lightning rod for trouble. I've seen a story about a 15-year-old Rollers fan needing stitches after being shot in the forehead with an air gun while sitting on the wall outside Les's home in West Lothian. He was charged but later cleared. Aside from Les, most of the negative press is about our fans, which is unnerving at first, but becomes commonplace. There's a story I just read talking about these 'monstrous girls' with stigmata arms where they've drawn blood, scratching 'Eric' or 'Les' with a pin and complaining when the wounds went septic. One of the papers reports a story saying that we don't play on our records, which seems to be a deliberate misunderstanding, and that leaves me feeling a little wary. It's pure bollocks; it stems from an interview Alan gave, where he mentioned the other musicians on our records. Al was talking about us bringing in a violin or trumpet player, but obviously it was reported that we don't play on the records at all.

In general terms, though, the press are enjoying the novelty of it all, like they've got this new toy. We're this commodity, a kind of daily headline-generating machine. I realise they could turn on a sixpence, but right now, there's this wave of hysteria, of sold-out shows up and down the land, so the press guys always greet us with a smile. The Rollers are an easy story, brash and colourful – even in printer's black ink – and presumably they're selling a lot of papers off the back of the madness around us.

You want to talk about upward momentum? Well, with six weeks at number one with 'Bye Bye Baby' and the new LP selling hand over fist, now that we're booked into these theatre shows – we could play every night until doomsday – with thousands of teenagers crammed in and these mad scenes outside in the streets, then this is it. This is that moment. The press call it Rollermania. The first time I see the word in the paper, I look over at Alan and say, 'Ach, we're a mania now.' He barely looks up from his plate of chips. Just says, 'Oh aye', dipping a burnt chip into a watery puddle of service-station ketchup.

I only ever heard the word attached to the Beatles before, so obviously it feels like a moment. Away from the shows, it's like nothing you've ever seen. We're getting practice in the art of stealth, such as climbing into the boot of a car and being carried incognito to the back of the theatre and bundled in through the fire exit. It's like we're spies, escaping from East Berlin, only in our case, instead of getting taken to a safehouse somewhere in West Germany, we're banging out the hits for the people who are trying to catch us.

My life is moving so fast, I barely have a chance to reflect. One major change is we're getting paid now. Not just our £20-a-week wages either. Money is coming into the Bay City Rollers' account from shows and records, a year's worth of hubbub, and shared five ways – an equal split for me and the guys – so we each opened a bank account back in Prestonpans, with Tam hovering over our shoulders. We got shiny new cheque books and bank cards, and our first statements say something crazy like £20,000,* making us feel like millionaires.

Tonight, 27 April 1975, we're on hallowed ground – Glasgow's legendary Apollo Theatre. For the record, there's 4,000 fans out there and it's a sight to behold. We're number one in the hit parade and you can feel the electricity. It's like the Mecca club nights are a thousand years into the past, because we're high, high, high – ten foot above the pit, kings of all we survey, and there's a smell of cigarette ash caught up in the plush velveteen seats, a hundred years' varnish blistering in the heat of all those bodies and from the hot lights bearing down on the chaos. The lip of the stage is too high to climb, but God loves a trier. They're still giving it a go. Leaping out of the darkness, you can sometimes see their flailing fingertips, the scruffy daubs of primary colour nail varnish, as they try, then try again. Occasionally, you'll see the black cap of a St John's Ambulance guy caught up in the soup of fans and tartan and unbridled joy – at least, I think it's joy – and pulling out some girl who's passed

* Equivalent to £250,000 in today's money.

out and fallen limp, a ragdoll, to be thrown across a hefty shoulder and carried out to safety. It's still just a tight hour-long set. Any longer and it's too dangerous. Sometimes, though, the local polis will step up on the stage and, with balls of pure steel, tell the crowd the show's over after 20 minutes. Not today though, but it's still hazardous out here – just not deadly. I'm dodging the shite that's getting thrown up on stage. Nothing malicious, just exuberance, I suppose, hoping something they touched might touch us or something. I've chipped a couple of teeth on this tour already. Grinning like an idiot – as I've been instructed – and some missile gets lobbed from Row 5. I took a direct hit from one of those disposable flashcubes and I'm a couple of weeks out from seeing a dentist, so need a bandage tied around my head like a comic kid with toothache. It's like the Odeon kids chucking fruit on stage, but now it's on a grander, more anarchic scale. There's discarded flashbulbs, high-street jewellery and God knows what else scattered around my feet. (Often, after a show and the curtain's come down, Alan will walk back on stage, start scouring through the debris to see if he can find anything of value, nibbling at the corners of something or other to see if it's real gold.)

Cast your eyes downstage for a second and you can see the ragdoll fans, who were pulled to safety, suddenly come to life and spring to their feet. They're trying to sweep past security and the St John's Ambulance people are taking off their caps and scratching their heads in befuddlement. As we come to the end of our show, I drop to one knee, giving it some, playing up to the crowd, doing my best to not get the scarf I've tied to my guitar strap caught under my heel and drag me down, as it has done a couple of times, half-strangling me, like a cartoon cat, and leaving me with egg on my face – and Al looking down at me, killing himself laughing.

I don't understand the logistics – why would I? – but this is the first house today, a matinee. Somehow or other, these 4,000 sopping teenagers are going to be ushered out into the chill spring air and replaced with another 4,000 fans, a second wave of tartan and teenage abandon. What chaos is befalling the Glasgow streets right now is someone else's concern, though from here, the constant singing that's drifting in through the dressing room window sounds like no one's having the worst day of their life.

B-A-Y, B-A-Y, B-A-Y-C-I-T-Y
With an R-O-double-L, E-R-S
Bay City Rollers are the best!
Eric, Derek, Woody too, Alan, Leslie, we love you,
With an R-O-double-L, E-R-S,
Bay City Rollers are the best!

We only hear it. We didn't see it on the way down. The band's new car, an imported AMC Ambassador station wagon, a big hulking thing with faux wood-panel trim like something out of *The Brady Bunch*, pulled up at the side of the road and we decanted ourselves into a high-sided white van with blacked-out windows to travel the mile from the city limits to the Apollo, seeing nothing, just hearing the sound, feeling the pounding on the side of the van, like we're murderers being driven up to the Old Bailey in a black Maria.

Without looking out, because I've seen it with my own eyes in half a dozen cities, I know there'll be lines of police, ambulances and scenes like an Old Firm derby being played out, a hundred yards from our dressing room, while we kill a couple of hours waiting for the second house to assemble. The DJ, 'Diddy' David Hamilton, will poke his head around the door a couple of times between now and then. Maybe we'll grab a word with Jake or Paddy the Plank, our security guy, but in every sense, we're prisoners here. We're pumped up on cola and the adrenaline from the first set, so none of us is paying close attention when Tam comes by and mutters something about us needing to put on a good show. 'The Americans are in town,' he tells us. 'Up in the balcony.' I make a mental note to look upwards during the second house. Then it's déjà vu for the next hour, for the second show of the day. It's the same scenes of carnage, only this time, the crowd has spent an extra few hours in the queue, fainting and whatnot, and they've a lot more pent-up emotion now. Then finally, the house lights go up, Les lets out a throaty 'Thank you and good night, Glasgow' and we're done, herded back to the dressing room for this meet-and-greet.

We're accustomed now to having local dignitaries dragged into the dressing room by Tam. Watching him bow and scrape to the mayor and his lovely wife or hauling in some raincoated dick from the local press and a bald smudger who wants to make sure he gets a picture of everyone flashing their pearly whites. We smile for photos for the paper, make a wee bit of chat –

the mayor invariably talks about the new bypass and shopping centre – and then they're whisked out again. This meeting's different, though. Even I can tell that there's something in the air, that Tam's ratcheting up his fawning, minding his p's and q's and making a show of being urbane, like he's washed the potato muck off his hands and he's now mingling with showbiz royalty or something.

Tonight, we're meeting this Clive Davis guy, who's jetted in from New York to sniff the thick Glasgow air and to find out what all this Rollers hullaballoo is about. He's stepping across the threshold, tripping over his Grammys and music biz baubles. He's forty-something, wears a fine-tailored suit and is bald beneath an unconvincing combover. His sharp eyes are covered by a pair of designer spectacles that probably cost the same amount as a family car. Clive's the head of Arista Records in New York and he's stepped away from his plush Manhattan office a while with Mike Klenfner, his head of A&R,[†] who looks like he's dressed for a round of pro-celebrity golf – canary-yellow EverPress trousers and a professional smile living in the shade of an impressive, bear-pelt moustache. There's a third figure in the doorway too, this big, imposing guy, Sid Bernstein, the New York impresario. None of these faces or names are familiar to me, but I'm told that Davis is the king of the music industry – big fish, big pond – and Sid is the man who is famed for bringing the Beatles to the United States in 1964, jumpstarting the British

[†] Later, Mike would go on to play himself as the record company executive in *The Blues Brothers*.

Invasion. He's probably dined off that for a few years now and looks like he hasn't gone short of a meal these past ten years. His suit is stretched over his heaving frame, looking like an expensive sack of elephants, and on his feet are a pair of hand-stitched Italian loafers. Sid mentions the Beatles. Then he mentions them again, in a thick New York drawl, like a bad guy out of an *Ironside* or *Kojak* rerun. No one's discussed this with us, but I put two and two together and realise he's maybe hoping he can repeat that Beatles trick with us.

'Wild crowd,' he's telling us, hooking a thumb backwards over his shoulder and shaking his head in disbelief. We look at each other and shrug. The insanity around us is normal and we need to take a beat to remember that, for an outsider, it probably does seem wild. For us, this is just like any other day, but he's gushing, in full flow now. 'It's like 1965 all over again,' he says. We're smiling, playing along, telling him 'Oh aye', and he turns to Clive and says something about us being the new Beatles and Clive's nodding sagely. I'm wiping away the sweat with a towel, half an ear on what's being said. There's talk about us breaking the States, making it big, real USA big. The guys are frowning, not serious, but that kind of frown where you're showing someone you're listening closely but hardly following what's being said. I'm nodding along, but feel my mind wandering as soon as they mention the USA. I'm not ambitious, I don't have a masterplan, beyond just carrying on with this ride, seeing where it's going to take us. Consequently, I've no fear. The idea of us cracking the US just seems like a logical progression and I start to daydream about what's to be. I'm thinking about hotdogs, hamburgers and milkshakes, about trips to Central Park, *Starsky & Hutch* and Hollywood like a starstruck teen would – which is fine, because that's what I am.

In no time, we agree to sign a deal with Clive Davis. Arista have bought out Bell Records and we're his star prize. Another six albums, no problem, I'm thinking, and I'm half-mapping out my future in my own head. Our accountant's set up a company and we're signed to Arista via that company. He could explain the reasoning behind it to me a thousand times and I'd still find my mind wandering off the point. I'd be thinking about what's for my dinner or whether we're getting a day off. I need him to go back to the start and explain again, no matter how many times he laid it out for me. Once the deal is signed, we pose for a few photos for the trade publications, and maybe one for Clive's wall of fame, and don't think about it again.

Chapter 13

A WEEK IN THE COUNTRY

The doctor gnaws the end of his pen before scribbling something down on his clipboard. A doctor's scrawl, indecipherable to mortal kids like me. He looks like a doc out of a *Carry On* movie, an absent-minded Dr Nookie or Dr Kilmore or something – white coat, National Health specs and enough Brylcreem to wax a floor. I'm standing barefoot on the metal scales, my feet freezing. He smiles reassuringly, then takes a squeeze of my arm. It's skinny as you like, a candy cigarette hanging limp at my side, covered in goosebumps from the draught. Together, we look down at the scales and I've barely registered. I'm nine stone soaking wet. There's not a stiff breeze that wouldn't knock me down. He mutters something to the nurse and she offers me a neat, professional smile. I throw her a lopsided grin and look back to the doctor. 'I'm just wanting to put on some weight,' I explain, and I see a look of relief pass over his face. He realises

I'm not mental and tells me they can probably help. 'It's usually the other way around,' he smiles, placing my file back on his desk, a giant mahogany affair littered with prescription pads and dog-eared copies of the *Lancet*.

Outside in the halls, the nurse accompanies me past a dozen or so overweight guys in white cotton robes, captains of industry on their way to the gym or the sauna. These greased, sweating bastards, sent here for the good of their tickers and in the hope they'll be starved enough that they don't crush their wives or secretaries when they take them to bed. In the main reception, I'm handed a pile of white robes and some paperwork, given a room key and I'm off up the grand stairs to my room. I nod at Eric and Alan, sitting patiently in the waiting area, a cheeky thumbs-up that it's going to be okay. They look up as I pass, neither of them looking particularly happy. But why should they? Alan and Eric have been sent here to Hampshire – to Forest Mere health farm,* a big old stately pile, halfway down the A3 – to shed some of those unwanted pounds. Al and Eric, Tam notices – because he's got an eye on us every minute and notices everything – have gotten a bit doughy, like they've been enjoying life a little too much, getting a taste of the highlife. Neither of them are happy to go, but I'm thinking, *Why are they getting a free holiday and I'm not?* I ask Tam to add me to the booking and make sure they know I'm looking to pile on a few pounds. I'm still rake-thin. I've been eating Mars bars constantly and drinking these protein drinks you get at the chemist and they're doing nothing. I could challenge Desperate Dan to a pie-eating contest every day between

* What we used to call a 'fat farm'.

now and the millennium and not put on an ounce, so I'm sent along with them, see if the doctors can help me bulk up a wee bit. I'm treating it as a holiday, a week of R&R. Meanwhile, my bandmates are acting like they've been shipped off to a stalag somewhere in 1940s Germany. I imagine them requesting rooms on the ground floor, so they can start work on escape tunnels.

When I arrive at my room – oak-panelled walls, sweeping views over the countryside, like a misty landscape painting out my window – I hurl myself on the bed, rummage a while in my bag, remembering they took my crisps and chocolate when I arrived, placing it in a cardboard box marked 'contraband'. All that's left is a week's worth of underpants. While I'm waiting for Alan and Eric to be signed in, hanging about for the clang of the dinner bell, I scan the notes the nurse handed me, a list of activities – walking, walking around the lake, fuckin' horse riding, more walking, a steam – and my diet plan. I think maybe I'm expecting it to be a list of cream cakes and mince and tatties dinners, something like when the Bash Street Kids have a slap-up lunch. Pies and wobbling jellies, teetering on silver salvers, while moustachioed waiters stand to one side, trying to not look disgusted at me as I scoff it all down. I'm scanning the list of food, still daydreaming, probably thinking about a T-bone dinner, with a rind of fat as thick as your neck, but all I can see is salad. It's probably an error, I think, and my belly turns over slightly, like it's been wakened from a slumber. It doesn't cross my mind this place might have a 'one-size-fits-all' approach to this health malarkey. I mull over the idea of calling reception, alerting them to their mistake, but decide against it.

For want of anything better to do, I stare out the window. I find myself thinking back to my comic-book days and reading the classified ads for Sea-Monkeys and X-ray specs and seeing Charles Atlas in a leopard-skin loincloth alongside a comic strip, some skinny kid getting sand kicked in his face by a musclebound beach bully. Send away now for Charles Atlas's free guide to getting a *real* body. I look down at what there is of me, just skin and bones, and decide I'm going to give this health spa thing a go. It's only a week. I can do that standing on my head, I think. That optimism lasts for maybe an hour.

It's five o'clock now. Weak with hunger, I drift down from my room for dinner. I follow the sound of cutlery and the bustle of kitchen staff, and take a seat with Alan and Eric. They're scanning the room suspiciously, eyeing the waiters, trying to get a look at the platters they're parading around the room and setting before the fat CEOs and middle managers. I pull up a seat, it screeches loudly, and all the fat guys throw me a look: what's this skinny fucker doing here? Across the tablecloth, Alan and Eric are already getting ratty with hunger, telling me their bellies are groaning, as the waiter suavely places three plates in front of us. There are a couple of lettuce leaves, a stick of asparagus and half of a pale, practically orange tomato neatly arranged on the white china. Alan says, 'Are you joking? Ah'm starvin' here.'

The waiter is unruffled. He's used to this reaction, I guess. He's probably had the same thing on four other tables tonight. I stay quiet. Half of me is thinking there's some real food coming. I've heard of side salads, so I'm still expecting a second plate to come over. Something with chips, maybe some scorched meat or something. But no. I watch the waiter leave through the double swing doors to the kitchen and slowly allow it to dawn on me. The side salad is dinner, I realise, and my heart sinks. While my friends gnaw on some grass, and wash it down with warmish tap water, I call a waiter and he arrives with a click of his heels. 'I think this is a mistake,' I say. 'I'm here to put on weight.' He pulls out a tiny notepad. He checks my name and room number, and tells me it's no mistake, before adding, 'Enjoy your meal, Mr Wood', the sarcastic wee shite. Eric and Al are killing themselves laughing watching me pick over the rabbit food with the tip of my fork. I'm staring down the table, hoping against hope they'll serve up a basket of bread, a couple of knobs of butter, but they don't. Not even brown bread and marge, the stingy bastards. I feel my stomach let out a weak murmur of disappointment, something like whale song.

'This won't do,' Alan tells me. 'This is like fuckin' prison.' We've been here six hours and he looks gaunt, tired already. But he has a faint glint of determination in his eyes. 'Ah'm breaking into the kitchen. Who's in?'

Eric keeps his own counsel, won't commit, but I tell Al I'm in and we agree to meet at midnight. It's a long haul, incidentally, between dinner and bedtime. I've eaten nothing since a service-station breakfast as the sun was coming up over Berkshire – greasy eggs and a couple of cremated strips of streaky bacon. Thinking about it now, I wish I'd gone back into the buffet queue and loaded up again, because now I'm bent double with hunger and the memory of that Happy Eater fodder is now looking like a king's banquet in my mind's eye. It's okay for Alan and Eric, I think. They've piled on the pounds, got a bit of excess fat to burn off before their bodies shut down. I'm here burning off muscle.

Another day of this and the nurses will be opening my room and finding a tartan-clad fuckin' skeleton stretched out on the divan, I think, as I step out into the corridor, hoping the floorboards don't creak underfoot.

When I find Alan in the hallway, he shushes me like we're in a haunted house and we quietly make our way into the bowels of the building towards the kitchen. I'm imagining making myself a giant *Scooby Doo*-style sandwich, standing in front of a massive fridge, groaning with roasted chickens and desserts. I can feel the saliva pooling in my mouth already. I make to turn the lights on, feeling my way up the edge of the doorframe and Alan shushes me again, telling me not to move.

'You hear that?' he whispers. There are mice here. Maybe they're rats, because I can hear cupboard doors creaking on their hinges. I start to walk back the way I came, heading back to the room, but Al grabs my arm and bids me to follow him. Up ahead, there's Eric, already ransacking the kitchen for food. He probably senses our presence, goes quiet and crouches behind a cupboard, his jumper stuffed full like he's been collecting tennis balls. The room is dark, just a spot of moonlight coming through the windows as we creep across the tiles. It's my turn to shush Al as I sneak up behind Eric and let out a loud 'Boo!', and watch a jumper full of apples, oranges and whatever else he's managed to acquire spill everywhere.

Al and I are laughing our heads off, but the hilarity doesn't last long. We're dead set on finding something decent. We're at a health club, so it follows that there's no biscuits – I can see that now, but in the moment, we're devastated. Still, we frantically set about opening cupboards, filling our dressing gown pockets with bananas, like cheeky monkeys, before traipsing defeated back up the stairs to our rooms.

'Just another six days to go,' I say, for a joke. A spot of gallows humour, but no one's laughing. None of us laughs for six days, in fact. We just walk, and squirrel away all the banana peels and apple cores we've left over from our night-time raids. There's no tunnelling to freedom, because none of us has the energy to lift a spoon, let alone a shovel.

Finally, our last day rolls around and we're gaunt, broken wee men. Whatever extra timber was showing on Eric and Alan has fallen away, along with the twinkle in their eyes. To be fair, probably the only difference between those guys and me is that they were here against their will. I'm unhappy because I actually volunteered for this shite. While I'm mulling that over, Muriel Young, our TV producer, calls. She's been going through the rushes of the show, editing our nonsense down to a palatable 25 minutes for teatime viewing, and she suggests we call by tomorrow, Sunday, for a roast dinner. I think about crying, but I manage to keep it at just 'Och, that'll be great, Muriel' and it takes all my strength to put the phone down without passing out. I pull my pillow over my head, dreaming of roast tatties and gravy.† It's 12 hours 'til check-out and nine hours until breakfast – half

† I still remember to this day sitting round the dining table with Alan, Eric and Muriel our host, eating what seemed the most amazing food ever. I never used to like Brussels sprouts, though that day Muriel had converted me into loving them . . . they were roasted in butter! A magical meal indeed.

a grapefruit and some more lukewarm tap water and back into my civvies, which are hanging off me like I'm Robinson Crusoe. I'm thinking we're back at Granada on Monday, recording more episodes of the TV show, playing shows everywhere and we're all looking like refugees, right off the boat.

After breakfast, I'm standing on the scales at eight and a half stone, the Brylcreem doctor smiling. 'You've lost half a stone!' He cocks an eyebrow, adjusting the weights, double-checking his figures a final time. I remind him I came here to put on weight, but it's like I'm talking to a brick wall. He's smiling at me, dead-eyed, like my words just don't compute. 'You've done very well, Mr Wood,' he declares. It's only my weakness from hunger that stops me from trying to strangle the guy.

Chapter 14

DEATH ON THE ROADS

June 1975, Oxford, England

A show somewhere, some Odeon or another, I don't know. What I do know is, everyone's gone mental. Sure, that's standard for us. As happens every night, a couple of fans have gotten past security. They're on stage and I'm trying to – gently – shake one of them off my back, but she's clinging to me like a rodeo rider, until she's eased off me by someone, Fred or maybe Paddy, and ushered off stage. As she's bundled away, she throws her arms up in triumph, showing the baying mob what can be achieved with just a little dedication to the cause. I don't think too hard about it. It would probably be weird if I *didn't* have a wild teenage fan hanging off my back like a knapsack at some point in the show.

As I said, this is all standard for us now. But listen closely enough and that sound you can hear over the screaming is the metal scrape of wheels coming off the wagon. That's Les up there, swinging the mic over his head like a cowboy trying to rope a steer in a Western. At first glance, he's bringing his usual A-game, standing imperious above the orchestra pit, a bunch of press photographers at his feet, their cameras trained on the fainting masses in the maelstrom. As ever, he's got the girls eating out the palm of his hand, it seems. Then he casts a look back my way and the mask slips. Just for a second, but I can see it clear as day. Take a million photographs of the guy and he'll sparkle like paste jewellery, not quite a diamond, so the change is noticeable to scholars of Rollermania. And as someone who's been living here in the eye of this storm, I consider myself a scholar. Despite all my academic shortcomings, I could take an A-level on the subject, no problem. I can see immediately that he doesn't look right at all. In this moment, he's like a wee lost boy and I feel bad for him. All the bullshit, all his alpha-male bravado that's caught up in his being – let's be honest – a class-A frontman, is forgotten for a second. He's a shitty person, a stone-cold narcissist. He has my hackles up most of the time now, so much so that Tam keeps us apart and doesn't even suggest the two of us sharing a hotel room. Possibly it's because we're the youngest, the most likely to get into mischief maybe, but mostly it's because there's a cold divide between him and the rest of us, me and him especially. Still, while he can be an arsehole, when we're up on stage, it's kind of like he's our arsehole. All the times he's acted like an entitled dick get lost in the ether. The million times he flicked me on the back of the head on long car journeys south, every demand for special attention, like he's a princess who found a pea under her mattress . . . For a moment, it's all forgotten. The mic is spinning above his head, like he's about to do a Mary Poppins and fly up into the skies, but if you strain your eyes, you can see it. He looks like he's going to start sobbing, poor bastard. Then it happens. One of the photographers is craning to get a shot, right under Les, who crashes his mic right into his face. Even over the screams of the crowd, I think I can hear the bones in his nose splintering.

Les says after that he was doing it for the fans, that the photographer had it coming, standing there trying to get a picture of some distressed kid in the crowd, blocking the St John's Ambulance guys. But I think he just wanted to clout somebody. I'm watching the photographer, clutching his face, a claret bib forming on his shirt and it's pretty fucked up. All the while, I'm expecting a big hook to appear at the side of the stage and yank us off, but no. Two songs later, Les is straining to sing and you can see the tears in his eyes. I'm smiling and waving, because that's my conditioned response now. There's actual blood on the floor in the stalls, tears on the stage and I'm taking my bow amid howling feedback. Finally, the show is stopped and we exit the stage.*

So, how did we arrive here? The long and short of it is, a couple of days back, Les killed a woman while driving in Edinburgh. Euphemia Clunie, aged 76, a sweet lady neighbour of his, was hit by Les's blue Ford Mustang, his pride and joy, while crossing Corstorphine Road. He'll later be cleared of causing Clunie's

* Les is later fined £1,100 by magistrates for assaulting the photographer.

death, but found guilty of the lesser charge of driving recklessly and dangerously, fined £150 and banned for a year. The day after the accident, Les rejoins the tour. We're expecting his usual preening self to arrive at the hotel, but it's like a light's gone out inside him. Rather than postpone the dates citing personal reasons – you'd think people would understand, right? – it's like Tam checked the bottom line and simply shrugged, took a glance at the schedule, a diary full of shows and obligations, and figured it would all come out in the wash. I want to say we're all on side, all pulling for our bandmate, but if I'm entirely honest, like when Derek and Alan's mum passed away, and I know this is terrible, it gets lost in the storm somehow. We've all been brainwashed to the point where the idea that 'the show must go on' is running through us like the message in a stick of rock. It's just pragmatism, a form of self-preservation, doing whatever you have to do to keep the show on the road. Although you can see the change in his persona, even Les is like that after a while. Three days of trauma, followed by looking like butter wouldn't melt. Just days later, everything's been internalised, a wound he's going to have to nurse himself with whisky and whatever else. On the surface, though, it's like nothing happened. To all intents and purposes, he's the same guy he was. Wouldn't piss on you if you were on fire.

Chapter 15

THE FARM

September 1975

I'm wiping the sweat off the inside of the window with my sleeve. 'They're still there,' I tell Eric. I should probably sound more solemn, only I've a mouthful of crisps.

Eric Faulkner brushes biscuit crumbs from his lap, gets up from the sofa to investigate, leather creaking. He's got a world-weary look on his face – like, what is it now, because it seems like there's always something going wrong here. Honest to God, this place is cursed, I think. We're both at the sill, white knuckles, shaking our heads in disbelief, staring out. Both of us wondering what they're doing out there. These strange human beings, out here in the middle of nowhere, the real back of beyond, peering back at us through their old man's binoculars, like David Attenborough scouting locations for a new BBC series. The cars pull up at the roadside, a convoy of Austin Maxis and Ford Escorts, setting up their camping chairs and laying out picnic blankets on the boundary of our land. You can tell they're not birdwatching because the tartan is a dead giveaway. In fact, there's tartan as far as the eye can see, like there's a dragoon of Scots pipers on the horizon. They're lined up at the edge of our farm, an encampment of teenagers and patient aunts and uncles who ferry them here in droves every weekend morning.

My dad always told me that if I ever came into any money, I should put it into property. It sounded like a decent shout to me, but what do I know? We had a meeting with our accountant in London and he's talking about tax and setting up shell companies and how that works, and I mentioned my dad's advice. All eyes were on the accountant, who starts muttering something impenetrable about tax complications, and kind of hypnotises me into changing my mind. Essentially, the message is, they're the adults in the room and I'm to take their advice over all others. Whatever the reasons, whatever the tax implications, ultimately we don't take their advice. We figure we're adults and it's our money to spend as we please, so Eric and I decide we want to get a place regardless. We want to build our own studio, so we ignore the adults in the room and tell Tam we want to buy a farm.

This is what we came up with: Dykefoot Farm on the outskirts of Carnwath, a wee village straight out of *Dr Finlay's Casebook.* If you need to run the numbers, it cost £34,000, but I've no understanding of the mechanics. We just saw the place and said,

'That'll do', signed a few documents and someone else wrote a cheque on our behalf. This place here, 30 miles or so outside Edinburgh, with the tartan army camped out on the fringes, is all ours, curses and all. We're in the middle of no place and that's just how we want it. We want to be isolated, to have a kind of decompression chamber outside the madness of the world. Admittedly, it's not much to look at. Set back from the road, something like 400 metres from the traffic's boom, it's grey stone, with a bunch of ruins amid the mud piles and cowpats, but we have an idea it can be something.

It's my first home away from Marchmont Street and my mum was very upset to see me go, but I told her I'd be back every other day most likely, just to have my tea. I've a room on one side of the farmhouse, Eric has his on the other. The rest of the place is a work in progress. It's scruffy – what you might call a fixer-upper, not that we do any fixing up. Maybe sometimes my mum will come by and hoover my room, but Eric's room looks like a tartan nightmare, just piles of dirty shit and what have you, like a tornado just swept through the place. Outside, there's a courtyard where the band rehearse occasionally, and a few outbuildings, which we plan to convert into a recording studio. We're not talking about a reel-to-reel tape recorder and a few eggboxes stuck to a wall in the cowshed here. We've asked some serious people to work on the designs for the space. The architects and designers commit our vision to paper and we're completely engrossed in the idea. In our heads, we see it as a place where orchestras can come and score movie soundtracks and we've an idea that we can record the next Rollers LP here and that the place can become a destination studio for some big artists.

Because we're nouveau riche, apparently, and despite the place being run down – a shell, basically – the farmhouse is kitted out from top to bottom by Harrods. Eric and me walked around the store with a personal shopper saying, 'One of those, two of those, oh and can we have it all delivered?' That was a sight, three or four Harrods delivery trucks getting down the track to the farmhouse, laden with sofas and white goods and, for some reason, a huge brass set of kitchen scales that neither of us will ever use. Any burglars passing by would have taken note. And, let me tell you, they have all taken note. The first time we leave on tour, the place is ransacked. We're out in the sticks, miles from the nearest police station, an easy mark.

After getting hit that first time, we get an alarm fitted, but it's about as much use as an ashtray on a Kawasaki. It takes the bobbies half an hour to get there, by which time the thieves have had it away into the night – or even broad daylight, they're so blatant about it. They strip the lead off the roof, and take the brass taps and fittings from the bathroom and kitchen. Anything that isn't bolted down is gone.

After a couple of burglaries, Eric and I regroup. It's obvious we're going to need to ditch the plans for the recording studio. It's just throwing good money after bad. We can't make a move without it being reported on the radio or in the newspapers. Every headline announcing our movements becomes an open invitation to the criminal fraternity of Scotland to just come by and fill their boots. These are the dates we'll be gone. This is when we'll be back. Make sure to wipe your feet when you come in and help yourself to our worldly goods, you bastards. It's not just Scotland's Neds who are making themselves at home, either.* We came home from a show, fair knackered from the trip, and Eric shouted for me to 'Come check this!' There's a fan asleep in Eric's bed, like fuckin' Goldilocks, only without the porridge.

I passed my driving test a while back and pushed out the boat by buying a second-hand Mini. You only live once, right? It cost me £60 and after a week it's covered in mud and shit. When you've had a couple of number-one hits and there are two Rollers albums knocking about the charts, you'd probably expect something a bit more glamourous. A bright-red Lamborghini or something, with one of Pan's People sitting next to me as we drive down to Saint-Tropez for the weekend. But no. There's no funny business on that front. It's like we've been conditioned to not even think about the fairer sex. Most likely I'd be too scared of getting found out by Tam to even consider meeting up with a girl. Just the idea, it's like a thought crime or something. Tam has spies everywhere. At least that's what I think, like I've got Stockholm Syndrome or something. I'm scared of the guy, but simultaneously don't want this journey to end. So, instead of chasing girls, Eric and me embark on this weird sitcom kind of life together.

It's the battered Mini and me and Eric running the gauntlet of tartan on our way to the local shops for a pint of milk,

* In Scottish slang, a Ned is a hooligan, lout or petty criminal.

Eric covering his face as we pass the girls. I don't know if that's because he doesn't want to be seen, or if he just doesn't want to be seen in my car. Probably the latter, now I think about it. Fortunately, Eric's embarrassment isn't a long-term concern. Following a mishap with a pothole on a routine trip back home, the subframe collapses and we have to abandon her at the side of the road. I remember thinking, 'That's country roads for you' as we climbed out and started walking down the main road to our driveway. It's probably a mile or so, and it's getting dark, and I'm thinking that if we cut across the fields and walk back, kind of as the crow flies, we'll be home and roasting by the fire in no time. Eric shrugged and said, 'Sure, why not?' You can see the farmhouse from here, it's probably a 1,000-metre hike. It was a bad idea. I recognise that now. I probably realised this after a few hundred metres, because we were mired in heather and reeds and mud and shite, all these bored cows lowing in the fields around us. I can't see his face anymore, but Eric's cursing me under his breath. 'Woods, you bastard . . . fuck . . . we should have gone up the road.'

Because I'm this eternal optimist, I'm telling him 'Ach, it'll be fine, you'll see' as we descend deeper into the marsh. In the back of my mind, I'm imagining the headlines in six months' time when they find our skeletons among the reeds and the discarded tartan scarves. We find our way through the first field, then a second, and we're both dead weary, and it's black as pitch now and you can hear these eery, hacking coughing sounds, like something's escaped from hell and is now walking among us. 'What the fuck is that?' Eric says and you can hear the fear in his voice.

I'm staggering, feeling my way like a blind man and there's that guttural coughing sound again. I think about it a minute. Feeling the cold wetness seep into my shoes, I realise. 'It's the cows. The fuckin' cows are coughing.' We're laughing, cold to our bones, staggering into the farmhouse. The next morning when we track back, we find that someone's nicked the wheels off the Mini. The day after that, the carcass has been stripped completely.

Eric comes round to my idea the place might be cursed soon enough. The other guys come over to rehearse in the courtyard and, halfway through our run-through, there's a chip-pan fire in the kitchen. We're running through a couple of numbers in the courtyard, giving it a bit of 'Shang-A-Lang' or something, and there's these black plumes of smoke engulfing us, like we're playing in the middle of a warzone. Everyone's looking at me, so I walk into the smoke-filled kitchen. I can't see a thing, just a very faint orange glow, the fire in the frying pan. I manage to drape a damp tea cloth over the flaming pan and start choking to death on the kitchen tiles. Somehow, I manage to crawl to safety, poking my head out of the galley window, soot all over me, like a cartoon character that got exploded, but by then I'm thinking maybe when the accountant says 'Don't put your money into property', I'll be more inclined to listen to him next time.

16

AMERICA AWAITS

13 September 1975

It's getting dark here. The fact dawns on me slowly, slower than I'd like to think. Maybe my reflexes are dull, but you'll forgive me that. I'm trapped beneath a pile of teenagers, the studio lights getting blocked out, a haze of pinks and reds, and something like claustrophobia has me in its grip. Some lucky punter has a good handful of my hair too, by the feel of it, tugging just hard enough to make me wince. At first, I can hear the screams, but after a second, the sound is blotted out. It's like being underwater for a minute. Then everything goes black and I think I slip into unconsciousness for a second. All I can hear is the sound of my own heart beating, the blood pumping in my ears. Then there's a break in the tangle of limbs above me and I take a sharp breath of air that tastes sickly sweet, like Parma Violets and excitement. Through a fan's lank hair, Vosene-clean, I can see the arc light flickering a moment, then the light is blocked out entirely – a stray leg or arm across my face, squishing my nose against my cheek, like a journeyman fighter who went down in the second round one too many times. I'm reaching out an arm, hoping someone will pull me out from under this heaving mess of humanity, but no help comes. Through the muffled sound of a dozen breathing fans, their abrupt, heaving laughter, I can hear Les and, like me, he's struggling for air. I think I can see Alan too in the stew of people. He's fighting for breath, laughing, sinking deeper into tartan waters. This scene is probably played out over 30 seconds, a minute maybe, but it seems longer, like I've been here a month, a dozen sticky hands held against my chest, pressing me down. I'm drowning, I realise, but I don't feel fear. My heart is pounding with adrenaline, sheer boundless excitement.

Then a familiar voice emerges from the fug of perfume and pent-up emotion, the squirming and wriggling fans, their sharp elbows finding my ribs and hips as they jockey for position. A gruff, authoritative tone immediately reassures me. I discount it as a dream, unintelligible cockney noise, as I feel his rough paws at my collar and Fat Fred drags me unceremoniously to safety. He picks me up and lands me square on the studio floor, right side up finally, and I blink hard against the light, dazed by the hot studio lights.

I automatically check for an injury, but I've received no wounds, just mussed-up hair and tartan tatters that used to be clothes. No drama here. Just a regular day at the office, I decide. As my vision returns, I should be running for safety, but I catch a look at the cameramen. I'm seeing two of everything, like

Mr Magoo, and these guys are all standing stock-still, cameras locked on this third circle of hell. They're watching this insanity unfold, recording the moment for posterity, making a mental note to tell their wife they witnessed true madness when they get home for their supper. I stand there for a minute, catching my breath, looking on as Fred and the TV security guys drag Les and Alan from the tangle of legs and nonsense. I see Tam Paton across the stage. He's sweating, turning his white suit grey with perspiration. He's smiling, got dollar signs for eyes. From his perspective – and, if I'm honest, from ours too – tonight couldn't have gone better, even if we'd planned it this way.

Usually if you want to break the US, you settle in for a year, maybe eighteen months, and knuckle down. You conquer the place territory by territory, slowly converting people, winning hearts and minds, city after city. Maybe you favour one coast over another, but if you want to make it there, eventually you will have to cover all the bases. Not us, though. We're prime-time and this is how the Bay City Rollers are unveiled to the US public. Live by satellite, beamed across the Atlantic somehow for the big show on ABC – *Saturday Night Live with Howard Cosell*,* the legendary sports broadcaster taking his shot at presenting a variety show. We're 3,000 miles away in London, yet – through a combination of Sid Bernstein's promotional nous and Clive Davis's undeniable savvy, an innate ability to sniff out a hit – it's like a grenade has been lobbed across the Atlantic.

* Not the *Saturday Night Live* that runs to this day on NBC. That show would debut in October 1975.

We've seen these scenes a hundred times now. We're battle-hardened. But for a virgin American audience, settling down for some mild, scheduled distraction from the Vietnam War to see them through until the late-night talk shows, this is something new. Sure, it's only a couple of hundred fans in a TV studio, but some new madness took hold of them. Maybe they were up too late waiting – New York is five hours behind London, so it's a long haul for some – but those feral teens can take some of the credit for what comes next. You could probably tell someone about this Rollermania thing until your throat bled, but here we are, thanks to these fans, showing them, in full-dimension colour in their living rooms, this strange phenomenon from across the pond. Thirty million Americans, TV dinners in their laps, and this is how we make their acquaintance. It was only meant to be a brief set, a quick run through a bunch of our hits, finishing just in time for the satellite hook-up, with our debut US 45 – appropriately enough – 'Saturday Night', handpicked by Clive as our first stateside single. To us, it seems a curious choice of song, like he just plucked the idea out of thin air. We all figure 'Bye Bye Baby' is the track, but we're talked down from that ledge. 'It's a Four Seasons song,' Clive tells us. 'A big hit here already. You'd be fools to go with it.' He has us back in the studio recording a new version of an old flop for release. After the Nobby version stalled outside the hit parade, we don't even play the song anymore. It's been left to die on the vine. But Clive's forgotten more about the music business than we'll ever learn, so we go along with his masterplan. His is the final word on the matter and will always carry sway over ours. Maybe he has a point, though. Just now, before the riotous scenes, it sounded every bit like a smash-hit record.

In the aftermath of the broadcast, Fred guides us back to our dressing room. Les and Alan are grinning, maybe slightly concussed, but happy enough. Then the door closes and the sound recedes, but I can still hear my blood racing around my brain. Tam's rubbing his hands together, beside himself, while we survey the damage to each other. Eric and Derek made a clean getaway. They saw the danger before the rest of us but, in truth, we're all fine, laughing and joking while Tam makes a call, then another, then another.

'Who are you calling?' I ask, helping myself to a warm Pepsi. My voice sounds weird, like I'm speaking for the first time, and I tap myself on the side of the head, like I just got out of a swimming pool with an earful of chlorine. Tam looks me up and down. 'I'm calling the papers,' he says, like the answer was obvious. I don't think to wonder why. I still have a finger buried in my ear, waiting for my hearing to return to normal. The morning comes and we're off to the airport. As we pass a chemist, Tam tells the driver to pull up. He jumps out and returns five minutes later with plasters and bandages, and a pair of drugstore sunglasses, which he tells me to put on. 'The papers will love it,' he explains. The next thing I know, I'm being swept through the terminal, looking like the invisible man.

We arrive at Edinburgh airport, get off the plane and we're suddenly surrounded by paparazzi, answering questions on the fly, telling them I'm okay following my near-death experience. As soon as I get into the car, I whip off the disguise, shaking my head. We have a couple of days at the farm to decompress and to pack our things for the flight to New York City, all under the watchful gaze of the Rollers day trippers out at the farm's boundary. Obviously the story of my brush with death is in all the papers the next morning, just as Tam knew it would be, as well as the news of the show's impact in the US. Whatever you want to say about the guy, and the fact he treats us all like shite, he understands promotion. He knows what makes a good story.

Chapter 17

THE LIMO INCIDENT

One week and maybe 3,500 miles later, the driver pulls out into the afternoon traffic. Outside our Midtown hotel, a mob of American fans cheer us on our way. There are a few shouts of 'I love you Les/Eric/Alan' and suchlike, much to the confusion of the doorman. His life was normal yesterday; maybe he took himself across the street to the Rockefeller Center, or to Central Park to feed the pigeons, or he complained to a hotdog seller about the Jets. But today he's caught in his own personal Twilight Zone, this surreal bubble of frantic, weeping teenagers asking, 'Where are the Rollers? When are they coming back? Can I use the restroom?'

Mere days after the satellite link-up with Howard Cosell, it's as if every available yard of tartan in New York state has been bought up and is draped around these kids' shoulders. Like the doorman, I'm similarly bemused, but also kind of delighted. I didn't plan any of this. None of us did. We could easily have arrived to zero fanfare, but already I've got this Spidey-sense that we're on the cusp of something here. It's like home, but madder somehow, and everyone's vowel sounds are more drawn out.

We're in a stretch limo, the space in the back as big as a football field, and we're sprawled out across the seats, gawping out the window, while Paul, our driver, in between honking his horn, points out the various landmarks as we cut through the city traffic. Not that we need anything pointing out. Everything here is iconic, seared into our brains from years of telly and movies. The Empire State, the Brooklyn Bridge, the World Trade Center. It's all just outside the window, big as life. Probably bigger. The limo has become a home from home, practically since we arrived. That was quite a scene, a couple of hundred press photographers and teenage fans chasing us through the terminal, proving that the Rollers virus has gone airborne, that it travelled across the Atlantic with us. We're good soldiers and we stop, wave, smile, answer the hack questions on the fly. You know the drill by now, I'm sure.

When we're not in a genial Mexican stand-off with the feral hordes, fighting jetlag, we're holed up in the hotel, this world of ornate columns, chandeliers and fussy concierges pleading with us to not approach the windows of our suite. We're here to meet the press and that's what we do, only here in the States, it's a 24-hour a day job, speaking to folk across Eastern, Pacific and Midwestern time zones. If we get some time to ourselves, maybe 20 minutes per day, we can't go out, so we're confined to quarters, ordering room service and clicking through a thousand television channels. On every other New York station, there's a guy with a side parting and thick glasses standing outside, with a hundred fans behind him, all chanting, 'We want the Rollers!' in thick New York accents. The rest of the time, we're in this stretch Lincoln half of every day, getting ferried from one grey building to another, greeted by a different tartan scrum to the one we just left behind at the last place, getting acquainted with the New York City traffic. These pissed-off New Yorkers are so close that you could land a kiss on their cheek as they stick their heads out their windows and shout at the clouds.

Between rehearsals for *Saturday Night Live with Howard Cosell*, we're swept into Clive Davis's offices on Broadway, given the dollar tour of the building, before posing for some pictures for the trades. I'm looking about the place, taking stock. The fact is, we're all staring like slack-jawed tourists here. The walls are lined with gold and platinum, like King Tut's tomb, and there's a hundred neat rows of black-and-white photos. The great Clive Davis is mugging for the camera in every shot, an arm thrown around the shoulder of every famous pop singer you care to imagine. The record is in stores, Clive's telling us, and he has high hopes. On the back of the single, there's an LP, a kind of compilation of our last two records from back home, a primer for the US market, he says. He's talking fast, I realise, like he's got a tee time to make. Then his secretary tells him it's time for another meeting and calls the elevator, and we're whisked away on a VIP tour of the city. Paul takes us on a jaunt around his Harlem neighbourhood, rolls back the roof and we're waving like visiting royals from the limo and all these black kids are flipping us the bird and catcalling us and it's hilarious. We're taken on a ride-along with the NYPD, given honorary certificates – Captain Stuart Wood and Lieutenant Eric Faulkner, that kind of thing.

It's 99 per cent great, the stuff of a kid's dreams, but the outstanding 1 per cent is a pain in the arse. That pain is Les. He could barely get his big head through the doorways back home, such is his ego, but here, where showbiz is king, where they congratulate you for being a bighead, he's gone from difficult to unbearable in the time it takes you to check in at a Manhattan hotel. I think since the moment we arrived at JFK, he's had his chest puffed out, like he's finally arrived. Really, it's a wonder he managed to get his ego through customs. That's okay in some respects. You expect a frontman to be a bit of an attention-seeker. I always laugh when I remember the first photoshoots we did. Les elbowed us out of the way so he could be in the middle of the shot, before realising he was going to be the one with the staple running through the middle of his face, so modified his behaviour, pushing one of us to the middle, just in case. Still, I can't help thinking, in his mind at least, this promo trip is just Les McKeown and his backing band. Maybe he's heard Tam telling me how expendable we all are so he's started to believe it. Except when it comes to himself, of course.

We've been in Manhattan a couple of days, barely stopping to catch our breath, taking calls from our hotel suite, schmoozing the radio jocks, recording on-the-hoof station idents – five-second soundbites of us saying 'Don't touch that dial . . . You're listening to WYNY FM . . . and we're the Bay City Rollers' in accents no one here will ever penetrate. It's the same as back home, I guess. We've done radio interviews before. No one is looking to hear your innermost thoughts. No one wonders if you have a solution to the Israel–Egypt conflict. They ask us about milk and teddy bears and the usual shite. While we talk, the cream of NYC's disc jockeys, magazine writers and TV crews are all standing in line, wondering what the fuss is, awaiting their ten-minute audience with the Rollers. The same questions, just different confused, frowning faces. The only difference here is probably that our hotel room has a telephone in the bathroom, so you can sit on the loo and speak to a hundred thousand New Yorkers on one line, while Eric speaks on another, sprawled out on the king-size bed, giving his arse a good scratch while he ponders the question about his favourite baseball team.

Given the flying-by-the-seat-of-the-pants way our career is managed back home, it's curious to see things so regimented. During rehearsals for the big TV appearance at the weekend, our lawyers, Arista's lawyers, Tam and the accountant Steve Tanenbaum descend on our dressing room and we each take it in turn to sign the new deal with Arista. We're assured by Tam and our lawyers it's all good. None of us has any questions. We're not popping on a pair of reading glasses and going through the clauses and sub-clauses with a fine-tooth comb, because no one has a minute – literally. Straight after the contract is flashed under our noses and while the ink is still wet, there's a knock on the door and we're told we're needed back on stage to check the camera angles for Saturday's performance. It's possibly a sign of Clive Davis flexing his muscle on our account, or maybe it's Sid

Bernstein seeking to recapture the Beatles glory days from a few years back, but whatever it is, every second of our lives here is accounted for. We're moved around the city with something like military precision. The new record, 'Saturday Night', is everywhere and it's like they've moved all these various pieces around a chessboard in anticipation of something.

In my mind's eye, I've got a picture of us having a top 40 hit, maybe even top 30. That'd be something exciting to tell the folks when I get home, but Clive isn't looking for a modest hit. He's got his eyes on bigger prizes. Really, I have no idea what's about to happen. The same goes for Tam. He has no better understanding of the US music business than the rest of us, and he's a pure passenger from this moment on, I think. He's along for the ride, enjoying the plaudits and money, having his ego fluffed by acolytes, but he has no idea of how it's working or how he'd make things better if they're not. If the Rollers was a movie, this would be the moment he was discarded, replaced with someone with more business sense, but this isn't a movie, so his berth here is secure. Aside from Les and Eric, the rest of us are still held under his spell to some extent, and he knows that better than we do, but when I think about it, he's neither use nor ornament now. We just haven't worked that out.

So, we're in the limo and it's the big day. Our 'in person' US TV debut. The partition is down and Paul is upfront, carving through yellow cabs. It's like we're passing through a swarm of bumblebees. To his right, leaning back over the seat, giving us a final pep talk, is Mike Klenfner, the A&R guy, Clive's man on the inside. He's pointing out various landmarks, making professional chitchat about the radio reaction to the single, and about the upcoming TV appearance. 'They got a great idea,' he's saying. 'Scots pipers playing and Howard's gonna announce you. Camera swings across the stage to a big fucking tartan package, marked "To Saturday Night Live – From Scotland". There's a couple of pyros, then the walls will come down to reveal you guys. It's going to blow their minds!'

We're all hanging on his every word, except Les. He's in a world of his own. He lights a ciggie, filling the car with blue plumes of Marlboro smoke. He shuffles into Alan, gives him an elbow to move up the long seat. Alan just cedes the ground, rolling his eyes. Les is enjoying the extra love he's been receiving at all the press calls, the few extra screams of his name as we pass out of the hotel. We're used to the dynamic by now. The singer, whatever the band, will always generate a little more heat. We understand the weird hierarchy of fame and we're fine with it. You do that in front of the cameras, when you're in a radio studio, sure, but once the show is over, once the curtain's come down, you're meant to return to factory settings, go back to being a regular member of the band. Unfortunately, Les doesn't have a reset switch. He's starting to believe his own press and it's pure annoying for those around him. Over the past year, he's found all our buttons and he'll press them whenever he needs a distraction.

From my perspective, I've been putting the Les thing to the back of my mind, trying to ignore him, but he makes it hard. He's hardly said a word to us since we landed, barely a 'Good morning, couldnae gae a fuck how you're doing', but we're heading up towards Broadway, and he turns to me. 'Woody.'

I don't answer for a second. I'm listening to Mike with half an eye out the window. I can feel Les bristle, getting impatient, as he says my name again. 'Woody. Woody. Woody.' Each time he says the word, he administers a flick to the side of my head, like a spoilt child. He's done the flicking thing before, when boredom has got the better of him on long road trips, but just now I'm not in the mood and, in a half-second, I launch myself across the seats at him. I don't know why. It's just pure red mist and suddenly we're piling into each other, just fists and feet flying, dust swirling around us. Derek, Eric and Alan are just keeping out of our way, not even laughing. We're pounding each other for maybe 30 seconds, full-on. I'm shouting, 'Fuck you, you fuckin' arsehole!', getting a few good stomps in, and him swinging these wild punches, screaming, 'I'll fuckin' kill you!'

It would still be going on now, I think, except for Tam, who's just mortified, embarrassed. I hear him clear his throat, like he's about to shout at us, like we're naughty wee children. When we got in, his only instruction to us was that we don't touch the limo's drinks cabinet, and now he's realising he should have also told us not to go to fuckin' war with each other. Instead of screaming at us, he lets out a tired-sounding 'Ach, I'm sorry about this, Mike' as he pushes the button to close the partition between the front and rear of the limo. Mike turns and faces forward. Somehow, Tam and the guys have managed to separate us and calm has been restored just in time as we pull up to the Ed Sullivan Theater. I look across at Tam and he looks like he wants the earth to open up and swallow him.

Chapter 18

COLLATERAL DAMAGE

If I were to spend an hour on an analyst's couch going over the events of the past few months, I think I'd come out of it okay. In my mind's eye, I can practically see the psychiatrist, frantically scribbling, wondering what's wrong with me, while I cheerfully run through a list of things I'm completely fine about. I'm barely old enough to shave but have got asbestos skin, so I'm oblivious. I can't say the same for everyone, obviously. The casualties of fame are often unexpected. Take my parents as an example. They've become collateral damage in the whole Roller madness. I don't see them often enough, but whenever I hear something from back home, it's generally bad news – some nonsense that's sprung up from my sudden fame and they're the ones bearing the brunt.

Whether I'm home or abroad, there's usually something, some pebble in my mum or dad's shoe. Even now, with Eric and Yours Truly living away at the farm, there's still this weird encampment outside my parents' house, a line of fans that needs to be passed through. Mostly they're nice people, just a little exuberant, but there's graffiti in the stair and the doorbell chimes every fifteen minutes. Just now in New York, we're holed up in a green room, about to appear on coast-to-coast TV. Just as Clive Davis planned, 'Saturday Night' reached the top of the Hot 100, was followed by a number-one album and another top-ten hit, 'Money Honey', a Faulkner/Wood original, so we're in demand. Every TV show with a three-minute blank spot between commercials are all vying to have the Rollers fill that hole. We're a couple of minutes from airtime and Tam Paton saunters in, a vision in white. He's wearing a $500 suit that plummeted in value the moment he got one leg in the trousers. He's had it on all week; it's his new look. Once he's got our attention, he clears his throat, set to deliver big news. Probably another appointment being added to our mysterious itinerary, I think. An hour less in my bed tonight.

'Your hoose is on fire,' he says, finally. He's grinning, like he just told the funniest one-liner in a *Laugh-In* re-run. We're looking at him, waiting for him to elaborate. It takes a moment for him to catch on, to specify. 'The farm,' he explains, trying to summon a serious expression at the same time as he's wiping away a tear, from laughing so hard.

Eric and me, we're on our feet, frantic. I can see Eric, holding himself back from grabbing Tam by the collar, wanting to shake more details out of the bastard. Maybe it's the glint of anger, I don't know, but Tam composes himself and runs through the story. This band Rosetta Stone – this other young band Tam's taken under his wing – had a mishap and set the kitchen ablaze. Our kitchen. As he's painting the picture, there's a tap on the door. A researcher tells us we're up next, asks us to follow them out to the studio and I switch to autopilot, walking onto the stage, painting a phony smile on my face for the people watching at home. I've no memory of the subsequent show, just of calling my folks when I'm back at the hotel. My dad fills me in on the rest. He sounds broken, just plain exhausted. After finishing his nightshift at the post office, he tells me, rolling home before dawn, he got a call from the local bobby in Carnwath, telling him the fire was under control, but he should come out and survey the damage. Half an hour later, he's standing in our kitchen, more charcoal than brick now, and the walls throughout the farmhouse are flecked with air pellets, where the wee bastards out of Rosetta Stone used our home for target practice between rehearsals. According to my mum, my dad has to be held back from taking a swing at them when he sees them. 'Why d'you even let them in the house?' she asks. 'We didn't,' I tell her. Tam asked two weeks ago and we told him no fuckin' way. He just did it anyway. How'd he even get the keys?

We're halfway through 1976 and, as you can imagine, my folks are done with Rollermania. It's so sad. These two amazing people who brought us up and instilled us with great values, and they're having to deal with all the shit by themselves because there's nothing in place to protect them. After much soul-searching, they make the sad decision to finally leave Marchmont Street. It's been a year of insanity and it's too much for them. I've only been making flying visits. A night here, maybe a quick afternoon stopover to get my socks washed, so for me it doesn't feel too much of a wrench, but I feel for them. They don't say anything but, naturally, I can't help feeling a little guilty when they up sticks. It's no reflection on the fans, but the day-to-day exhaustion of having to deal with dozens of screaming girls has taken its toll on the rest of the Wood clan.

It's my mum who's most anxious. She's old-school. She worries what the neighbours are thinking of her and imagines the curtains twitching and the street corner gossips tearing into her reputation. It's getting to the stage where she feels like a prisoner in her own home. Just something simple like taking my wee brother to school in the morning is completely surreal. The fans in the stair scrawling graffiti, standing vigil every day and night, pushing the buzzer every five minutes, making everyone's lives miserable. There comes a point when you realise it's not worth the aggravation. They probably meant well, the fans, but my mother was a nervous wreck. They had to change the telephone number a dozen times because within a week, someone would get hold of the new number and be phoning my mum and my dad. As the Rollers became more popular around the world, the calls start coming at all hours, from every time zone. Usually it's benign – kind of 'Is Woody there? Can you tell him that I love him?' But not always. One time, my dad gets this message from one of his workers to get back to his office as someone's on the phone saying something's happened to Stuart. My dad flies into a blind panic. When he got to the phone, it was a fan.

'Why did you say something had happened to my son?'

'It was the only way I could think to get you to come to the phone,' she said.

She probably thought it was harmless, but my dad was shaken. He didn't sign up for any of this, so I understand. But that was the straw meeting the camel's back as far as he was concerned. After that and the kitchen debacle, they make the decision to move. It's sad for them to leave the old house behind. It's the place I grew up, the place I kept my heart all these years. I buy them a nice, detached house on the outskirts of Edinburgh, away from the noise and constant tartan traffic. No one can find them there. Even me. The move happens when I'm away with the Rollers and I've no idea where they've gone. I only get to talk to them once a week maybe. Tam's watching the pennies and scrutinises every hotel bill like he's studying for his Masters in being a dick, so I can never get away with using the hotel phone to check in with them as often as I'd like. By the time I get to see them next, I drive up the A1 and realise I've no idea where they are. They've been settled in for three months by the time I find them.

The new place is bought with Rollermania in mind. It's situated on a main road on the outskirts of town, with a long back garden, which I can access via a side road. It's a little off the beaten track, so no more having to do the Grand National across everyone's gardens just to get in the back door. I can call ahead, drive my car into the garage at the bottom of the garden and come in undetected. It doesn't take long for the jungle drums to get the word out that my folks have moved, and they track the Wood family down, but it's less stressful for my mum. It's a house with its own front door, so we're not sharing the entrance with five other families and my mum doesn't worry so much. After a fortnight, there's still an army of fans holding the line at the front of the place, but the back way in is a mystery to them, so I can come and go without losing clumps of hair at least. My mum relaxes enough to take out cups of tea and wee plates of biscuits when it gets cold because that's her personality. They were making her life miserable but, at the same time, she's worrying that these wee girls are catching their death of cold out there.

Chapter 19

THE DEAD GOLDFISH

May 1976

The phone rings. It's Tam. I tell Eric to turn the telly down. After the last burglary, this is a new TV – and a new everything else. 'Urgent meeting,' Tam's saying, his voice rising to a panicked whine, like air escaping from a lilo. 'Get down here now,' he says. I'm surprised Eric wants to come. Our most recent trip to Tam's place was traumatic, as I'll explain, but I guess if Tam says it's urgent, we just go. We're in the car within five minutes. I've dispensed with the services of the £60 Mini; its carcass still sits at the side of the road a ways down towards Edinburgh. I've a Range Rover now and she's a beauty, battle-damaged from my driving skills, and spattered with mud and cowpats. Funnily enough, a psychic warned me the car was cursed, but I ignored her warnings. The first day I got it, practically the minute I drove it off the lot, a car drove into the side and scrunched the door. A week later, I'm arrested for sleeping at the side of the motorway. I woke up to the sight of a traffic cop tapping on the window, but if I hadn't stopped for a rest, I think I would have fallen asleep at the wheel. But he wrote me up for something called 'dangerous parking'. Not long after, I was in a head-on collision with a drunk driver. Thankfully no one was injured. They just found the drunk driver stoating about, 50 yards from his battered car.

As we pull away, Eric's already digging his nails into the plastic moulded dash because he's a nervous passenger – only when I'm driving though, I notice. Possibly I'm in too much of a hurry, gunning the engine, down the track and onto the main road. There's a tiny encampment of wee girls at the edge of the farm, tartan blowing in the cold wind as we head out. I resist the urge to give them a wave.

'Did he say what it was?' Eric asks. His knuckles are stark white now. His eyes are glassy, like he's just been saying a wee prayer to himself. A 'Please God, don't let Woody kill me' kind of thing.

'Nope,' I say. Up from second, a crunching gear change to fourth, feeling the clutch grinding under my feet, imagining I'm Jackie Stewart or Fangio at Monte Carlo or something. Radio 1 is playing, probably too loud. 'He sounded like he was in a state,' I say. 'Proper meltdown. Something serious.' We're doing 70 now, my comfort zone, and the countryside is a greenish blur out the windows. Twenty minutes later, there's gravel under the tyres and we skid to a halt outside Tam's place. Eric finally opens his eyes and checks he's still got a pulse.

Tam's moved away from Prestonpans and his old mum's chips and his dad's spittoon, and has a place outside Edinburgh – Little Kellerstain. It's his fortress, security up the wazoo. You can see the airport from here, smell the jet oil from the DC10s and whatnot. He's here in the shadow of a grand old mansion, standing in stark contrast to his place – a right ugly prefab-looking, flat-roofed eyesore that someone built in a single afternoon. The architect was either drunk or a child because it looks like it will fall over in a stiff breeze. Still, it's maybe five bedrooms and it's on a big chunk of land, with a big wooden aviary out back, filled to bursting with primary-coloured budgerigars, rustling their plumage and chirping away in the darkness – and shitting all over the stone floor.

If I'm honest, I'm surprised Eric's come with me today. We were here not so long ago. Eric claims the overdose was accidental, but only he will know the truth. I only know when it happened, not how. We'd flown up from Heathrow with the newsreader John Craven for an interview here at Tam's. After the interview, we went our separate ways. Or so I thought. But apparently Eric had gone for a lie-down in one of Tam's many rooms and helped himself to a bunch of his sleeping tablets. Tam says he found Eric unconscious and immediately called an ambulance. Call me a cynic, but the press arrived on the scene so swiftly that I wouldn't be surprised if Tam called the papers before he dialled 999. I file away the memory, marking it up in my brain as a cry for attention, or maybe he can't face getting on the plane with us to the US this coming week. The sad truth is, I don't know either way. I can't fathom the depths of Eric's mind – and, let me tell you, he is a deep person, inscrutable. I'd love to tell you I'd noticed the signs, but he's a closed book to me, to all of us. He's often quiet and withdrawn, because that's his character. You ask if he's okay and he says, 'Ach, I'm just thinking, Woods', mulling over an idea for a new song, or away somewhere in his own world.

Anyway, Eric is back at the scene of the crime and we're staring out of the car, breathless, peering through the cast-iron gate, and Tam's dogs are barking at us from the other side, going mental, just adding to the drama. I click the buzzer once, then again for good luck. After a minute, Tam's boyfriend appears at the front door. The poor kid lands right in Tam's predatory sweet spot – not a boy exactly, but not a man yet. Tam's given up on the pretence now. All of us knew all along, but he doesn't hide the fact that he's gay. It's curious, I suppose, because back in the day, he made a lot of effort to put himself across as a tough guy, always the first to roll up his sleeves and start swinging whenever there was trouble. Maybe he was overcompensating, just trying to convince those around him he isn't gay. He's open about it now, but still cautious. He's got a lot of friends in high places – well-connected bastards everywhere, people in the press and wherever – so I'm sure he's got a plan in place to stop the word from getting out.

So, Tam's boyfriend. He's eighteen or nineteen, maybe. Eric and I give him a wee wave, relieved we're not going to have to shin up the wall and go up and over the barbed wire at the top of the wall, like I had to do last time when Tam lost his clicker for the gate. He comes over and there's the creak of metal and the gate starts to swing open, and we drive up to the house, past the workmen who are busying themselves around the grounds.

Tam greets us at the door. He's got some face on him. 'You want something? Tea or something?' he asks, leading us through to the kitchen, shuffling across the floor in his tartan slippers, a collie dog doing laps of the lino around us. He's wearing his new white suit. The kettle goes on, throwing steam up the tiles, and we're standing there waiting for the announcement. Tam's guy is skulking by the door, not going to speak unless spoken to. I've got a feeling in my guts whatever we're here for, it's not good news. The butterflies in there are doing somersaults, so I know it isn't news of us topping the charts in Poland or appearing on *This is Your Life*.

Obviously, he's got the heads-up that the world is coming to an end tomorrow, I'm thinking. A fiery comet spotted in the skies above Galashiels. A proper extinction-level event, like they have in the movies, and he's got word of a bunker nearby for us, his best boys. Beside the sink, there's a dead goldfish from Tam's pond. 'Just a second,' Tam says. He picks up the pasty fish and runs it under the cold tap a minute to try and revive it before, twinkling like a cabaret comedian, starting to give the dead fish mouth-to-mouth. When he sees we're not laughing, he pops the poor fucker on a dish, opens the back door and hands it to one of the guys who's working on his house. 'There's a fish for your dinner,' he says, and comes back laughing like he should be on the telly. He dismisses his guy and nods us over to the lounge. Eric and I take a seat on a big doughy sofa. There's a wall of awards and gold discs behind us, needing a polish.

'It's Alan. Something really bad,' Tam says, like the guy shot someone in the face on national TV or something.

'Okay, what is it then?' I ask. Tam hands me a mug of tea. I'll not be drinking that, I think. Hate the stuff. Eric takes a sip of his, but kind of screws up his face, like it's been brewed from piss and vinegar.

'I got this in the post this morning,' Tam picks up an envelope from the coffee table. A teenage girl's writing is on the front – primary-coloured felt pen, hearts over the i's, a wavy line underlining and SWALK probably written on the back. 'He's been seen around town. Drinking in pubs, if you can believe that?'

I'm thinking, *Yes, I can believe that. A grown adult having a pint in a pub*. I'm about to pipe up that it's probably not a sacking offence, but Tam's already heading me off at the pass. 'He's been out galivantin' and now, to top it all off, there's this . . .' He takes a grainy photograph from the envelope and shows it to us. There's a guy standing at a bus stop. I squint, get Tam to move his fat thumb out the way so I can see the face. It's Alan in his civvies, a leather jacket, T-shirt and a pair of blue jeans. The grainy figure is smiling, his arm around a woman.

'Alan has been photographed with *a bird*,' Tam says, his world crumbling around him, actual tears in his eyes.

'A bird?' Eric says. He's smiling but trying to frown. Got to look serious here.

'Alan? Away with a bird?' I feel panic rising. Realising that Al is getting kicked out of the band, and at the same time thinking, *Well done Al for getting a bird*.

'Aye,' says Tam, shaking his head solemnly, returning the photograph to the envelope. He looks like he just had the doctor tell him he's stage four. Terminal. 'It's a catastrophe. You realise that don't you? A fuckin' disaster.'

He leans back in his chair, picks up his briefcase and takes out a couple of pills for his palpitations. Then his expression shifts from heartbroken to pragmatic in a second. 'So I've told him he's sacked.'

He can see we're not amused, stuck here in the first stages of grief – denial, and moving into anger – but he's already moved past stages three and four and is on to five: acceptance. 'Ach, he's lost interest anyway,' he says, and then starts a shitty chart rundown of the reasons he's out. 'He disnae like the music. He won't wear the tartan gear. He's getting too old for this anyway.' He says Alan's too old a lot, as if at 28 you're suddenly aged out of this pop music malarkey.

'What are we going to do now?' I wonder aloud. I'm not pretending to frown anymore. I've got an upside-down V practically carved into my forehead. Tam places the envelope neatly on the table and leans forward, raising his hands like, *This is fine.*

'Dinnae worry. I've got this sorted. I've already hired a replacement,' he says, like my pal was a kitchen lightbulb. Not, 'I've found someone to try out, you understand. Let's get him down for rehearsals and see how you guys gel.' Nope. Nothing like that. Just, I've already hired a replacement. He's on the plane for the Canadian tour.

The next day, we meet again at Tam's. Alan comes along to hand in his gun and badge, and Eric and I drive him home, the drive of shame. I'm not exactly great at judging people's moods. He's trying to play it cool, taking it square on the chin, but maybe he's gutted. I can see him shifting around in his seat, like he's making room for his tail between his legs. Outwardly, though, he's playing it lackadaisical, because that's his nature. 'Ach, it'll be fine,' he says, but his eyes are telling another story. He knows he's dead in the water, like that fuckin' goldfish yesterday.

Ian Mitchell is the new guy, one of the wee fuckin' arsonists out of Rosetta Stone. Tam tells us he's keen and interested. He says 'keen and interested' a lot. Keenness and interest are always at the top of Tam's list of requirements, but usually he means pretty or malleable, or maybe a combination of the two. That's the subtext. If someone's pretty, it means the girls will like him, the same way Tam does. Still, Ian is okay. We meet him at rehearsals a couple of days later. He's a nice kid. Good guitarist. Never a dull moment. He's a year younger than me, so I'm not the baby anymore. He's here when we reach the crest of the wave in the US, but he's less inclined to put up with Tam's shit and won't bow down the way we have, so fair play to the guy.

Chapter 20

THE HOTSHOT

The offices of Clive Davis, Manhattan. A brief stopover with the money man before we head north to Canada. The door swings open and we're introduced to the new producer, Jimmy Ienner. Clive does the formalities and tells us that Jimmy's the main guy, a real hotshot. 'You should listen to Jimmy,' he tells us, so we listen. He shakes everyone's hand, simultaneously running through his resumé, spells working with Three Dog Night, Grand Funk Railroad, Blood, Sweat & Tears, Air Supply, the Raspberries and Eric Carmen – half of the songs we're hearing on FM radio, essentially. Then he starts telling us his plan.

'We wanna record the screaming,' the producer says.

'Oh yeah,' I say. 'Why they wanna do that?'

Across the office, under lights that shimmer, reflecting off a thousand Grammy awards and gold records, the producer just shrugs. He gives me a look – ruffled brow, feigned confusion –

that says, *Why are you even voicing an opinion here? Hey kid, you're not supposed to speak here. Just listen.*

'At the start of the song,' he says, slow and deliberate, like he's talking to a child, 'we wanna hear the fans screaming, you know.'

In an instant, I realise Jimmy's used to having the floor, so I don't interrupt again. He's worked with every fucker going and he has a *vision* to evolve the Rollers' style, he says. He wants the records to sound sleeker. More orchestration than a weekend with Mantovani. A middle-of-the-road sound to appeal to the US market. The Bay City Rollers aren't sleek, though, and we know it. At heart, despite what you might think, we're a street band, rough around the edges. My bandmates Derek and Alan, who founded the group in their teens, used to practice in their mum and dad's cramped front room in Edinburgh and were later forged in Tam Paton's potato shed. But Jimmy wants to hear lassies screaming, so we better do what he says, I guess.

'Sounds great,' we tell him. Just go along with it. Going along with it is probably our Achilles heel, but it's too late to change our DNA now.

'So, you'll be doing an appearance in Toronto,' he goes on. 'At – um . . .' He peers down at a folder in his hand. '. . . Nathan Phillips Square. Not a show exactly, not performing. Just show your faces. Wave to the girls. Ten minutes. Fifteen tops. Let 'em all see you. Exciting, right? And we'll set up the mics and record them. Sound okay?'

'Yep. Sure. That sounds fine. We'll do that.' *Just say yeah*, I'm thinking. *Nod your head.* A sarcastic part of me thinks having us standing and waving like morons in an open square won't cause any problems. I consider raising a hand, to clarify. Then I figure *Don't rock the boat.* We're not on home turf here. It's a whole new ballgame now and we're minded to be on our best behaviour. That's new bandmate Ian Mitchell, Les McKeown, Derek Longmuir – who has taken the news of his brother's ousting the way the rest of us react to getting served a Pepsi instead of a Coke, with a shrug, essentially – and me, all present and correct. Just the one notable absentee, you'll note. Eric Faulkner is missing. Eric is in Scotland, still recuperating after his overdose. We're a man down in a strange country and the Eric thing is playing on all our minds. Maybe not Les, but Les doesn't really think about anyone but Les because Les is like a universe unto himself – and probably a borderline sociopath. The rest of us, though, are concerned and it's there in the background, like a low, loud hum. Once Jimmy has made his pitch, we're back down to brass tacks, deciding which tracks we're gonna record for our next album. We all have sheets of paper to write down the names of the tracks Clive is about to play to us. The plan is that we'll mark them out of ten and the ones with the highest totals will be contenders for the album.

I wish Eric was here, though. None of our own songs are represented and he wouldn't stand for that. All the material is stuff Clive has suggested because he's accustomed to getting his own way. If he doesn't like something, he's quick to veto the idea. Eric would have had something to say about that, but the rest of us aren't sure how to express our annoyance. We're conditioned to pipe down, to keep our powder dry. Tam made sure about that. Just in practical terms, with our crazy touring and publicity schedule, there's very little time left before recording is scheduled to begin and for us to write anything new. Still, we do manage to shoehorn a couple of our own songs on there in the end. We've broken most world territories doing things our way and we're in high demand. Everybody wants a slice of us and, here at Arista, their job is to make sure they get it. They'll probably all end up with more than a slice.

As we file out, heading down to the limo, Paul is leafing through the *New York Post* and smoking a crafty ciggie, which he stubs out on the pavement as he opens the door. Les says to me, 'So, this Nathan Phillips Square? Do they have a McDonald's?'

Chapter 21

THE BATTLE OF NATHAN PHILLIPS SQUARE

27 June 1976

It's day two in Toronto and we're booked to appear on CHUM radio – a 'Hey, how are you guys doing, here's a blast of the new 45, stay tuned for more Rollers after the traffic' kind of deal. I'm not exactly immune to our success, but maybe a bit glib, a little entitled. The records here are selling in droves because, well, why wouldn't they? We are indisputably the biggest pop band on the planet right now, so it tracks that we're selling a lot of records. And shows. What do they say on this side of the pond? Oh yeah, *Forget about it!*

Every show is vast, like a friendly war, with thousands of casualties, but they're all smiling through the pain somehow, having the best time of their lives. I don't even think about it anymore. If I'm thinking anything, it's that I'm distracted, probably hungry, and there's a wee bell ringing in my brain. What is that? I remember the tour manager saying something, some obligation or other, but whatever it is, it's swept under a tide of in-car conversation and a pervading sense of hunger. I should probably eat something, I think, and my mind wanders. I forget about the ringing bell. I look across the seats at my partners in crime. Eric has flown in to be with us and that's a good thing – it seems more like the Rollers somehow, despite Alan getting the sack. I give them all the once-over. They're all similarly lost in their own worlds – except Ian, the rookie. He's not been christened yet. He isn't battle hardened like we are. Hasn't got the same armour we all have, but it will come. Either that, or he'll fall by the wayside and the Rollers juggernaut will carry on without him. He's peering out the window and he's looking scared. I have to put myself in his shoes a minute. Take myself back eighteen months, explain that this is all perfectly normal. Just another day in paradise.

The driver drops the divide between us, tells us this might take a minute and we all crane to see what's ahead of us. I'm expecting a bunch of Canuck roadworkers, steel caps and cigarettes hanging off their bottom lips, telling us to turn back. Or maybe a couple of Toronto cops. But no. It's a siege. The radio station is crawling, alive, like a termite mound. Derek shrugs. Eric and Les light a ciggie. I look back to Ian, screwing up his eyes, his jaw falling open. 'Is . . . is that for us?' he says finally. The car edges forward a couple of metres and we're caught up in a sudden mudslide of females, badges, banners and smudged shopping-mall lippy. Colour drains from Ian's face and I give him a nudge in the ribs. 'Ach, it'll be fine,' I tell him. I mean it too. Then the stretch Lincoln reels slightly and we're caught in the undertow of maybe 2,000 tartan fans, every ounce of daylight suddenly subsumed, like someone forgot to pop a shilling in the meter. We're sitting in the half-darkness in the back of the rocking, shaking car. There's pounding on the roof. It sounds and feels like a sledgehammer, and the ceiling starts to cave in above our heads. Ian is skittish, smiling nervously, trying to not let the fear show. The rest of us are fine, just waiting patiently for security to sort it out. A minute passes. Then it's five, and I can see the driver checking us in the rear-view, dabbing the sweat from his brow with a monogrammed handkerchief. Then to the right, there's a thud, and a giant bear paw sweeps some of the humans off the glass like they're not even there. The Canadian security guy. He's lumberjack-strong and could carry a mounted policeman and his horse on one shoulder, but even he looks battered and bloodied. He has two words for the driver: turn back. The driver doesn't wait to be told a second time.

Next morning over breakfast, the tour manager is talking to me while I load a plate with pancakes and syrup. Something about Nathan Phillips, he says, and I'm wondering who that is. I hear that bell ringing again. Maybe it's the besieged CHUM DJ from yesterday. He senses that I'm not listening so tells me again. 'Nathan Phillips Square,' he explains, and I remember the meeting. Jimmy Ienner, the hotshot producer. The 'We wanna record the screaming' guy.

'So where is it?' I ask.

'Downtown Toronto.' He smiles nervously. The scene of the crime from yesterday. 'The car will be out front in five minutes,'

Above left: Me, my mum, Ronald and my dad.

Above right: My big brother Gordon and me.

Right: Me and my dad early BCR days, before the tartan.

Left: At home with my mum.

Top left: My second band Wot's Up.

Top right: My 'W' jumper, hand-knitted by a lady in Cockburn Street, Edinburgh.

Above left: One of Tam's publicity stunts with sunglasses and Bandaid hiding 'fake' injuries.

Right: The classic five back in the day.

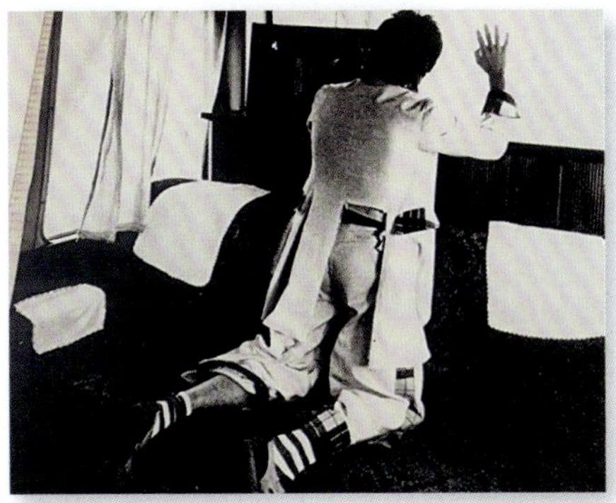

Top left: Part of the 'Tartan Army'.

Top right: Almost wearing one of the jackets made by our seamstress Bambi Ballard.

Middle left: Japan airport mayhem ... waving out the back of the bus with my jacket in shreds, while Mr Ono stops Taxis.

Left: Les, Gary the tour manager and Tam with his briefcase.

Nathan Phillips Square, 1976, where we appeared for a few minutes.

Above: Montreaux studio engineer and Harry Maslin ... he was great fun to work with.

Below: The sax I won from Harry in a bet.

Above: My custom-made 'White Knight' bass made by John Birch.

Above left: The good old days when there were record stores.

Above right: Thankfully two toy guns.

Karu playing to 12,000 in Jabulane Stadium in Soweto in the 1980s.

Top left: This was the Celtic music period.

Top right: Me with blond hair and beaded braid until my mum cut it off without me knowing.

Middle right: Tam with his friend at our wedding on 8 March 1997 (keep your enemies close).

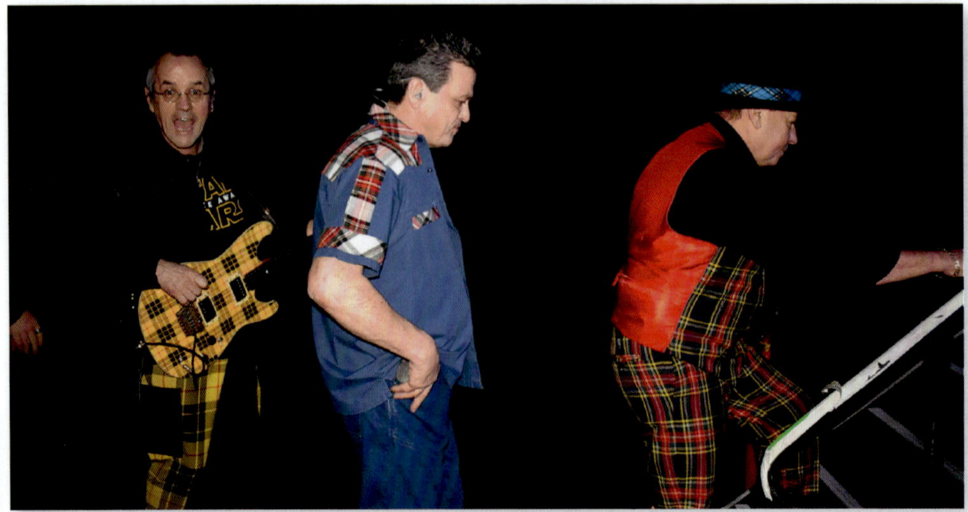

Every picture tells a story.

© Brian Anderson

Left: The legendary Barrowlands Ballroom gig in Glasgow that sold out in less than three minutes!

Below: Myself with Rod and John after the amazing Edinburgh Castle gig we guest appeared at in 2023.

© Brian Anderson

© Gemma Leigh

© Richard Jezek

Middle left: *Star Wars* ... which it very much was.

Left: The current Bay City Rollers line-up. *Left to Right*: John McLaughlin, Mikey Smith, Ian Thomson and Jamie McGrory.

Top: On our honeymoon in the south of France being French.

Middle left: Our 21st anniversary.

Middle right: The day I met my wee dug Elvis.

Left: Heading to the beach.

he adds, almost embarrassed. If I could roll my eyes back any further, I'd be staring out the back of my head about now.

Five minutes later, as we move off into traffic, I half-expect to see Ian crossing himself for good luck, whispering a silent prayer, but he looks like he's recovered from yesterday's trial by fire. He's got an ear cocked in Eric's direction. 'You hear what Les did yesterday?' Eric says. Les pulls a face, as if he was embarrassed. 'There was this guy at the hotel with a Corvette. Amazing looking car. Fuckin' Les asks the guy if he could have a go in it. Poor guy said yes. Les took it out of the hotel to take it for a spin, but he didn't know they have trams here.'

Derek's laughing, Eric's thwacking his open palm against his knee. Across the floor, Les opens his mouth to say something, then thinks better of it and folds his arms defensively.

'So, trams are everywhere in Toronto, right?' continues Eric with a grin. 'They don't make any noise. They're electric. You can drive across the tramlines, but you got tae make sure there's not one coming. Obviously Leslie here, he never looked, did he? Just fuckin' pulls out of the hotel and drives straight across a tramline and a tram was coming the other way . . .' Eric holds up an open palm, clenches his other hand, smashes them together. 'Crashes right into the Corvette. Massive dent all down one side. They're paying the guy off and it's gonna cost a fortune.'

Les is staring out the window now, muttering. 'Ach, that's bollocks . . .' He trails off, the sound drowned out by a familiar noise, that of thousands of young voices screaming as the limo edges nearer to Nathan Phillips Square.

We want the Roll-ers! We want the Roll-ers!

The car slows. The first splashes of tartan begin to appear on the pavements, start spilling into the road.

'Here we go again,' says Derek, shaking his head.

We're hustled out of the limo and taken backstage, outside still, roped off in a holding area, peering out onto Nathan Phillips Square, this strange city-of-the-future sci-fi deal with its high, gleaming walls of glass and concrete. Yesterday's DJ from CHUM is already on stage, warming up the crowd for our arrival. He could be playing Beethoven. Or heavy metal. Or anything. But you still wouldn't hear it over the screams.

We want the Roll-ers! We want the Roll-ers!

Some young guy in a headset finds his way to us, starts talking at 500mph, tells us he's the promoter, but who can tell anymore? He'd be better off using sign language, the noise is so loud.

'Hiya, hi – Les, Woody, Derek – great to see you guys!' He leans in close to be heard, yelling at the top of his voice. 'Great! Hiya Ian, hiya Eric. Look, we got a big turn-out here, guys! I mean BIG – three times what we figured. Could be more. So, we gotta do some crowd control first, okay?'

We all shrug, even Ian. The calm at the eye of the storm. It's the folk around us who tend to get bent out of shape. They've never seen anything like it, but for two straight years now, we've seen nothing else. We're acclimatised, numbed right out. We stand watching the promoter outline his plan, throwing the occasional thumbs-up his way, just for encouragement. His eyes, though; he looks like he's not ready for this.

We want the Roll-ers! We want the Roll-ers!

'We gotta stop them pushing forward, right?' the promoter's saying, but no one's listening, certainly not me. 'I've got Chris on stage right now, yeah, doing the warm-up. He's gonna do that, then he's gonna introduce you, and then you go on and you just wave at the girls, okay?' He looks to us uncertainly.

'Sure. That'll be fine, I'm sure.' I'm looking around, making sure there's someone ready to press 'record' on the tape. I'm not coming back here if they forget to tape the crowd noise, no matter what Clive or the producer says.

'Great! So, yeah, if you guys could stand at the side here and wait, and when Chris has done the announcement and the introduction, you just go straight on, okay?'

Ian gives him a half-hearted thumbs-up.

We want the Roll-ers! We want the Roll-ers!

I don't hear our introduction. I can barely hear myself think. There's just a jab in the ribs from one of the stage crew and I'm stepping forward into the afternoon sun. No one's saying 'Rollers' now – it's a primal, indecipherable howl. I'm already wilting in the heat, sunshine bouncing off the concrete and glass buildings, making it like an oven in here. As my feet reach the raised stage area, a makeshift thing built of balsa wood and blind optimism, I feel a sudden breeze land on me and, for a second, I feel okay, happy to be here. Without prompting, I begin to wave and smile. I can feel the guys around me doing the same. But the stage lurches under my feet, like a clipper ship taking the Cape of Good Hope, and I suddenly feel seasick. At my feet, Canadian policemen in white shirts with peaked caps and brown leather gun holster straps across their chests form a line in front of the stage.

Immediately, the girls catch sight of us, lurching forward as one and the line of white shirts bends and buckles under the pressure of the surge. I look out and it's unreal – a swaying, shrieking tartan sea. All around the plaza's edge are police cars, with four or five ambulances lined up at the back. The teenage girls at the edges still have a little space to jump around – I can see them clutching at each other, screaming in delight like, 'This is it, the moment we've been waiting for'. The girls at the front are less fortunate. They couldn't swing a mouse by its tail, let alone a cat. They're jammed in so tight, trying to stay upright as the tide of humanity sweeps around them. I'll be honest, even I'm finding it scary. What if they can't breathe? What if one of them gets swept under, crushed underfoot somehow? It looks like it would be almost easier to die here than to survive. One of the white shirts in the square must be standing on a box, or maybe some sort of ledge. He stands out like an island in the swaying waves of faces. At least he can see what's going on. I see him signalling to someone in the wings, a big urgent gesture with both his arms thrown forward, pointing away from the stage. I don't read sign language, but the meaning seems clear: get them to get back.

One of the white-shirt cops strides onto the stage past us, takes the microphone and starts trying to give orders to restore some calm. 'Everyone move back! Move back!' He's like that olden-days king, shouting at the sea, telling the tide to retreat. Get back to France, you fucker. No one can hear the cop, but no one could move even if they wanted to. The girls at the lip of the flimsy stage have nowhere to go but under. The screaming is something else now. It's not even a sound. We're way, way, way off the spectrum. Only dogs can hear it.

'This is a very important safety announcement! Everybody MOVE BACK AT ONCE!'

I glance across at Chris the DJ. He's starting to look scared. I've seen crowd problems a few times before but have always taken them in my stride. We've had to stop shows while the venue staff tried to get control before somebody got hurt. I've stared upwards watching Victorian balconies heaving, threatening to give at any second. But the heat here, and the huge numbers of fans, make this feel different somehow. Then I clock more white shirts assembling in the wings. Some guy with more stripes and more epaulettes and who seems to be their leader walks onto the floundering deck. He takes the mic and somehow makes himself heard. The screaming now is less a sound than a pressure building up around him – and his voice cuts through.

'You must move back! Move back or the band will have to leave!'

I'm finding my sea legs now. I see a young fan, barely out of her teens, with long dark hair and holding up a tartan scarf. Her eyes lock onto mine; she doesn't even try to smile at me. Not waving here, she's drowning, practically. There's no way she's having a good time. Then a bunch of policemen come marching onto the stage and it veers to port and back to starboard, and they signal that this madness needs to stop right now, if not sooner. A strong pair of arms pulls me away, drags me down to the wings and someone else grabs a fistful of my collar, like I'm a football hooligan, and pulls me back to the limo. There's Ian. He looks like he's done a tour of duty in 'Nam.

'Fuck's sake,' he says.

'Yeah,' I say. 'I know.'

'Hope they got their recording!' He cracks a smile. Then the car peels away and starts picking up speed. Les and Eric are shaking, lighting up, cupping their hand around the flame as they each light a cigarette. I'm thinking this is too much. We need to get this under control. Then the familiar numbness returns, kind of a grim balm that makes me forget it as it's happening, a kind of anaesthetic against the insanity of it all.

Chapter 22

SCREAM!

November 1976

Back home in Britain, there's the first flushes of something they're calling punk rock, but we're out on manoeuvres, caught in the Rollers bubble, entirely unaware of this existential threat. We have bigger worries right now. We've taken our peculiar brand of madness global now. We're sprawled in the back of this slick black limousine, a stretch Lincoln, a kind of slow-motion crawl to our hotel, right in the heart of downtown Melbourne. I'm looking forward to getting an hour's peace before our show later today. But that was probably a fool's errand, because the scenes here have been wild since we touched down in Australia a few days ago. Rollermania at the airport and determined fans scaling the walls of our hotels like wee ninjas. We've grown accustomed to these kind of things, only now the scene is playing out on the far side of the world.

The plan is that we're going to arrive at the front entrance of the hotel, but the driver's clueless, or got the wrong information, or it went in one ear and out the other. He's pulling into the underground car park at the rear of the building. I mean, that's fine – only there's something like 4,000 Rollers fans waiting for us. In the rear-view mirror, I see the driver's eyes switch from chilled to panicked as we're swept under a tide of tartan and bubblegum. The screaming – fuck's sake, it's something. It's like being underwater or waiting for your ears to pop when you're on a plane and the cabin just decompressed. None of this is new to us, but you can see the driver has not seen the like. His last gig was probably taking a few sad mourners up to the cemetery, smoking a sneaky ciggie during the burial, doffing his cap and sucking on a Tic Tac when he sees the sad-faced family trudging back towards the car. Poor guy. He's in the grip of a panic attack. His knuckles are turning white, and he's going green around the gills, like he's taken his last breath of clean air. I'm staring at the back of his neck. He's a big guy, a real brick shithouse, bullets of sweat pouring down over his shirt collar. He was the personification of Australian machismo when we climbed in the car, but now he's whimpering like a sickly pup. He's the only adult in the room and he's a quivering, shivering mess. I wouldn't mind, but it's getting serious out there, like a zombie movie. But they're not staggering slowly, easy to avoid; they're running at us like wee gazelles. It's an endless stream of them, pouring into the parking lot from the street above, like liquid tartan.

The teens have turned. They sense the driver's panic. They can smell his fear and they do not give a fuck. A dozen of them break free from the pack, run up the hood and land squarely on the roof. Above our heads, there's a sound like thunder, then I realise it's metal creaking. The roof is coming down on us, about to fold in on itself and squeeze the band and driver, like we're the last traces of toothpaste in the tube. We slip down off the seats and onto the floor. The roof is now six inches lower than it was a minute before and I can't see out the window beyond the teenage girls. I can't breathe. The driver is up front, white as a ghost, loosening his collar, scrabbling around for a rosary or something so he can pass into the next life having made his peace with his god or something. Maybe I'd join him, I think, but then I catch a glimpse of something. The windows are covered in sweat and spittle, and white gleaming thighs and arms, but in the distance, I can make out a group of security guys cutting a swathe through the cloud of perfume and perspiration. They're trying the door but it's buckled, concertinaed under the weight of teenage wildlife. We're pushing on the doors ourselves, but there's not an inch of give. There's a thousand souls pressed into a space maybe 30 feet square and it's like we're battling against the crowd and the laws of physics all at the same time.

Then there's a chink of light and I see a security guard who's built like a grizzly bear. He's completely unperturbed, got teenagers hanging off him like Christmas tree ornaments and he's swirling his index finger, the universal signal for 'Roll your fuckin' window down ya daft wee shite'. Naturally, I comply and he's pulling us out, one by one, passing us back over his shoulders and over the heads of the fans like parcels at a sorting office. It's only 30 seconds of my life, but it's among the maddest. I'm kind of crowd-surfing, getting passed along a human chain towards these big metal fire doors, getting bits and pieces torn and snatched from my Roller clothes as I go. Then, before I know it, I'm on the other side of the metal door leading to reception. The last man in the chain dumps me not-ever-so-gently to the ground and everything is suddenly quiet, aside from the soothing piped muzak the hotel has playing in the lobby, the kind you hear in an elevator. Just now, after all that, it sounds a bit surreal. Five minutes later, all the guys have suffered the same fate, but are safe in the hotel lobby. Time to check in. The hotel receptionist has this frozen gaze throughout. 'Do you have the room key for Wood, please?' I smile.

I don't know what you call this kind of thing. I call it a Tuesday.

I guess if this was a corny movie, this would be the montage: a map of the world with a tiny plane flying over it, a neon dotted line marking its trail; flashes of nation's flags, overlaid grainy footage of fans lining the roadside, fainting in the aisles and 'Bye Bye Baby' playing in the background. Because that's kind of how it feels. It's not real life and there's no consequences. We're walking the same earth as you, breathing the same air, but we're wrapped in cotton wool, bundled into cars and waiting vans and I can tell you right now, it's absolutely okay with me. Despite the danger to hide and hair, it's exciting, you know.

Following this slew of sell-out November shows in Australia, our next stop is the land of the rising sun, a chance to draw breath. Japan is a calm, respectful society, nothing like back home or the US, so we all have our guard down. We have a chemical memory of the Beatles playing shows here to quiet, reverent crowds and that's what we're expecting for ourselves. I'll be honest, it's a nice feeling, an opportunity to have a breather. I'm leaning back in my seat, resplendent, like a teenage tartan king, smiling at the air hostess as she passes up and down the cabin, telling us to fasten our seatbelts. It's like a recalibration, after seeing this madness take over the world like an airborne plague in an old B-movie.

Heading down the steps on the runway, it's 6am and I just want a shower and to fall into bed. I want to climb into the car, roll my jacket up into a neat ball and use it as a pillow, and have the driver take me to the hotel suite. But no. There's a huge group of press, shining Pentax cameras in the morning sunshine. They don't care that you're knackered. They want a wave and a smile, so I switch to autopilot, start doing the thing that God made me to do: making nice, while the shutters click and the flashbulbs pop. I've got my eyes peeled, staring out on the tarmac, a thousand-yard stare, thinking there's a car coming. Behind me, Eric mumbles something, reminding me there's a coach waiting for us out the front of the airport. *Oh yeah*, I think, looking up at the terminal building. From here, it looks like the glass and cement are alive. A billion ants are making the edges seem fuzzy. When I narrow my gaze, I can see it's not ants. Of course, it's not fuckin' ants. That'd be mad. It's something like 5,000 Japanese teenagers with their wee faces pressed against the glass. They wave scarves and banners, handwritten signs with declarations of forever love: 'Love you Woody', 'Eric you so dreamy', 'Les is very good' . . .

I turn back to Eric. 'So, how are we getting to the coach? We're not going to go through them, right?'

Eric thinks about that for a second and looks over his shoulder for a responsible adult because, right up ahead, there's a line of fans that the Light Brigade couldn't get past. 'I dunno, Woods,' he tells me at last. He's got that look in his eye – Michael Caine at the end of *Zulu*. He's mustering a stiff upper lip but knows in his heart that this is the end of the road for us. Then it's us, tearing across the tarmac, once more unto the breach and we're running at this army, getting them all riled and hot under their collars.

Somehow we get into the terminal, but that's the easy part. We're now in the building with the fans and it's pure bedlam in here. Security have no idea what to do; maybe call them insecurity. Hold the line? You must be joking. They're subsumed by tartan and oestrogen. Everyone's crying, like they flicked a switch in their heads, went right up through the settings and landed on 'hysterical'. I'm two steps inside the door, feeling the blast of the air conditioner, making out the vague, alien-sounding announcer's voice, picking out maybe every third or fourth word if I'm lucky, and I can see the crowd barriers toppling over like they're made of balsa wood. There are some smiles, some actual joy, but something else too – like a wildness, the moment in the comic book the shitty character drinks the potion and has unlimited powers and decides they can do whatever they please. Only they're crying and screaming and I'm not Peter Parker or Mister Fantastic. I'm the skinny kid who lived in the stair and I'm fighting for breath, fighting for my life as I scramble through the meat grinder of people expressing their love for us in this – let's be honest – fuckin' weird fashion. I'm underwater ten minutes? Fifteen? I don't know, but I step out into safety somehow, through luck not judgement, and I'm in tatters. My gear has been lost to the tide, my clothes are hanging off me – wee tartan ribbons. Then I see them emerge, one by one. Les. Derek. Ian. Eric. We all look like we've been in a war zone. Automatically, we all turn and face the army that almost bested us, and we wave, and we smile. Watch the footage and we look happy, because that's in our DNA now.

We're dusted down and marched out the front, finally, laughing. Mine's a manic, just-cheated-death laugh, like when you get off a rollercoaster, and we're led to the kerbside by some flunky. Like every good schoolkid, I make my way to the back of the coach and we pull away. If this was the UK or the US, we'd be out of trouble now, in a safe space, but out the back window, I can see the crowd spilling out of the terminal building and they're hailing cabs, climbing into cars. A mile down the road, I pull back the curtain. I should be taking in the sights of this amazing new world opening up before us like a flower, but we're getting trailed by hundreds of minicabs, like a weird Japanese take on *Wacky Races*. Every cab is carrying four or five Roller fans and their scarves arc trailing out the windows like streamers as the cars duck and weave through the rush-hour traffic across the two lanes.

Mr Ono, our Japanese promoter, is prowling the aisle, his face a mask of concern. He's 50 maybe, but he's carrying these worry lines like he's lived a thousand years but never saw the like of this. Ono-san is telling us to draw the bus curtains closed, but it's already too late. I cast my eye down the seats and there's Eric waving at a cab. Two seats further down, there's Les doing the same. And Ian and Derek. I give in to the inevitable gravity of the situation, give Mr Ono a shrug and start waving at the nearest cab, buzzing around us like a bumblebee. 'Close curtains, please,' he tells us, with an economical bow. Then there's some shouting in Japanese, Mr Ono strides towards the driver and I can feel the bus slowing down and coming to a halt in the middle of the highway. There's an immediate cacophony of car horns blaring as Mr Ono demands the driver open the door and to allow him to leave.

'Wait here,' he says and there's a pneumatic hiss as the door opens. We're exchanging looks, double-taking like mad. We're old hands now, with two years of madness making us think we've seen everything. But this is all entirely new to us. I peel the curtain back a smidge and watch in wonder as Mr Ono strides to the back of the bus and adopts this curious they-shall-not-pass stance: legs akimbo and a hand held up, the international hand signal for 'Stop. In the name of God, stop!' There's a screech of tyres and the two lanes of traffic come to a confused, angry halt. Up front, the coach driver is peering into his side mirrors wondering what the hell he's going to do, when Mr Ono signals for him to go, like he's going to hold off the convoy of taxicabs by sheer dint of his will. It's an act of self-sacrifice worthy of an old movie and, if I'm honest, it looks entirely futile. The driver shrugs, puts the coach in gear and we're moving away. Beyond the curtain, Mr Ono is still standing there, his hand held up, as a hundred cab drivers simply start up again and drive past and around him and take up the pursuit. I can just make out the heroic sight of Mr Ono falling to the ground, clutching his arm as we get up a head of steam.

We beat the traffic to the hotel, pass through reception and find our way to the Rollers suite, panting like dogs on a summer's day, occasionally peering out the window to watch the taxis pulling up and the fans spilling onto the concourse, handing over fists full of yen, bowing politely at their drivers before starting an impromptu, 5,000-person vigil on the roadside. It crosses my mind that maybe our idea that the Japanese fans were going to be sedate might have been wrong. A couple of hours later, Mr Ono arrives in the suite, his broken arm in a neat cast. He looks understandably shellshocked. We're expecting a welcome speech, a breakdown of the itinerary but the only thing he says is, 'Please keep curtains closed. And no waving from windows.' He offers up a weak bow and with that, he leaves.

Chapter 23

BRAIN DEAD

Maybe this is the high watermark, I'm thinking. Don't get me wrong, it's still a thrill, this Rollermania game, but there's something not right about things. In some senses, we're at the top of our game. A second wave of mania over in the States – albums and singles, a cavalcade of hits – then, as the rest of the world woke up, a wild third wave Down Under and in the Far East. At the tail end of the year, and into 1977, the albums pop into the chart – top 30 now, rather than top ten, which was the case at the start of 1976. They have a wee look around and then make their way to the cut-out bins. The last album, *Dedication*, is still a sizeable hit, just not nearly as massive as the hits we were scoring a year ago. The accompanying singles – a cover of Dusty's 'I Only Want to Be With You', 'Yesterday's Hero' and 'Dedication' – peaked on the Billboard chart at 12, 54 and 60 respectively, marking a visible downturn.

At the heart of the storm, though, we barely notice. If I had a minute to take stock, maybe I'd see more clearly, but our foot is pressed so hard on the gas, everything is a blur. Back home, they're selling Rollers scarves and even knickers in Woolworths and there are factories churning out mile upon mile of tartan for the kiddiwinks, teens, aunts and grandmas lining up to fill their wee Jennie's stocking. So, on the surface, it seems the same. It'll probably go on this way forever, I figure, and I start to develop a thicker skin, a goldfish memory. I know in my heart that flatlining here at the top and never coming down from this peak is a ridiculous notion. Endless shows, a month-long sell-out tour of the US, Australia . . . Everywhere the same scenes, only different accents.

The madness around us has been normalised. Maybe – although, here in the eye of the storm, I'm not looking too closely – if I really strain the grey matter, I'd understand it's not quite what it was. Over the course of a year, Les disengages from the band completely, dropping the matey pretence entirely. If I were going to go forensic on what happened there, what was the root cause, I'd probably trace it back to the car accident and the death of his neighbour. He was a pain in the arse before but, from that moment on, he's become a different person. I can't speak to what drives him – and, in his defence, maybe we've all withdrawn into ourselves a little.

Personally, I've started to worry about my sanity. I'm enjoying this life. Parts of it, at least. I still get to play music, to make that connection with the fans, and Eric and I are still throwing ideas back and forth. When we're in the studio, we're like this well-oiled machine. Everyone hits their marks, understands what's expected of them. Only I feel numb, like I'm on this treadmill that leads nowhere and everywhere all at once. I wake up wondering *What city this is? What country? What am I doing here?* I don't remember what I had for dinner last night or where I played. I'm picking up magazines, reading about these shows, and I've no idea. I'm on the tour bus, peering over the open pages of a magazine, got my face screwed up, wondering if this event, or that one, even happened. It's been going on a while now. I read about a show at the New York Palladium at the start of the year. The usual scenes: wild fans taking to the stage, hanging off us as we played; Derek keeping a beat while he's got fans all over his back, hanging there like a tartan rucksack. I've no memory of it, so I ask Eric if it really happened. He trawls his memory banks, takes a long draw on his ciggie and tells me, 'Aye, Woods. It happened.'

It's okay at first, but after a few months, I start to think I need professional help. Beyond the flashes, stark pictures in my mind's eye, every day is the same, becoming blurred around the edges while it's happening. There are whole weeks of my life that seem lost to time. I feel a bit brain dead. It's clear to me that Rollermania is levelling off. It most likely peaked with the US tour. The fans who were mad for us are still there, but the initial impact has subsided.

The flashes, though, they're great. Maybe that's all any of us remember about our lives, like funny, weird snapshots from someone else's life:

Standing at an open hotel window in Copenhagen, a crowd of hundreds serenading us with a version of 'Wonderful, Wonderful, Bay City Rollers' and us conducting them from the balcony.

The band just mooching along Mulholland Drive, getting spotted by a gang of fans and chased around Beverly Hills for the next hour.

Tam chasing a group of lads through an airport, wheezing away, red-faced and furious, after they called us a 'bunch of poofters' and the rest of us bent double laughing at the scene.

A brief promo tour of Australia, followed by a couple of days' relaxation on Lindeman Island, and Tam losing his fuckin' mind when one of the hotel staff tells him Eric's been spotted holding hands with a girl.

Me freezing on stage at the Budokan, forgetting the opening piano chords to 'My Lisa', my mind going blank, and 15,000 fans staring back at me and the guys in the band wondering *What the fuck?*

The US shows, strutting around on stage in a stars-and-stripes catsuit.

Arriving at the Mallory Park Radio 1 Roadshow by helicopter, looking down at this floating stage in the centre of an ornamental lake, realising there's 47,000 people there, and it dawning on us that *Jeez, we're a really big deal now*, before escaping by powerboat after hundreds of teenagers tried to swim after us.

Eric and Yours Truly having a barney on the autobahn, getting pulled over by the polizei and having to explain, 'No officer. No one's been kidnapped. We're pals.'

Turning on a hotel TV in Italy, catching the final moments of the San Remo awards show, and the hosts announcing we'd won something or other and suddenly realising we'd left too early.

The time I had to hide my pack of cigarettes during a photo-shoot for an anti-smoking campaign.

A flight into terror, from Vegas to Los Angeles, inducing panicked scenes as our plane is forced to make an emergency landing. All our knuckles are white, and we're shaking, but still making it to Hollywood in time for the final segment of *The Mike Douglas Show*.

The band landing at Gatwick, caught in a press scrum, with wee tape recorders held under our noses, like they're administering smelling salts to a fainting maiden aunt. The press guys walking backwards, as we stride through the terminal building, 25 men in raincoats, moving in perfect synchronisation, like a single being with one shared brain. They're shouting questions. Nothing interesting – they're not looking for insight. Just a blurb that says Woody likes milk, Les is looking for love, that kind of thing. Alan's at my hip, keeping pace with me and I give him a nudge. 'Let's see if these mugs will follow,' I say, and we steer away from the rest of the guys. There's a modest recalibration from the hive mind of the press around us, and we splinter away, walking down a flight of stairs, taking a dozen of these guys with us, shouting inane questions before stopping, realising we're in the gents' toilet.

In terms of actual, tangible events away from the screaming, things that don't happen every day, the main takeaway from these numb days is that I don't seek counselling. I don my suit of armour every morning and face the day, like I underwent a factory reset while I slept. If I can't sleep, Tam is a walking apothecary. He has a ready supply of sleeping pills, and if I can't keep my eyes open, he's got something else rattling around in that briefcase of his.

There's a conflict between Ian and Tam, a real personality clash. Ian's a strong character, got some steel to him, and I think Tam's got some buyer's remorse there. I realise as soon as I see the signs, but there's nothing I can do to shape events here. I just woke up one morning, strolled down for breakfast, carried out a headcount and we were a man down. 'Got too much for him. Couldnae stand the heat' is all Tam says about the matter, chugging down a handful of uppers like they're fuckin' Smarties. Ian lasted eight months, all told. The line-up reshuffles a while. This young guy Pat McGlynn, another Edinburgh native, gets roped in for a few months. He was with me in my old band, Kip, a hundred years ago. He's a good player and fine to hang out with, but he's an uneasy fit. He's never a fully fledged Roller, gets paid a wage, never a share. One day he's there and the next he's gone.

Chapter 24

THE RETURN OF SHANG

After Pat's departure in May 1977, followed by a couple of big tours as a four-piece, a change is required, something to restore a little balance, to maybe right the ship. I'd been pushing to get Alan back in the Rollers for a while now. I missed my friend but, more to the point, the band missed his personality on stage. After a show, I'd be drumming up support for the idea and eventually I think I ground them all down. I'm older now and don't want to drink milk anymore, and Alan's my best pal, the one I like to have a drink with. Jake's been acting as the band's road manager, Tam's consiglieri, doing the day-to-day grunt work, getting us where we need to be, so Tam hasn't been in our daily lives so much, and we're starting to think for ourselves a bit more. We're older too, not so easy to control. Maybe the 30th time I suggest bringing Alan back into the fold, the other guys relent, if only to shut me up. I figure Alan will be up for another go around the block of pop. He tried his arm at launching a solo career. It was a good effort, but it didn't set the world on fire, so it's obvious he misses the thrill of it all.

I stayed in touch with Alan throughout, keeping his chair warm on the off-chance he might come back. If I'm given a free day north of the border, often I'll drive up to his secluded house, Shelter Hall, in Dollar. Dollar stands ten miles outside Stirling, and a hundred years into the past, a quiet, bygone-times kind of place. He likes a drink, so we'll share a dram or two in his local, the Dollar Arms, where everyone refers to him by his nickname, 'Shang'.

A while back, a local bobby caught him driving home from the pub one too many times, so he has a workaround now. I'll park up and Alan will ride down to the pub on his horse, a retired racehorse, part of this menagerie of his, and hitch it to a post outside, like he's Clint Eastwood. We'll hang out, reminisce and bitch and moan about Les and Tam before heading back. Sometimes it takes a couple of us to get him back up and into the saddle; sometimes he's up and over in one smooth movement, like a true cowboy. One time, a bunch of rowdy teenagers give him some hassle while he's making his way to his homestead and he chases them up and down the street, swinging a horsewhip over his head. Just everyday retired pop star antics. When we're back in his kitchen/zoo, both of us slightly worse for wear, we'll sit there watching the dogs chase the goat and the goat maybe turning the tables and chasing the dogs out the house. It's always nice to see my pal. He's been a worry to me this whole time he's been kicked out of the Rollers. Not long after the shit hit the fan, Alan's girlfriend phoned saying she couldn't get an answer on his home phone. In a blind panic, I got in my car and made the 50-minute trip to check on him. Knocked on the door. No answer. I'm banging now and there's no response. When I peer in through the window, I see him flat out on the floor, a half-empty whisky bottle beside him and a couple of dogs licking his face. I'm banging on the window, terrified he might have done something stupid, remembering the time he stuck his head in the oven, saved only by the fact he didn't have any money for the gas meter. So, I'm banging on the glass, screaming through the letterbox, and he finally stirs. 'Oh, Woods. What the fuck are you doing here?'

After Al's return is rubberstamped, I arrive at his door and tell him to get the tartan out of storage. He joins us out in Montreux, recording our new LP, *Strangers in the Wind*, with Harry Maslin producing again. Harry produced our last record – and lost a saxophone in a bet with me. The long and short of that is that I'm the band's designated sax player now, and I've got another string to my bow. The studio becomes a sanctuary, a little respite from the mania we're seeing wherever we go. With Tam on the fringes, and Les drifting into his own world, I can hear myself think again now.

We're holed up in a new studio, a feat of the modern age, a technological wonder, but Tam probably lined this up to avoid paying too much tax. There are a few meetings I dozed through, where I didn't pick up on the fine detail: a guy in a suit saying we need to stay out of the UK, record someplace different. But I'm a guy in a band, not an accountant. You could stay out of the country for a certain amount of time, he said, and come back for maybe a week, but I thought fuck that. I want to be home. It's too complicated. I just want to enjoy my life, carry on touring, making records and developing as a band.

The new songs are pretty decent. More of an AOR kind of feel, hopefully to reflect the fact that our fanbase is starting to grow older. Because our success is staggered around the world, getting big at home, then a while later in the US and Japan, I don't know if I can see it yet, but it's definitely on a downward path now. Can I see it though? I doubt it. Tam brings me a fax from the record company in Japan, expressing their concerns about the band's popularity beginning to wane. There have been newspaper reports about Les's behaviour with female fans – bunches of teenage girls in his hotel room – and him hassling executives or hotel staff to get him dope. There's a list of things we can do to right the ship, but it's kind of lost in the background hubbub. We're spread so thin, touring these other territories and leaving the UK to dwindle on the vine. We've taken our eye off the ball back home and, despite the excitement of rocking up in a new city or a new country, often I'd rather be there. In a parallel universe, maybe the Rollers remained true to the British fans and just stayed and played and played, but who knows? Back home, half the bands we came up with – Mud, T.Rex, David Cassidy, the Osmonds – are all struggling to make the charts. Everyone's star fades at some point, I suppose. It's the nature of fame that it comes and goes, even I know that, but from my standpoint, it's better to be a has-been than a never-was. Now, everything's getting swept away by the new music and that's fine. Not everyone sees it that way, of course.

It's great to have Al back, though. He and I slot back into our old routines we had before, like he hasn't been away. Getting a seat near each other on the tour bus. Drinking buddies after every show. We're like brothers, but without the bullshit. He's the kind of friend you can push into the pool and he'll get out with a smile on his face, rather than looking to thump you one. Some nights we're incognito, jacket and jeans. No one even notices you. Eric will tag along sometimes, although he's never been a drinker. He used to get stupid with it, so usually he'll excuse himself after a couple and make his way back to the hotel. Other times, there's a big hullaballoo, the waiters falling over themselves as if it's a state visit and we're ushered to a private room or a table that's off the beaten track, away from prying eyes. We have a different drinking culture in Scotland to the rest of the world. Some nights we'll head out with the express intention of getting completely wrecked; others, just a couple of wee drinks and a chat. But for the first time in a while, it feels like a good time to be a Roller. A good time to be me.

Chapter 25

THE KROFFT SUPERSTAR HOUR

Late summer 1978

We touch down in LA. We're here for maybe four or five months to film our first – and probably last – US network TV show, *The Krofft Superstar Hour* with Sid and Marty Krofft, these American TV performers. I signed on the dotted line thinking it was going to be a breeze, a nice way for us to broaden our appeal in the US of A, but that's possibly my eternal optimism at play, because nothing's ever as simple as it seems. Outside of Japan, where it sells hand over fist, the *Strangers in the Wind* album is a bust. It barely registers, even on the fringes of pop culture. The record stalls outside the Billboard 100 and doesn't even dent the charts back home. It might be more mature-sounding, but the three accompanying singles – 'Where Will I Be Now', 'Another Rainy Day in New York City' and 'All of the World is Falling in Love' – don't get any airplay and the record sinks without trace, so we're open to the idea of getting our faces out there again.

I'm imagining an American version of our previous TV show *Shang-A-Lang* – a few songs and musical guests – but this is straight-down-the-line under-10s stuff. Sid and Marty are US kids TV stalwarts, and they want a band, probably any band, to come on for the new series, so we're signed on to do just that. Not that there's much of a discussion, of course. Tam mentioned it in passing when he came to the sessions in Montreux, but fuck knows if anyone's taking in half of this stuff anymore. We're not taken to a studio in Burbank and pitched by a bunch of execs, seeing if we're interested. It's just, 'You're recording, doing some promo, getting on the radio . . . Oh, and there's this TV show you're doing.' 'Oh aye. What's that then?' 'Don't you worry about that. Oh, it's four or five months' work, incidentally and it's locked in the itinerary.' You'll forgive me for not paying attention, I hope. By now, every meeting is a kind of dull haze. I think we're only listening out for the words 'day off'. Everything else is just static.

The band has reached a plateau; maybe we're coming down the other side even. It's clear to us all, but there's still some sunshine, still some hay we can make between now and our bedtime. We could do a big world tour or throw together a greatest hits album to maybe cement the legacy of the past few years, but there's no plan. As I mentioned before, between us, we've decided we want to move the band towards a more mature sound, the idea being that we're getting older, and our hardcore fans are getting older with us. Most of us agree that's the path forward, so this kids' show seems like another backward step. We want to know if we'll be back in the UK again. We see the letters from the fans back home saying we've abandoned them for the US and we're losing that foothold.

Tam is still getting his percentage, but he's become a peripheral figure in our lives. He was a decent promotions man, helped get us up the mountain, but he's no businessman. I think he worked that out a while ago. We're all grown adults now and the truth of the matter is that, now he's not living in our pockets, he hasn't got us in the same iron grip as before. His influence is starting to wane. We all know it, and I think he's realised too. He's not around so much, punting his new band, this bunch of malleable teen boys, Rosetta Stone, including our erstwhile colleague Ian Mitchell, who must be a glutton for punishment. I imagine Tam is getting a kick out of telling them to wave and smile, and how he can kick them out at a moment's notice if they don't toe the line. He's not the puppet master he once was in RollerWorld, so maybe this is an opportunity for him to get his claws in nice and early with another bunch of fresh-faced scamps. In terms of his control over us, the tide is starting to turn slightly, so it's possible, if the older guys had dug their heels and said no way, it might have been different, but who can say? It's a moot point.

When we're told it's in LA, no one's thinking that making a kid's TV show is going to be a bind – answering the call every morning, hair and make-up and all that shite – because we're all thinking about the Hollywood lifestyle, the palm trees and the lovely food and girls we'll find there. If I put a positive spin on things, it's a break from the old routine and we can put some of our recent headaches behind us. Not so long ago, we had a big legal mess to untangle. I'll not tire you with the gory details, but the business side of things has started to unravel. Like I said, Tam's no businessman. Anything related to the business, he's out of his depth, preferring to trust the money people. Consequently, some time ago our accountant advised us to set up a bunch of companies. In theory, it was fine. You have a company in your name as an individual, one for the band, and various other things. It made sense. Then we discovered the accountants were double, triple and quadruple dipping, charging us for maintaining all these separate accounts, auditing them quarterly and rinsing us for every penny we have. In the end, the accountants' bills for their services were six times what they would have been if they'd just kept one set of accounts. Because of the multiple accounts, Arista stop paying the band their royalties. The money's there, they tell us, they just don't know who to pay. It's like they found a neat loophole to not pay us for the work we've done. At the behest of Clive Davis, we're told to sign a letter indemnifying Arista. After we're informed the companies are now bankrupt, we don't sign. If we take the owed royalties, the money won't come to us; it will just fall into this pit the accountants have left us with. It's a total headfuck, so I'm just looking at being in LA as an opportunity to put some of the nonsense in the rear-view a while. Only then, just prior to filming, Les calls an emergency band meeting. He tells us we're heading in the wrong direction, and he wants to take the reins. We're all accustomed to Les laying down demands, so none of us take it too seriously. A week later, we get a letter from Les inviting us all to leave *his* band. I mean, I had no idea I'd been working all these years in Les McKeown's backing band. It's the sort of thing I usually notice.

The letter reads:

Dear Eric, Derek, Alan and Stuart:

I have given our situation a lot of thought since our discussion last Wednesday, and I am more convinced than ever that you are doing the wrong thing in trying to change the artistic direction and image of the Bay City Rollers. You are making decisions that are detrimental to the band as a whole and to my career as the lead singer and front man.

I want you to know that I am not bound by your decisions to change the artistic direction and image of the group, and I'm not going along with it. If you want to continue along those lines, then you can do it on your own, but not as part of the Bay City Rollers.

If your decisions are final, and if you won't go along with my views as to the creative and business direction of the Bay City Rollers, then you should all leave the band immediately. I will get another group together that will have the kind of attitude and artistic outlook that will assure the Bay City Rollers of the tremendous success they have had in the past and the greater success they deserve to have in the future.

Sincerely,

Leslie Richard McKeown

Following Les's first letter, there's a hundred more. Drip, drip, drip, like a kind of water torture. If I'm honest, I understand there are different pressures for the perceived frontperson of a group. It's like a dividend that needs paying. I'm not naïve. There are a few more photographs and interviews, and there are people who *do* think of that person as a kind of avatar for the band, but we've always been careful. It's one of the things I give credit to Tam for: to portray the band as five individuals, five stars, not just one guy and his interchangeable backing group. But it doesn't matter what I think. We're here on foreign soil, in the middle of a full-blown band meltdown, but expected to entertain, sing a few songs, play in a few skits, you know, typical mom's-apple-pie wholesome bullshit. The idea is that there are millions of kids munching on their cornflakes on a Saturday and maybe we can wrench some of their allowance money from them and keep the hits flowing. It's no surprise that none of us is in the right headspace about now. We're all wondering what to do. We saw the guy this morning and suddenly we're only communicating via mail, which is ridiculous, obviously, but it's the hand we've been dealt. Following a quickly assembled band meeting, we reply to Les's letter as follows:

Dear Leslie,

We are in receipt of your recent letter regarding the Bay City Rollers and its artistic direction and image . . .

As you are well aware, the Bay City Rollers is not an individual, but a group, of which we are all members. Although we certainly respect and value your opinions, and you are always free to render opinions, nevertheless, decisions will be made by the majority and not by your dictates. This is the only basis on which a group can operate.

We feel that your course of conduct to date and your failure to follow this procedure has caused considerable damage to the group and that this course of conduct cannot be allowed to continue.

This letter is to serve as our notice to you . . . that we wish to meet to discuss your withdrawal from the group at a time and place that is mutually agreeable to you and us, all in accordance with the present commitments of the Bay City Rollers.

Very Truly Yours,

Eric Faulkner, Derek Longmuir, Alan Longmuir, Stuart Wood

Obviously, there's cats and pigeons everywhere now and it's a pure mess. It's half-comical, as well as depressing. I don't think anyone realises until the first day on set that we're on a puppet show, which from the outside probably just makes the situation more funny, more depressing. We're playing against these *H.R. Puffnstuf* characters – Witchiepoo, Weenie, Dr Deathray and Hugo, and the other Sleestaks and dinosaurs from the *Land of the Lost* – and I'm thinking, *Jeez, this is a long way from the Mecca in Doncaster. And not in a good way.* People don't talk about us as a band, I get that, but we're wanting to mature, to grow with our audience, and this is just putting us back at square one. Bubblegum TV instead of bubblegum pop, but aimed squarely at small kids. I know Eric and Les had their doubts before the get-go, but I'm going with the flow, I guess. Still, five months is a big chunk of time to take off for a US Saturday kids show. Are we spreading ourselves too thin? We could be touring Europe, Japan, Australia. We could be really making a killing. Probably. I don't know.

While the letters are going back and forth, we're staying at Marty Krofft's place in North Hollywood, over Laurel Canyon. It's a nice six-bedroom pile – swimming pool, jacuzzi, pool table, the whole nine yards – and it feels like we're insulated from the bullshit flying around us. Well, a little. We're occasionally besieged by fans, who've found out where we are, and every day or so, you look out and see someone climbing over the wall, trying to break in. We only see Tam one time. He comes by to see how we're settling in, finds Al and me in the jacuzzi and climbs in. We're ripping the piss out of him for his hairy back and he climbs out before coming back with some hair removal cream and asks Alan to apply it. It's like smearing axle grease into Hugh Hefner's carpet. Five minutes later, the cream has burned its way down to his pasty skin and he's screaming and hollering, running to the shower and we don't see him again the whole time we're here. After he's gone, Al and I laugh for an hour solid. Not one of those polite giggling laughs either. Proper, snot-streaming-down-your-face, ach-I'm-dying, howling laughter.

After a week in – let's be honest – paradise, Les decides he's had enough of communal living, so he moves to the Chateau Marmont on Sunset Boulevard, to hang out with Britt Ekland and the international jet set who have taken him to their stony hearts. The shift in his personality is almost instant. Wherever he goes, he's treated like a visiting dignitary, given access to whatever his heart desires. Parties every night, getting wined and dined by some fat fuck or other. Either that or he's with one of his new buddies. Maybe John Bonham or Keith Moon, who knows? They're out there raging into the LA nights, because that's going to work out fine for all of them, I'm sure. I suspect Les has been using alcohol as a crutch since he killed that woman back in 1976, but there's a lot of cocaine in LA these days, a proper blizzard. Maybe that was always the case, I don't know, but he's never the same again after this point. There'll be no bringing him back from the brink. As far as I'm concerned, it's one less person in the hot tub at least. He's their problem now.

Then, a week after Les moves out, Eric wants his own space, so he's away now too. I wonder who's paying for all this extravagance. The record company? The TV folk? Then I remember. If it's coming out of someone's bottom line, it's ours most likely because that's the way it works. Everything is offset against what we're paid. It feels like free money when you get it, like it's fallen out of the skies, but you need to remind yourself that the money going out is yours too. It only *feels* like somebody else is footing the bill.

Every morning in the Canyon, for those of us who remain, it's the same routine. They've got us on a course of vitamins. Not just a couple either. We're on a 26-pill-a-day course – nothing untoward, I gather, but everything from vitamin A to Z – like we're members of a cult or something. Maybe we are. This is Hollywood, after all, so we're rattling like Tam's briefcase half the day. Jake's knocking on our door at 6am, a quick bite to eat, go to the Hollywood Y where the production company has gotten us a membership. I'm still in shape, but maybe some of the lads have got a bit doughy, carrying a wee bit of timber, I don't know. We should be on tour, burning off the day's nervous energy, taking a big gulp of adrenaline, but instead it's this weird workaday existence. We wait around half the day for someone to set up a shot and are done and dusted every day by mid-afternoon, so maybe there's one too many steak dinners being eaten. Steak dinners, though, are probably the least of our worries.

Still, the rest of us do a 6.30 workout each morning before the car comes to take us to the studio and we're on set each morning before 8, waiting for Eric and Les to roll in. When you arrive on the soundstage, you can smell the fresh paint where the set decorators have been working all night to make a backdrop, plying everything in bright primary colours and glitter. The people working on the show are all nice as can be, so despite the tedium, we're making it work as best we can and our hosts are most gracious. We never think our Scots roots are a problem, but the producers are a bit wary of our thick accents, so they have us work – day in, day out – with this guy Jonathan Lucas. He's a dialogue coach, brought in by the network to temper our accents. We're too Scottish, apparently. They probably have a point. Jonathan has us lined up, saying 'how now brown cow' or whatever, and we're trying not to laugh, but he still can't understand a word we're saying. He's there, tearing his hair out, telling us to enunciate and to slow down, and wondering how this is going to play in the Midwest.

We've been given a couple of cars to get around LA, and we have our own chef, providing meals at the drop of a hat, but I eat most nights at the Imperial Gardens. There's no mince and tatties here, but I've got hooked on the hot lobster salad and the shabu-shabu. I don't speculate about what Les and Eric are getting up to at nights, but I know they're not sitting around watching telly – Les in particular. From the letters we're getting, you get the idea that he's got half the Los Angeles cool set in his ear, telling him he doesn't need us. That's probably the case with most lead singers, I guess. They all have a little devil on their shoulder, but they don't always listen to them. That's the difference with Les. You don't have to be too good at reading people to know that – he's got it written all over his face when he swans in every morning. Every day, it's the same: him smoking a ciggie. He'll take a few final drags under the giant NO SMOKING ON SET signs, daring the wee guy with the combover and headset to come over and tell him, 'Excuse me Mr McKee-own, would you put your cigarette out?' Les scoffs, rolling his eyes like a teenager getting called down to a plate of liver and onions. Without a word, he scrunches the cigarette butt into the freshly painted floor, like a total egocentric prick.

If that's not embarrassing enough, he's telling anyone who'll listen he's not going to do the upcoming tour of Japan, issuing all kinds of demands and generally being uncooperative. It comes as no surprise to me when it turns out his hotel isn't being covered by the production company or the record label, so he's demanding we pay his $6,000 bill. He's pissing folk off, left, right and centre. There's a moment in Marty Krofft's office where Les is barking at him and Marty winds up grabbing him by the scruff of the neck. He's got him pressed against the wall, having to control the urge to batter him senseless. I don't think any of us would have stood in his way, now I think about it. That's not to say none of us were without fault, but in terms of our mental health, it's a miracle we make it to work every day to face the guy.

Despite everything, I think we'd be fools to grumble. There are tougher gigs, I'll be honest. After a few weeks, with the Rollers as the main draw, the show gets rebranded as *The Bay City Rollers Show*. We're getting bussed around LA to various theme parks, miming to one of the hits, getting dressed up as cowboys, chasing each other around like Keystone Cops, throwing buckets of water at each other or scooting around on wee bikes, while one of our records plays in the background. It's not hard labour, but it's not a comfortable fit for us. Our TV show in the UK was made for a teen audience, whereas *The Bay City Rollers Show* seems to be squarely aimed at preteen kids. I'm not trained in the dark arts of market research, but it seems to me that's a misstep that could be avoided, but the deal's signed and, from that moment on, we've no control over our destinies. We're having to learn hackneyed dance routines and doing weird performances over a laugh track. One week, you're doing a mental '50s rock and roll routine, all of us getting our hair swept back into a DA style that's all ass and no duck, bopping around with a bunch of girl dancers and Erik Estrada (Ponch from *CHiPs*) and wee Chachi from fuckin' *Happy Days*. Another week, we have Twiggy as the special guest and, during this routine, we're lined up, holding our arms out in front of us, holding her up while they get the shot. She's dipping in the middle and the director is shouting at us to 'pull her up by her fanny'. We're all looking at each other like, *We're not doing that*, when a runner comes over and explains that fanny has a different meaning here in the States.

Maybe punk and new wave are getting up a head of steam in the music papers back home, sweeping away all the glitter bands, but here in LA, pop music and showbiz are so adjacent, it's like none of it matters anyway. It's stupid, but it's fun. But I'm glad when it's over. I keep a positive outlook. I mean, maybe we might have been good dancers or decent actors, and this was the only way we'd find out. And we do find out. We're not good actors. We're not good dancers. When we finish our last day filming at the soundstage, filming links to go out during the ad breaks – 'Stay tuned, we'll be right back' kind of stuff, direct to camera – the director asks Les to hang on a moment. He tells him they have a surprise for him and Les has his chest all puffed out, because obviously he's the star and deserving of extra special treatment. He's there smirking when this guy walks onto the soundstage with a beautifully wrapped gift box. There's a wee ripple of applause and Les is like, aw shucks, preening away, as the guy tugs on the ribbon, removes the lid of the box and takes out a custard pie. Apparently, he's a professional pie thrower hired by the production crew, if that's even a thing, and he takes the pie out and pure smashes it into Les's face. You can actually hear his bones crunching it's that hard. There's a small audience of kids, the whole crew and production staff and us, and everyone is cheering, rolling around the floor laughing. Really, you'd have to have a heart of stone to not find it funny.

Eventually, though, the piper needs paying. After wrapping the final show and the back-and-forth letters and the frosty atmosphere, we assemble at the house in the Canyon. All of us, save Les, that is. Jake calls him up for a final bout of clear-the-air discussions and it goes about as well as you'd expect it. Jake's there, taking down notes, and we're hanging on trying to listen in to the call. Les has gone full-blown megalomaniac by now, his narcissism on full display.

'I want out of this band YESTERDAY . . . I'm more important than these guys . . . I'm where I am because of me and the Rollers are where they are because of me . . . If they want me to sing with them, they'll have to pay the price for that . . .' Referring to the $6,000 hotel bill, he says, 'If Marty Krofft doesn't pay for it, then *they'll* have to pay it . . . The Bay City Rollers have breached a partnership agreement by bullying me by not paying my expenses.'

Possibly there was a chance we'd find a peaceful way out of the situation. But after that call, everyone agrees Les is more trouble than he's worth.

Chapter 26

SAYŌNARA

September 1978

In the end, none of us really knows if Les jumped or if he was pushed. It was probably somewhere in the middle, like he sacked himself. I hear word from a couple of people that he's only gone because he can see the writing on the wall and wants to get out, to launch himself as a solo star before everything goes tits up, but who's to say? We're just happy to see the back of him. Whatever people think – and all our fans have their favourites – I think it's testament to years of Les being a prima donna that we'd all rather fail without him than succeed with him. After the pie-throwing incident, we have ten days pre-production and rehearsals for a run of Japanese shows and it's like a slow death march. Les doesn't show his face, but we do the work, hit our marks and make the best of a bad situation.

Prior to getting on the flight to Japan, the last word we get from Les is when he tells us 'I will fulfil my commitments on my terms', so we just assume he'll be there. No one seeks Tam's counsel. He's back in Scotland, in his counting house, giving mouth-to-mouth to his goldfish and God knows what else. Because he's not there for the day-to-day stuff – driving us from the shows, bawling us out after a gig for not moving about, making deals and making a pig's ear of sorting out the money – he's losing his influence over us and, let's be honest, he's as pissed at Les and his antics as the rest of us.

The Japanese shows go ahead as planned. No one would be any the wiser what was happening behind the scenes because we're all sweetness and light up on stage. Les is acting a little less like he's God's gift, as if he's suddenly experiencing some uncertainty, like a rare moment of clarity. When we arrive at the airport, he has this guy, a representative working out of Tam's office, and he's Les's consiglieri and sherpa rolled into one. We're picking up our bags from the carousel and Les strolls past to greet the waiting crowds – because, despite everything, there's still crowds here – leaving this guy to pick up his matching luggage and carry it out to the car. Thinking about it now, I rarely remember Les picking up his own bag. That's a lot of Holiday Inns. Him just walking up to his room and leaving his bag for someone else, or maybe a bellboy, to do it for him.

Still, it's curious to see him like this. I don't know if he's expecting us to fall to our knees and accept his attempted takeover of the group, but there's no danger of that. We're completely united in wanting him gone. We don't have a crystal ball and can't possibly tell whether it's going to leave us dead in the water commercially, but in terms of our well-being as human beings, as members of a band just wanting to make music, it's important that he goes. He was a handful before we got to LA; now he's completely unmanageable. In his head, he's a superstar. He's got his own security in place, his own dressing room at all the shows and is ferried around in his own personal limousine. I hear talk that he's telling folk that the personal security is to protect him from the rest of the band, which would be funny if it wasn't so insane, but he ends up receding into the background, getting himself fitted with that rod for his back he's been working on, while the rest of us let our hair down and try to have fun. We only see him now on stage. All of us are on autopilot, genuinely enjoying ourselves for once and looking at him upfront. He's still good at doing that thing, being a frontman. But it's such a fine line between charisma and egomania. By all means, have an ego but leave it on the stage – but he never can. When you're on stage, whatever baggage you've been carrying around with you, whatever bickering's been going on, suddenly you are brothers again. Off stage, though, the atmosphere is frosty, just mild passive aggression, but we're in separate dressing rooms: one for us, and one for Les and his wee entourage of shits. He'll drift in, all high and mighty sometimes, like he's being absent-minded, strolling into the wrong party or something before remembering he shouldn't be here. That or he'll say something snidey to Eric. A cola bottle will go flying, Eric trying out his throwing skills, hoping to catch Les square in the face and barely missing. At least they have that, the two of them.

Les and I, we're strangers now. We've barely said a word to each other since the US tour last year. There was a show, probably the third or fourth in a row, when I get the spotlight for a sax solo. It's only a minute, but it ruffles his feathers every time, so he always marches over like a wee toddler, stands between the bright spotlight on me and the audience. Once was funny; the second time, less so. Come the third time, he's pissing me off and I tell him after the show, 'Maybe let me have my moment. The rest of the hour is all yours, pal.' Because he's a dick, he doesn't listen. He does it the next night too, because that's his personality: never learning, never growing. So, this fourth time, he's jigging around in front of me, I take two steps towards him and boot him off stage. Through the onstage monitors, I hear the sound guy speaking through the static: 'Nice one Woody.' The security guys, who would normally come rushing from the wings, are much slower, grinning and giving me a cheeky thumbs-up before dragging Les out of the swirling soup of teenagers. And, just for a minute, he looks suitably humbled, his jacket in tatters. He doesn't do it again, but whatever traces of camaraderie that still existed between us were lost in that moment.

While we're playing out Les's farewell tour, some old faces from previous tours come by. Our loyal Japanese promoter Mr Ono has offered to cover our bar bills, thinking we're still on a milk-only diet. But it's a five-star hotel and no one told him that Al and I have developed a taste for whisky and sake, this expensive Japanese wine. The bar bill comes in at thousands of dollars. He's there studying the fine print of the drinks bill like he's been handed a warrant for his own death. As ever, there's the usual magazine, radio and telly people coming by the suite to interview us. If we're on a plateau, or coming down the other side, it's hard to tell. The Japanese fans have come out of their shell and the shows are well received. I don't know if it's a reliable metric to measure things by, but based on the sheer weight of gifts we're given and the crowds waiting outside for us when our flight arrives, you'd think we were still right in the heart of Rollermania here. The fans are frantic, but simultaneously reserved. They go mad at the sight of you, but usually you can stop and chat, and sign a few things. And when you explain you need to go, the crowd parts like the Red Sea and they let you go about your day. Usually.

After one of the shows, Alan and I polish off a bottle of whisky in our hotel and decide to go for a walk. It's the first time I've been out by myself in Japan without security. It's around 3am and pouring with rain. A couple of hundred yards down an alleyway, we spy someone crumpled on the ground and wander over to investigate. It's a young woman slumped on the narrow road. As we draw closer, Al stops in his tracks. I'm peering into the darkness and he's groaning, telling me she's dead and we're looking up at the tower block she either jumped or fell from. There's blood and guts everywhere, pure heartbreaking. I grab an umbrella and hold it over her while Al dashes back to the hotel to get help. I'm looking down at her, shielding her from the rain, but there's no signs of life. Finally, the police arrive and ask us a few questions, before we're sent back to the hotel, both of us completely shellshocked. The next day, we're due to play in Osaka, meaning an early start to catch the bullet train. I'm feeling dreadful, a bit hungover and the memory of that poor soul is hanging heavy on my mind. I'm processing all this, allowing it to percolate while we're told there's thousands waiting at Osaka station, and we're to stay in our seats until the local police give us the okay. When we pull into Osaka, I stick my head out the train and see them, held back behind barriers like cattle. The plan is, when we get the 'Go', we're to run down four flights of gangways to get to our transport on the ground floor. There's a voice in my head telling me to get up and run like fuck, and another telling me not to puke in front of the fans. I spew a little as I get up, then I run like fuck out of there, two security guards at my shoulder, following the directions of the police until I reach the safety of the van. The guys are way behind me, though, and the crowds have swollen, like I made them aware of our escape route. So, by the time the rest of the guys are bearing down on them, the barricades have been broken and I can see them getting swallowed up by the crowd. It's pure George Romero zombie movie stuff. It's only two or three minutes, but it feels like hours I'm waiting for them to get themselves free.

The tour isn't a disaster, but it leaves a bad taste. Suicides and zombies. It's not what anyone signed up for. It's probably a fitting epitaph for the Les era. We play our final show in Tokyo and we take our bows, followed by separate limos back to the hotel. We meet later at the hotel bar. I'm nursing a drink. Alan too. We're in a wee booth, away from the crowd, but close enough that we can hear the jazz band that's playing just over yonder. Someone's doing a decent take on an Oscar Peterson number. There's no hoi polloi here, unless you count us. We're up here among the gods of Tokyo, sucking up the rarefied air – just Japanese society's elites, all bow-ties and evening dresses, and us, leather bomber jackets and jeans, waiting around to call last rites on the Les McKeown era of the Rollers. The place around us is bustling, waiters whizzing past us with luminous cocktails held above their heads on silver trays. We're up in the clouds, looking out over the neon skyline. It should be that we're all celebrating, but it's slightly tense. A sweet waitress brings me a drink, then another as the other guys find us. A beer and a whisky chaser. Jake, Alan, Derek, Eric and me waiting to see what will happen, but it's anticlimactic. There's 20 minutes of 'will he/won't he?' tension before, finally, the elevator doors swoosh open and Les saunters in, with his minder carrying his bags. Les is all smiles, friendly and warm, like he hasn't been acting like a sociopath for the past six months. We all shake hands. Good luck fellas, good luck Les. See you around the clubs, kind of thing. Sure, it's sad, but only briefly. Across the bar, the jazz band strikes up and starts playing that standard, 'That's All', the old Nat King Cole number, and it feels poignant. It's the end of something, but for the sake of our mental health, it feels okay. The feelings of sadness will be gone by morning, I think.

None of us knows how this is going to turn out. Not us, and not Les. I just know it's for the best. I've met a lot of famous people. They all think it's never going to end, but I've never thought that, that we're going to be this successful forever. Fair play to those guys, but I've never woken up thinking that. Even now, it's about the excitement of being in a band. Music is always the thing. I'm not hung up on fame the way Les is. I wish people could see that playing in a band is normal. It's just a job, like being an electrician or an accountant. It's the fame that's weird. Personally, if I ever had someone in my ear the way Les had, telling me I was the best or whatever, I'd think they were full of shit. It's the same attitude I had playing the old folks' home with Freezin' Heet but, for Les, I think it's his undoing.

Chapter 27

A FRESH PAGE

It's January in Dublin. The skies are grey and the streets are still damp from the morning rain. We're in the studio again, finally, doing band stuff, but a man down. With Les gone these past three months, the famous five are now trimmed back to four – but only fleetingly. After the misstep of the US TV show, it feels good to be on familiar terrain again, even if the band is going down the tubes, circling the drainpipe of pop. It takes maybe a minute for me to understand that our heyday is in the rear-view. It's okay. There are worse feelings, like the first time you see yourself staring back from a magazine cover, but in reverse. You feel weird that you're not on the front of the magazines any-more, but you only briefly feel the sting. There's a new blue-eyed boy getting the girls hot under the collar. It's an adjustment, a fine-tuning of one's ego, but fine.

Back in the States, the Sid and Marty show is still on the air, limping to the end of its run, cut from an hour to 30 minutes. As all of us probably suspected, it's not moving the needle on the band's popularity one iota. In the months since Les departed, the rat departing the sinking ship, we've changed the band name to the Rollers. Eric and some of the guys are thinking we might distance ourselves from the bubblegum pop sound we had, like there's a kind of guilt by association, some kind of stigma, and I agree. Ninety-nine per cent of our fans call us the Rollers anyway. Tam doesn't care and Arista couldn't give a fuck, so we put out word that we're looking for a new member, as we get to work on the new album. It's like business as usual, only there's not this malevolent force in our midst, sucking up all the oxygen in the room.

After the casting call, we've been sent a bunch of headshots, bios and tapes, and we've got them all laid out on the floor here at Dublin Sound while we get to work on this new record. The bio we've landed on is this South African guy, Duncan Faure. He's been in LA a while, a gifted singer and musician, with a good reputation in the business from his time in the band Rabbit. Rabbit didn't exactly make any waves away from apartheid South Africa, but back home, they were a big deal. They had a hefty teenage following, so we all figure he's got the constitution to cope with being a Roller and we have him flown over to meet us in Ireland to see if he's a good fit. He comes in and we're all friendly, maybe a bit poker-faced sitting up in the control room, just in case we have to say no and send him straight back to the airport.

Our first impression is he looks the part and seems a lovely guy, so we press the intercom button and ask him to do his thing.

He sits up at the piano, plays a while, sings a couple of songs. I don't know if we're all 100 per cent sure about him. Because he's South African, a *white* South African, we know that comes with a lot of baggage, most of which we don't understand, but we can see he's a real musician and knows his way around a studio, so we agree to give him a shot and worry about the rest of the crap later. He's a decent writer too, and after a couple of days with him throwing in ideas and us coming up with a track list for the new record, it starts to feel like we're turning a fresh page. I start to imagine that we can become the really good rock and roll group we aspire to be. Naturally we'd keep one foot in the pop camp and chuck in a few ballads. I mean, we don't want to throw the baby out with the bathwater, but this feels like a step forward.

The album is called *Elevator* and is one of our best records by a mile. It's more of a move towards power pop, with hints of mid-'60s Beatles, and we're all slapping ourselves on the backs for making such a genius left turn, outsmarting all the naysayers who said we're finished. Obviously, the record is a resounding flop. It turns out the idea of changing the name of the band wasn't one of our brighter ideas. Add in the ongoing issues with the record company, who promoted it as if it was the new album by a serial killer, and the record was ill-starred from the outset. We greet the news with a shrug. We're naïve, but not so naïve that we believe every record is a hit, like we have some pop music Midas touch. It's just nice to be normal again.

If you're wondering what's going on in with our former band-mate about now, the same time as we're unveiling *Elevator* to an indifferent world, Les releases a solo album, *All Washed Up*, on his own label, Ego Trip. If he's been talking shite about us in the press, I've not seen it, but he makes his feelings known in other ways. I'm back in LA when I see a copy for the first time. The cover art depicts a kind of sci-fi/new wave-looking Les, walking out of the sea, with a crashed plane behind him, sinking into the waters. Look closely and you'll see there's a couple of dead guys floating face down in the sea or speared on Flying V guitars and the plane's fuselage bears the initials BCR. The waves on the cover art are the only ripples the record makes. Like our own magnum opus, *All Washed Up* fails to light up the charts.

The next time I lay eyes on the guy, we're in Berlin playing a big show for *Bravo*, West Germany's premier teen magazine. We're lined up with a bunch of top-20 artists at the grand Schweizerhof Hotel, the kind of place Agatha Christie sets her murders. It's all chandeliers, dark brown oil masters hanging in gilt frames and bellboys sweeping about the place in wee scarlet jackets. We only agree to the gig on the proviso that Les isn't playing. Not that we're trying to rain on his parade; it's just we don't need the drama he inevitably brings with him. An old friend, Booby Heidleman, the photographer for *Bravo*, assured us there was no chance. It turns out Booby was full of shit. When we finish our short set, we discover the next act is Les. Booby was always a lovely guy – he took a bunch of pictures of us in our heyday – but he's burnt his bridges with us now. I find him in the hotel bar afterwards and tell him he's a fuckin' liar, that he had one job, just as Alan and Eric are walking into the lobby. That's the precise moment Les and his sidekick, this guy Scobie, are catching up to them, giving them grief. I can see this confrontation getting going, while Berlin's polite society are tucking into their neat triangle sandwiches and clinking teaspoons against the fine bone china. I turn my back on Booby and I'm sprinting across the grand foyer. The dispute is getting louder, more aggressive. Les takes a swing at me, blocked by Alan who smacks him one, and Les folds like a deckchair. Scobie is having a go at Eric, and I sprint through the crowd after him, all these vicar's wives clutching their pearls and calling over the waiters. Scobie shouts, 'If you catch me, I'll kick yer heid in.' I catch up to him and pull him to the floor. I'm like the dog who's been chasing a car – no idea what to do next. Derek has caught up by now, so he kind of shrugs and, because he's got this weird Charlie Chaplin gait, he gives Scobie this side-footed kick in the guts that wouldn't break an egg. There's polizei everywhere streaming into the foyer now and I can see all these waiters and bellboys pointing in our direction, so I slip off to my room, whistling in the elevator. Nothing to see here guys.

Despite our record's failure, Les has gone and it's like the sun's come out on a gloomy day. We're back Stateside, sheltering on the west coast and Duncan is a fully fledged Roller now. He's professional, hits his marks and is never a dick. Even with the suffocating Los Angeles smog, it's like a breath of fresh air. There are no camps anymore. We're hanging out, getting a kick out of being in each other's company. Most of all, it's stopped feeling like hard work. You wake up in the morning, punching the air.

Outside of the five of us, though, not everyone is happy. After the record stiffs, we're summoned – all of us bar Duncan – to

Clive's suite at the Beverly Hills Hilton for crisis talks. Essentially, this is Clive browbeating us for an hour, telling us to take Les back. We think about that a while, scratching our chins, casting our eyes around the vast suite, the kind of place an emperor would stay if he was in town. We're hemming and hawing and Clive says, 'Just think about it.' Clive's been a good friend. I'm talking in music business terms here, because no one's really your friend in these waters, but I've got his phone number and, while we're riding high in the chart, he always takes my calls. I think we've got that kind of relationship, like we're friends, not like he's my boss, so I tell him, 'Don't be an arsehole, Clive. It's not gonna happen.' He bristles, then smiles like he didn't hear me, like it's a glitch in the matrix. I realise that was probably a stupid move from me as soon as the words leave my lips and I want to catch them in a butterfly net, forget it happened. Clive is the main man, a total player, and here's me, just a kid, telling him he doesn't know shit from clay. In a split second, you could see us go from priority act to being dead in the water. After that, when I call him, his secretary just tells me he's out to lunch. It's that way for a year, like it's one long lunch. I'm too naïve to realise I've been put on the backburner. Fair play.

In a bid to forget my gaffe, Jake and I head out for a few drinks. We've hired a couple of classic Cadillac convertibles from 'Rent-a-Wreck', these great classic V8 cars, ideal for screeching around corners and suchlike. We're tearing around Hollywood in one of them, checking out the nightlife, when the car comes to an abrupt halt on Sunset Boulevard. Jake jumps out and pops the hood, wafting away the steam with his hand. I'm there, peering over his shoulder, scratching my head. The engine is molten hot, so I get an idea that I'll just kick the radiator cap off, rather than try to unfasten it with my bare hands. But, by then, physics takes over and the cap just explodes, soaking me in scalding steam. Jake's looking at me. 'Ya awright, Woods?' and I'm telling him, 'Och, I'm fine.' And I am fine. For five minutes. Then, I guess the shock wears off and I realise I'm in excruciating pain. Jake's telling me we need to get to hospital, Cedars Sinai, which isn't too far from where we're staying, and I don't know if it's bravado or the fact I'm a bit wasted, but I tell him no. I opt for us to head back to the hotel's rooftop pool to try to ease the burn, only the water somehow makes it worse. Jake gives me a look that says it's time to go to hospital.

'Okay,' I tell him reluctantly. 'I'll need to get some underpants from somewhere though.'

Jake's telling me the ones I've got on will be fine, no one's checking, so I have to explain I don't wear underpants and haven't done for years, so here's me, knocking on Alan's door, my leg and neck really starting to hurt and asking if I can borrow a pair of his pants. 'A clean pair, mind.' Alan's standing there bemused, holding out a pair of briefs at arm's length, as if what I've got might be catching. 'I'll not need them back,' he tells me.

Next stop is Cedars Sinai and, because it's the USA, you don't just get to roll into casualty and have someone see to you. There's a whole rigmarole to go through and they're wanting a credit card before they'll even sit me down. Lucky for me, Jake has a card and does the necessary. Finally, a wheelchair duly arrives and I'm swept away for an assessment. I'm looking down at my leg, at these vast water blisters bubbling up on the skin, and nodding out from the burning. The doctor gives me an injection and a bunch of pills to help with the pain and he mutters something about second-degree burns. I'm bandaged up like King Tut, feeling spaced-out, and sent home to the hotel. On the way up, I bump into a woman, someone who's been flirting with me on and off while we've been staying in LA, and she follows me to my room. I should have possibly just said a polite goodnight, but we make out for a bit, which is probably testament to the painkillers, and I have to apologise for the bandages and the water blisters popping all over the sheets.

When Alan comes by to check on me in the morning, he opens the door a crack and he's doubled up laughing, calling me The Mummy. Over his shoulder, there's Jake reminding me we've got a video shoot today. Fuck's sake, I think. I've second-degree burns here, groggy as hell from the painkillers and I can't get into my Roller gear. Al pops by a sportswear store and picks up a red tracksuit for me, and it's okay, bearable – except every five minutes we need to cut because another fuckin' blister has popped out and I need to push it back under the fabric.

Full disclosure here: I'm probably drinking too much and too often these days. Not just occasionally, but habitually. A few days after my wounds have healed and the payment for treatment has cleared, I'm back on the horse that bucked me. We've moved out of the hotel and into a rented house. I've been out and I'm staggering, feeling lighter than air. I'm not full pished, but close enough. These stark, hot Los Angeles nights are a lot to deal with. You drink because you're thirsty, then get up to leave and find your sea legs have abandoned you. I'm hot and sweating and decide to cool off. Strolling around the back of the house we're renting, I'm into a swan dive the moment I reach the edge of the pool. There's only one problem. The pool guy drained the pool earlier. Maybe he told us, but I don't remember. There's probably a note on the kitchen counter somewhere, or something stuck to the fridge, and I just missed it. I walk out to the end of the springboard, flinging my shoes hither and thither, one gentle bounce, then another and I launch myself into the hot California air. Then I see it, the ground looming up at me. I kind of recalibrate somehow, like I've got cat-like reflexes, and manage to not go face first. I steer myself to the edge so, rather than a direct impact on my face, I crash awkward-as-you-like into the steep sides of the empty pool. My clothes are ripped to shreds and I'm scratched to fuck, limping around the bottom of the pool, picking up all the money that dropped out my pockets on impact. The guys are all peering over the edge and I'm stuffing loose change and dollar bills in my trousers, telling them, 'Ach, I'm fine. Don't you worry about me.'

I mean, it could be worse. Les might still be in the band.

Chapter 28

SQUARE GOES

June 1979

A Berlin hotel room. Me and Al and a bottle of whisky, enjoying a post-gig game of chess. Usually, it's Eric and me playing to pass the time on tour, but after he showed an interest, I've been teaching Al the ropes. I love the game. Could lose hours playing, sitting in front of the board, strategising. Not so long ago, we had a mad plan to go with a chessboard motif for the cover of our *It's a Game* LP. Six pieces, representing the band and Tam. Eric, because he thinks he has the most power, was represented by the white queen, with me as the white knight, me figuring I like the movement, and the fact a knight can always catch you off guard. Pat McGlynn was the black pawn, Les the black king and Derek was the white rook. If you look closely at the finished album cover, you'll see we'll end up in a stalemate as it's black to move.

This was mine and Eric's idea of where the band was at the time. Never let it be said that we can't do subtext! By the time the record reached the stores, no one was paying attention to any subtext – not as close as before, anyway – so our in-joke was kind of lost. Pat, who's out of the picture now, had his face on the back cover airbrushed out. The main thrust, though, the reason I mention it here, was Tam. We had him as the white king. He's overlooking the board, the main piece, but holding no power.

So, Alan and I, we're in lockdown, seeing another night through until dawn, having checked in under the pseudonyms, Mr A. Southern and Mr S. Comfort, our usual trick for evading the fans. It's sedate, not exactly rock and roll, but we're relieved to get a night like this for a change. We came back to our room the other night to find half-a-dozen German women waiting for us. Tam's not in our day-to-day lives, micromanaging us, so we can act our age a bit sometimes. We can have a few too many drinks and meet the occasional woman. Without going into detail, hopefully to spare your blushes and mine, Alan and I didn't play chess that night. We paired off with a couple of women. Probably my main takeaway from the night's events was that Alan was done before me. I was still in the throes of passion and could hear Alan's companion teaching him German in the darkness – 'Eins, zwei, drei . . .' – like I needed a countdown.

Despite our years under Tam's thumb, subject to his determination that none of us get too friendly, it's curious that Alan and I now share a room voluntarily whenever we're on the road. The other guys do whatever they do, in the privacy of their own rooms, but we're happier in each other's company – talking shite all night, drinking whisky and playing chess. We're at the dregs of the bottle now, the last knockings, so we've been here a while. I'm winning, thanks to some sweet gambit I've had brewing these past few moves. Check. Check. Checkmate. Sweet. He's all like, 'Och, Woody', but smiling still, because that's Al. He's not got a mean bone in his body. We take a sip of whisky, lean back in our seats and he tells me he didn't see that one coming. Out of nowhere, I say, 'I'd like to take Tam out like that.'

'Aye. We should get rid of the fucker,' Alan agrees. He's looking around, wondering whether there's another bottle somewhere. 'Aye, yer right. Why don't we call him?'

I've been mulling it over a while now, this idea to take out the king. I've been tired of the control freakery of it all. It was manageable before, because at least he got things done. I'm probably like one of those people you read about in the old times who embraces a dictator because they got the trains running on time. I'm happy to ignore all the shite as long as I can get to work in the morning. Now the trains aren't even running, so I'm done. In terms of the Rollers, the train isn't even on the tracks anymore. Tam has one of his henchmen out here these days, useful as an ashtray on a motorbike. This guy's getting his hands dirty so Tam can do whatever it is he's doing now. Back home, the press got a sniff, picked up his trail, discovered he was harbouring a secret lifestyle and were set to expose him as gay. These are the times, I'm afraid. The same as it was for Brian Epstein, I suppose. Being gay is seen as a bad thing, so Tam and the press office came up with a counternarrative to torpedo the story when it came out. He announced his engagement to Marcella

Knaiflova and embarked on, well, what they used to call a lavender marriage.

Meantime, his eye is off the ball. The record company is pissed with us and the shows aren't selling. We're not exactly in freefall, but we're in disarray. Travel arrangements are getting arsed up. These are the meat and drink of a dictator and he can't even get those right. Things are fractious between us in a way they never were before. There's an argument waiting for you around every corner and even to me, someone who's not looking too closely, everything seems to be unravelling. We played a show a while back and Eric – who rarely drinks – was drunk on stage, making all kinds of mistakes. He was staggering about and even tried to leap into the audience. He fell short, catching some scaffolding right between his legs.

Alan, who'd earlier pulled a tendon in his foot playing football, was on crutches. He played the whole show seated, with his crutches propped against the amp. Every few songs, when we switched up, he had to be helped to the keyboards by the crew, but because Eric was all over the place, that fucked the running order, so whenever we started a song, Alan was stranded in the wrong place, waving hopelessly for help. The whole thing was a comedy of errors. Eric and I were shouting and swearing at each other as we took our bow. Jake was ushering us off stage frantically. He could see the fans and organisers scratching their heads wondering what was happening and it wasn't a good look at all. Meanwhile, Alan was struggling to keep up. Suddenly, like he'd been touched by a born-again preacher, he just threw away his crutches and pegged it across the stage to follow us into the van. When I caught up to Eric, I was fuckin' raging. 'What are ya fuckin' doing?' Eric was all red-eyed, slurring. 'Square goes when we get back to the hotel. Just you fuckin' wait. Square goes.' Next thing, Eric belts me a shot right in my nose, claret all down my tracksuit. He's running and I'm after him, raging. Bastard's hiding in his room. Square goes, he says, like we're still in the playground.

So, it's chaos and I'm placing the blame squarely at Tam's door. I don't know if it's the whisky, or if it's just pure bravado, but I pick up the phone by my bed, get an outside line and put in the call to the Potato Man. 'You know what time it is, Woody?' he says. 'For crying out loud.' He's wheezing, and there's the rattle of pills.

I've got the phone pressed to my ear. Alan's up close so we can both hear. 'Tam,' I say. 'You're sacked. Done.'

'What do you mean, I'm sacked?'

Alan and me are covering our mouths so he can't hear us laughing. I'm feeling so good. It's an incredible sensation after all these years of shite.

'Yer fuckin' sacked,' I tell him again and I run through a list of recent disasters. I'm ten minutes recounting the disorganisation, the petty bullshit. To underscore the point, Al takes the phone from me and says the same.

In the morning, Eric and Derek are hammering on the door. My head's foggy from the whisky.

'What the fuck have you done?' Derek asks.

'We just fired him. He's a useless bastard anyway.'

'We better get a lawyer then,' Eric shrugs.

Our lawyer jots down our list of grievances, noting that Tam probably has grounds to sue us for lost earnings if he is so inclined. But Tam, the great instigator of our fame, and a genuine 20th-century horror show, doesn't bat an eyelid when he's served the papers. He goes meekly into the night, like all bullies. The king is dead, finally. The king is fuckin' dead.

Chapter 29

JAILBIRDS

March 1980

It's a new decade and, about now, I'm finding there's something in that Warhol line about being famous for 15 minutes. It's feeling a bit like this is the 14th minute for us. Our previous album didn't stop the band's slow, downward trajectory one iota. It's a shame. We've a ton of experience in the studio and, like any band worth its salt, we want to do something a bit different, the same as when we showed Martin and Coulter the door when we got tired of working to their shuffle template. That was then, of course, but I don't know if anyone's paying attention anymore. Maybe they looked away a minute too long, and now the record company is running the ball to the corner flag, just seeing out the contract so they can be rid of us. They long since decided not to bother promoting the Rollers, so you can't find the new record in stores even if you tried. It's a real shame. Everyone's throwing in ideas and songs and it's a good feeling around us. There's a ton of good things to say about us, but now the volume's been turned down a touch, we're a lot like any other jobbing band you've seen a few times on the telly.

Duncan Faure is less trouble to have around the place than Les ever was. Probably the only strike against him is he's a real ladies' man, as we used to say. As we still say, for that matter. Les is still out there on the periphery of culture – and of our memories. He's in that same big-in-Japan bubble we seem to co-exist in. He's promoting another solo record and watching it sink like a stone. Duncan is probably the reason we're here in South Africa. He knows the ropes and how things work here. At least, that's what he says and I've no reason not to believe him. In terms of our career, we can't get arrested – although we'd soon find a way to resolve that. Just not in the way I might have hoped.

The last time I was here was for a dozen shows over Christmas and New Year. In the US and the UK, the mania has quietened to a dull roar, like a background noise, but the band isn't quite becalmed yet. We can still create a bit of a buzz in the colonies, especially here in the outer reaches, where the arrival of a band like the Rollers still generates a bit of excitement. If I was listening in history classes, I'd have had a better angle on it, but to me, it's the same as the other places, only you can go on safari after you've lounged a while by the pool. The shows over the holidays were decent enough. We had fun and it was like all the bullshit got washed away on the Cape Town beaches. While we were over for those shows, I reconnected with a girlfriend of mine, Danielle.

Most nights we were all out, enjoying life in nice bars and restaurants. One night after a show in Durban, Danielle brings her dad, Barrie St Clair, out for dinner with me and the guys. He's a big-shot movie producer. He made *Zulu Dawn*, the other Zulu movie, the one that doesn't have Michael Caine. He's telling us about his upcoming projects and, across the table, I can see Alan's ears prick up. He always fancied himself as a movie star. Before we even finish our entrees, Alan's pulled up a chair next to Barrie and they're huddled up talking about a possible movie project. Barrie's mulling it over, Alan's touting himself as the next Warren Beatty. 'Maybe I got something for you,' Barrie tells him and then sets about pitching this new movie he's getting underway in South Africa in the New Year. It's a drag racing thing called *Fat Takkies* – racing driver boy meets girl, faces adversity and wins the race and the girl's heart in the end. He looks across the table at the rest of us. 'You guys should be in it too,' he says. He's probably thinking getting the Bay City Rollers in his B-movie is a good hook and might put a few bums on seats, so we all say, 'Aye, I'll have some of that. Might be fun.' So we sign on, swept along on a wave of Alan's ambition.

That's all of us except Eric. He's had enough of South Africa by now and just wants to go home, so he politely declines. With the benefit of hindsight, he maybe dodged a bullet there. Meanwhile, I'm thinking, *Wow, an actual film. Maybe a premiere and a stroll down the red carpet.* It never once crosses my mind that I can't act for toffee. Derek, Duncan and me are roped in to play mechanics, glorified extras, while Alan gets to act out his Steve

McQueen fantasies as a racing-car driver. What could possibly go wrong?

Here we are now, a few months later, Duncan, Derek, Alan and I arriving on South African soil to start work on the movie, now going under the title *Burning Rubber.* Only one problem. Unbeknownst to us, since our last trip we've become wanted men. Someone didn't pay for the lighting rig or the PA, so we're practically on the run, from the minute we walk down the stairs off the plane. Someone's telling us we'll be filming some stuff on location at a drag racing circuit. Nothing too strenuous – maybe have a smudge of engine oil on our cheek, and a line of dialogue perhaps, but mostly we're going to be milling around in the background with a spanner while Alan does all the heavy lifting. Sounds good to me, I think, as we're taken down to the track. 'Oh, the police and the sheriffs are on the lookout for you boys,' the driver says. We're all aghast. 'You're wanted fugitives.'

We arrive on set in Magaliesburg, around an hour's drive from Johannesburg. We're staying in this sprawling hotel complex, in these wee cottages, completely cut off from civilisation. Every time we wander out from our trailer, someone gives us the nod to tell us we just missed the police, who are driving around South Africa with warrants for our arrest. They have an inkling where we are, of course, so we get these unscheduled raids every day or every other day. The track that takes you from the main road to our hotel is about a mile long, so we're in this ridiculous situation, having someone keeping lookout for police cars coming down the dirt road. A guy from the production crew stands on the roof with a walkie-talkie, looking out for plumes of dust, setting off this weird chain of Chinese whispers telling us to hide until the coast is clear. Every day when the cops arrive, the director kind of wanders out to the front of the hotel, shrugs and says, 'Oh, you just missed them.' The cops have a sniff around our hotel rooms and whatnot, scratch their heads that they've been outsmarted and head off. Once you see the dust clouds rising on the track and the cops heading back to town, the director shouts 'Action' and we all come out of hiding, safe until the next day. It's pure Keystone Cops.

After we wrap, we climb out of our mechanics' overalls and retire to the bar or keep an ear out for whether there's something happening in the hotel. It's a huge place, so often we find there's a disco or something. We're eating our dinner on Saturday night, and the waiters come in and start taking the tables away while we're still eating, with the disco starting around us finishing our meals. All the local farmers and their families start filling the hall and they're all in their finery – ballgowns and tuxedos – and the disco lights come on. The DJ's playing all this old-timey accordion music. It's like stepping back in time, watching them marching around the dancefloor. I'm wiping my mouth with a napkin and the table in front of me is swept away by the staff, so I'm 'Oh, I'll not be having pudding then' while the farmers and their wives are doing this kind of ballroom dance, the Langarm. We're in jeans and T-shirts, sipping whisky, rubbing our eyes at this strange sight. It looks like something out of *Monty Python* and I'm half-expecting them to start at each other with giant dead fish or something. We're rolling around laughing. Once we've drunk enough whisky, Alan and I link arms and get up, figuring that if you can beat them, join them.

There's something like three weeks of this nonsense and we're all finding it bemusing, but also kind of hilarious, outsmarting the cops daily, and being these rock-star fugitives from justice. The next time the police come, the fateful time, we're in this hotel nightclub for a band meeting. It's midday and the place is closed, with no one around, except us. Alan is late and Jake's running errands so we're sitting on our arses waiting to start the meeting. Derek is on the phone to Jake. 'Jake, I've got some grass hidden in my room. I need you to get in there and fetch it.' He pauses. Jake is saying something. 'It's in the bathroom,' replies Derek, 'under one of the tiles. Ach, no. You'll have tae stand on the loo seat to reach it man.'

We don't hear the other side of the conversation, but unlucky for us, there are a couple of press guys chasing the story of the Rollers on the run and they're eavesdropping in the corridor while Jake's frantically scrambling around Derek's bathroom. Grass is illegal here. Not that we're drug fiends or anything – I didn't just move up from milk and sweets to mainlining heroin. Maybe just a small joint every now and then. I've had a neatly rolled joint in the spine of my passport case for a couple of years now, untouched, just there for emergencies. Being tricky, I figure it'll be the last place they'll look. Tam isn't in our hair anymore and, well, it's pretty decent grass here, so why wouldn't you? The reporters let the cops know what they heard and they rock up and arrest Jake with the bag of grass. We've no idea this is all happening, but Jake's panicking, telling them, 'It's not mine, for fuck's sake. It's Derek's.'

Once they bring out the cuffs, the jig is up. Jake folds like a deckchair and brings the cops down to the band meeting.

Meanwhile, Derek's staring at the phone. 'The line's dead. You think he got it?' We're all saying, 'Aye, of course he got it because we're masters of deception.' The cops, even Sherlock Holmes himself, could never bring an end to our crime spree. I'm so confident that, as I'm taking a sip of Coke from a green glass bottle, I'm thinking that maybe we'll have a wee joint when Jake gets here. Then the door opens and in bursts a squad of armed police, handguns at the ready. There's 20 cops and one sheriff and they're not here for a glass of cola. One of the cops holds out the bag of grass and says, 'Is this yours?' I tell them no and look down the line. Duncan says no. He looks down the line at Derek, waiting for him to fess up. Instead, he says no as well. I'm watching in horror as Jake is taken away. One of the cops tells us he's going to be deported. Fuck. The next day, it's splashed across all the papers. The police and the sheriffs come back to the set and Derek, Duncan and me are placed in cuffs and marched at gunpoint to a line of waiting patrol cars.

Maybe you've noticed, but I'm an optimist at heart. However, pulling up at the Johannesburg Fort Prison is not something I saw in the cards for me. It's a proper prison, like you see in the films – bars on the windows, stripey suits and actual misery. We're bundled out of the cars, standing in line, waiting to have our prints and mugshots taken before being taken down to a holding cell. There's one line for black prisoners, another line for the rest of us. The prison guards make sure the black inmates get it harder. Even on the way in to getting their thumb prints taken, the guards are going at them with their billy clubs like total pricks. It's not exactly VIP treatment in our line either, but we're not shown any disrespect, at least. I'm just trying not to think about the smell, trying not to think I've not eaten since breakfast or that there's hundreds of bona fide criminals crammed into cells, just a stone's throw away from us. As the cell door clangs shut behind us, someone tells us we'll be out tomorrow, so there's a sigh of relief, but I'm still tense. It's a big grey miserable rectangle, with a stinking toilet in the corner, watched over by a moth the size of a crow. I'm wondering where the wall is, to protect my modesty if I need to take a shit, then I realise, it's meant to be like that, you just shit in front of everyone. I decide there and then, even if I'm here for a hundred years, I'm not using that toilet ever.

There are eight single beds, four fellow prisoners, the three of us and a prison cat that, the minute we walk in, jumps up from the stone floor and onto some guy's bed where it promptly vomits. The single big light in the centre of the room is kept on all night, fizzing with electricity and flies getting scorched on the hot glass every couple of minutes. Everyone falls asleep by 9pm. Not me, though. I'm awake all night, watching the other guys sleep, and with one eye on the other prisoners in the cell with us. We're not in with the general population – the real rough guys – just a group of political prisoners. There's a lot of that about over here, it seems. My bed is four feet away from the toilet, so I'm treated to the sounds and smells as everyone gets up through the night to take a leak or settles in for a dump. The guy who had the cat sick on his bed takes a turn for the worse himself and spends the night heaving into the toilet, puking until nothing else will come, just a dry, miserable heaving sound. Across the way, I can hear singing coming from the black side of the jail. Beautiful, spiritual voices, wafting across the stale stink of the air. Really, you can find beauty anywhere is what I'd say here, if I was looking for a positive spin on things.

Morning finally comes and the guys stir. It's 6am and there's much clanging of cell doors and sudden activity. Two guards, keys jangling off their belts, come in and carry the sick guy out on a stretcher. Truly, I couldn't tell you if he was alive or dead. Duncan puts pen to paper on a new song, 'Doors, Bars and Metal', to commemorate the miserable last 24 hours of our lives. I note, with some annoyance, that the crow-sized moth hasn't budged all night. It's still there, keeping its beady eye on us, a witness to our misery. There's breakfast, if you can call it that – like skunk shit: a pile of red stuff, a pile of white stuff, with a piece of bread on the side of a tin plate in case you want to mop up the gravy (I don't) – and then an hour's exercise. Even now, as we're marched through the exercise yard, segregated, like everywhere else in this messed-up country, I'm thinking, *Ach, this will be okay. We'll be out today. This'll be a funny story for the folks back home.* There are these big guys, the kingpins of whatever cell block, surrounded by henchmen, one gang on each corner of the high walls. We're milling around, kicking stones across the concrete and, I don't know, maybe word got out that there was a band in the jail, but a prisoner pulls out an acoustic guitar and hands it to me. Another guy hands a guitar to Duncan.

'You play,' this guy says. He's grinning, nodding toward us, and I'm looking at the guitar like I never saw one before. 'You play songs for us, yes?' I look at Duncan and he shrugs, and we start playing. We go route one on the song selection and play 'Jailhouse Rock'. What else are you going to play when you've wound up in prison? The other inmates start drifting over and we play the Beatles' 'Help', because obviously that's the second song you'd play if you were in a South African prison. We finish to cheers and are escorted back to our cell. We never hear from the cat-sick guy again, but our cellmates are quite chatty, so I start to relax a little. Not relaxed enough to use the toilet, but not as bad as I felt just before dawn with the guy dying from cat disease a metre away from me. We're out today, so it's not like I'm doing a 20 stretch.

Only we're not out today. This dawns on us slowly as the day passes, and the light from outside the bars dims and is replaced by the harsh light in the cell. We ask the guard, and he just shakes his head: no. What about a change of clothes? I'm still here in my civvies from two days back, pure stinking. Again, the guard shakes his head. We haven't been charged with anything, it turns out. The authorities are just holding us until they get paid the money we owe, so someone must be working on it, I think. Exhausted now, I finally fall asleep, thinking the moth is going to stretch its wings and come down and eat my face in my sleep.

The next morning, I'm a wreck. I tell everyone, half-laughing, that I had this dream about the moth coming down to devour me as I slept. One of the political prisoner guys says, 'Oh, right' and climbs out of his bed to walk over to the toilet. I presume he'll pick up the moth and let it fly out through the bars. Instead, he removes one of his shoes and walks up to it, like a snooker player sizing up a shot. He gives it a last look and there's a big explosion of powder. Bits and pieces of coloured dust and moth gunk and goo fall down over the toilet bowl and a giant smear appears across the wall where the moth once was. I'm like, 'Okay, thanks, I think.' The guy just looks at me. 'Fancy a game of cards?' he says. We all say aye. He teaches us a game called Grouch, which passes a few hours. It's fun, but I'm still thinking about the moth, and the dead-cat guy, wondering when we're getting out of here.

Not today, apparently. The guard comes and takes us off to another room where Duncan's brother Bill Faure and his lawyer are waiting to see us. Bill says the money's been held up and we're stuck here for the weekend. Eric's back in Scotland. He's got the money and he's sending our limo driver on the next plane to Johannesburg, but as for getting it over the weekend, forget it. Duncan is fuming. Derek and me are more used to the chaos surrounding our every move, so we just sit there like it's exactly what we expected, nodding while Bill explains the fine detail of why he can't pull any strings. At least the fuckin' moth is gone now, I think, as we get led back to our cell. Another two days of playing Grouch and wondering what happened to the cat. And I've had my legs crossed for three and half days now. Then on Monday, 6.30am, I look up from my bed. A guard is grinning a kind of lopsided grin at me.

'Today?' I say.

He nods. 'Today. Maybe.'

What can I say about the movie *Burning Rubber*? Was it worth going to prison for? Well, it isn't *Citizen Kane*, it's pretty much a

B-movie, although we signed up willingly. The deal was that we could take $15,000 up front or a percentage of the movie's eventual take. In an act of boundless fuckin' optimism, we all opted for a percentage. Now, I'm no mathematician, but based on my calculations, a percentage of nothing is not a lot, so it wasn't our most shrewd business decision. And that's a crowded field. If I'm going to be generous, Alan can act a bit and the Rollers theme song is a good tune, but I won't be signing up as an actor just yet. And I definitely won't be needing to hire a tux for the Oscars this year.

In Germany, they're marketing it as a Bay City Rollers movie. We should probably have made more of a fuss about that, but I think after the prison thing and all the record company stuff bubbling away in the background, we wound up just shrugging and accepting what they'd done. Maybe, I'm thinking, if we don't draw too much attention to it, nobody will notice it happened. When I see it finally, it's been dubbed into German, so it's hard to say, but I know I'm pure squirming in my seat watching it unfold. Funnily enough, though, I wouldn't change a thing.

Chapter 30

GERALD

1981

We're a year deep into this new decade and the Rollers have ground to a halt here in suburbia. The band is staying in Maple-wood – at 40 Crestwood Drive, way at the top of a hill, deep in New Jersey – while we record our new album, *Ricochet*. It's our third record with Duncan, a swig or two at the last chance saloon of pop, with us embracing our more mature sound. If only we had a mature outlook to go along with it. The previous Rollers record, *Voxx*, was a hotchpotch of songs we had knocking about. Something old, something new and borrowed, even a couple of Duncan's old numbers from when he was top of the pops in South Africa. It wasn't our finest hour, truth be told – just a contractual obligation so we could weasel out of our relationship with Arista, which went toxic after some idiot called Clive Davis an arsehole. It worked. We're free of Arista, but we're trapped here for a few months, going out of our brains. The only screams we're hearing now are coming from inside the house, which is a change at least. We're going about the business of rehearsing our new record amid rows of neat, detached houses with driveways and barbecues. It's a relaxed set-up but, like I said, it's suburbia, so not exactly the most rock and roll environment. We have our equipment set up in the basement to work on new songs for the album and, one flight up on the ground floor, there's a lounge with an open fire that no one can seem to get going. This leads to a kitchen, a small office, a table tennis room and a small bedroom, which becomes Eric's room. Alan, Derek, Duncan and Yours Truly take a bedroom each on the first floor, across the landing from a small library. The old house is topped off by a creepy attic. You get chills just standing there a minute, so we keep that door firmly shut. That's where Gerald lives. But we'll come to him.

We're recording the new record at the nearby House of Music studios in West Orange and, when we're not getting into scrapes, we're home most of our downtime, rehearsing for some upcoming tour dates. Initially, everything's fine. The usual rigmarole: wake up late, drift down to the studio for a few hours. Standard 9-to-5 for us, even if it's more like lunchtime until dark. The US singer Meat Loaf is in one of the neighbouring studios recording with Jim Steinman. He's a stone-cold gentleman. He's got one of the biggest records of all time under his belt, so he's bought an arcade game for the green room, Asteroids. He'll probably be able to retire on all the quarters I keep piling into it between sessions. When you catch him in the cafeteria at lunchtime, he has all these meat patties lined up in front of him, like a prize fighter bulking up before the weigh-in. Between mouthfuls, he'll always tell you to pull up a chair and tell him what's happening out in the sticks. In the next studio, there's another session for Kool and the Gang, the US funk and soul outfit. A great bunch of guys – always playing pinball in their downtime and a lot of fun to be around.

After the sessions, Al and I will likely find a wee bar and get steaming drunk. I don't want to say that drinking's becoming a problem, but my head's a fug most mornings. I could strike up a sponsorship deal with Anadin, because I'm probably keeping that company afloat about now. It's all a far cry from getting up at the crack of dawn to be driven down to the Hollywood Y for a workout during our US TV days. Most nights, we blow off a little steam at Doc Callahan's, a neighbourhood bar in Maplewood. I'm either needing smelling salts the next day just to get out of bed, or I'll find myself star-shaped, sprawled out in a disabled parking spot, with no idea how I got into this situation. One night at Doc's, we're several whiskies and beers into the night and, every now and then, the barman shouts 'Shooters!' and everyone at the bar necks a shot. There's a line of people, knocking back shots. A fireman, a cop, a dentist. Maybe the fourth time this happens, we get talking to these guys, getting interested in what's happening, wanting to try it for ourselves. As soon as they hear our accents, they're saying, 'Oh, you Scots love a drink, right?' The next lot of shots gets lined up and the barman shouts 'Shooters!' and we're knocking them back with the guys at the bar. We're not getting drunk under the table by anyone, we figure. It's our national pride that's at stake, so we're standing at this bar at two in the morning, lining up our 20th shot, waiting for the shout. I find my way home somehow. Alan knocks at my door in the morning and he looks like a fucking ghost. The barman who was pouring the shots was the last man standing, he tells me. He was drinking apple juice the whole time, while he was pouring grain alcohol for every other poor sap at the bar.

Because there's a sucker born every minute, Al and I turn up the next night and do the same again. Derek joins us, having finished his drum overdubs. We sink a few more, then, like idiots, get in the car back to Crestwood Drive. Al's behind the wheel, assuring us he's got this, and we go screeching off into the night. It's only four miles, a five-minute drive, but I start to drift away, lolling away in the passenger seat, feeling a bit icky. We'll be fine. Next thing, I'm woken with a jolt. The car's tearing around a corner, up on two wheels and I've leaned against the door somehow and spilled out, and down this grassy knoll – because it's the US and grassy knolls are very much a thing here. Alan, meanwhile, has slammed on the brakes and jumped out the car on the driver's side, without putting on the parking brake. He's rolling down the hill after me and the car is picking up speed. I'm so drunk that I'm picking a fight with a tree I just crashed into. A few feet from me, Alan is rolling around the ground having palpitations as the car comes to a halt. We both look across to see Derek, who has climbed from the back seat to apply the handbrake. Weirdly, this tail end of this scene is witnessed by the rest of the band, who coincidentally were coming back from the studio, all of them sober as judges, and seeing this little slapstick movie play out in front of them from the safety of their car. They arrive just in time to see Derek applying the handbrake, before calling an ambulance. The following morning, Al and I wake up in adjacent hospital beds, like characters in a bad sitcom.

When we're not at Doc's or getting into fights with trees, we're climbing the walls on Crestwood, finding mischief in the most unlikely places. We're rooting around in the cupboards and come across a cache of prescription drugs, left by the previous owner. We ask around and discover it was this old gent who succumbed to cancer. He died in the house, we're told, and I feel a shiver pass through me. We make use of all the pills though because it would be a shame to let them go to waste. There's all manner of painkillers and quaaludes and the like. There's so much that every now and again we have a special D-Day (drug day) where we (everyone except Eric) smoke a few joints and take the odd 'lude. I don't know that it's the best idea we ever had because we're half out of our minds the whole time, all of us on edge, like walking fuckin' timebombs.

Once we've played our hundredth game of ping pong and scanned the library for something to read, I set up a homemade Ouija board, using scraps of paper for letters and a wee upturned whisky glass. Eric can't hold his drink – he gets proper arsey when he's had a couple, and so he usually doesn't get involved – but I can always persuade Alan to join me on the road to trouble while Eric adjourns to his room to write a song or two. Alan and I occasionally mess around with the makeshift board, usually after we've sunk a bottle of something or smoked a joint.

I'll switch the light out and we're there by candlelight. I'll ask, 'Is there anybody there?' in my best spooky voice, trying not to laugh. We're touching the glass and it slides across the table to the piece of paper that says YES. *Jesus*, I think. *We're summoning the spirits here.* In truth, I can't tell if Alan's pushing the glass, and I get an inkling from looking at him that he's wondering the same thing about me. He's wearing one of the road crew T-shirts from the last tour, one that says, 'Blow me' on the front and 'Meet the band' on the back – or maybe the other way round. I can see him narrow his gaze, taking a slug from his glass.

'Okay,' I say. 'Who are you?'

The glass slides. It's spelling something. G . . . E . . .

'Fuck off, Woods. Stop pushing the glass.'

'It's no' me. It must be you, ya bam.'

I check the bottle. Not a drop left, so I go to my bed. Suburban life is getting to me. It's getting to us all, I realise.

The next afternoon, I've forgotten about our DIY séance, the fact the ghost seemed to be spelling something out. Duncan and I have just scrunched out a joint in the basement ashtray, got that warm, fuzzy thing going as we pick up our guitars and start going back and forth with a few ideas. Duncan clicks record on the wee cassette player and we're like that for an hour, exchanging riffs and throwing middle-eights out into the ether. We smoke another joint, then flip the tape over and go again. When we're done, thinking that we maybe came up with something there during our prolonged, slightly wasted jam session, we take the cassette up to the lounge and play it back over the hi-fi system.

We're getting another joint together, sitting in front of the big speakers. I don't know if it's the grass, but it sounds fine enough. Then Duncan turns to me. 'You hear that?' he asks, turning up the volume for maximum effect. I lean in closer to the speaker, shake my head. 'If we're both playing guitar, who's that doing the handclaps?' Duncan says. He's right. There are handclaps, completely audible on the recording. It wasn't Duncan and it definitely wasn't me. Slightly spooked, I get up and look around the house to see if anyone's home, but every room is empty. We're the only ones here. My head's a little foggy, so I put it down to a glitch on the tape, but Duncan's not so sure. Straight-faced, he suggests we might have a ghost.

Later, because we move in strange circles, I bump into this psychic, Bette Peters, and I show her a photo taken of me in the kitchen, with a blurry smudge over my shoulder, which she insists is a ghost. When I tell her about the phantom handclaps, she says we probably stirred something with our homemade Ouija board. I'm not exactly convinced. I still think it's a problem with the tape. When we play the tape back to the rest of the guys, they're all on the fence, so maybe the psychic was talking shite.

Then, maybe a week later, Duncan and I encounter more weirdness. We're in the library at Crestwood, scanning the shelves, looking for a book, when out of nowhere, I feel something. The best way to describe it would be as a kind of 'swooshing' sensation, like there's 'something' travelling from the front door at incredible speed right up to where we're standing. Neither of us see a thing, but we've got hairs standing up on our necks, all over the shop. 'It's the ghost,' Duncan says. I'm 50 per cent sure he's talking shite. I'm no maths genius, but I guess by the same token, I must be 50 per cent unsure. I don't think I'm scared, but we give the ghost a name, Gerald – he *was* spelling something beginning with G – E – possibly in the hope we'll make it seem more friendly if there is something trying to haunt us.

A few days later, our new manager, Al Dellentash, comes by to visit. Unlike Tam, he's not here to check we're all behaving, scrutinising the bedroom floors for girls' knickers lying about. It's just a courtesy call. Al arrives with his young son. This kid is maybe five or six, full of excitement, and just runs off into the house while we talk turkey with Al. When we've finished our business, Al shouts up to his kid to tell him they're leaving. The wee kid comes downstairs and asks, 'Who was the nice old man in the attic?' We all look at each other. There's no one upstairs. It must have been Gerald.

Another week down the line, Alan, Duncan and I are watching TV in the lounge and there's this sudden uproar from upstairs. We're slightly worse for wear maybe, getting to our feet slowly as Eric and Derek come tumbling down the spiral stairs, scrapping with each other like something out of a *Tom and Jerry* cartoon. We're scratching our heads, looking down at them, this crumpled heap of tartan strewn across the carpet. When I ask what happened, they both have no idea. They're blinking hard, like they just got snapped out of a trance by a stage hypnotist. *This fuckin' place is messing with the wiring in our heads*, I think. Next day, it's me and Eric going at each other in the kitchen. As I said, Eric's no drinker, but we're both drunk somehow and going stir-crazy here. We're squaring up and he's punched me, got a real good shot to my nose. It's literally a sore spot for me. When I was a toddler back on Marchmont, I fell flat on my face, made a real jam-and-bone sandwich of my face. The doctors said I had to wait until I'd grown more before they could fix the bone damage, rather than rummage around the middle of small child's face with a scalpel and pair of tongs. I've not long had the operation, so my nose is a sensitive area for me. When Eric catches me, I lash out and land a punch square in his face. The next morning, he's looking back at me across the breakfast bar with two black eyes, like a panda. 'We need to get out of this place,' I tell him.

The next minute, the phone rings. It's Bette Peters, the psychic. After all the shenanigans of the past month, I'm a little more receptive now. She's telling me she believes we have a ghost problem. 'Oh aye,' I say through a mouthful of pancake.

'There are negative energies in your house,' she says. I stop munching and look across at Eric, sitting there scowling at me.

'Negative energies, you say? Maybe you're right Bette,' I say. 'When can you come over?'

She arrives later and we're all completely weirded-out now. We've had some inexplicable encounters and, even for a band, we're all acting strange. Eric, with his panda eyes, and the rest of us all hang on her every word. Bette, this middle-aged mystic type straight out of central casting, all wild hair and bangles, is running around the place, waving her arms around mysteriously. We're following like tartan pups as she sprinkles salts across the thresholds. I'm wondering if she thinks we have a slug problem. She turns to me to explain. 'The salt has been blessed.

It will subdue any spirits.' I watch every move closely, keeping an eye out for any sleight of hand as she seasons the place, but see none. We're walking around with her as she closes her eyes tight and blesses every room, ridding it of any bad energy or entity.

As she departs, she advises us to gather the letters and numbers from my homemade Ouija board and burn them. I arrange a few pieces of wood and scatter the letters in the fire, the fireplace that none of us could get to work. Just like every other time we tried, the fire won't get going. The next night, though, we're finished in the studio and this fire starts while we're sprawled across the sofas watching *Family Feud*. We all rush over to watch the blaze, looking at each other, like, 'Was this you?' But none of us has touched the fireplace since we got home because we're all lazy bastards. The wood goes up just fine, but it takes an age for the scraps of paper to catch light. When they do, they don't burst into flames, as if they're hanging on for dear life. The paper just grows darker and darker – like the map at the start of *Bonanza* – before crumbling to ash on the floor. Oddly, though, the house does feel better. It's like a weight has been lifted and the atmosphere between us is immediately less paranoid and tetchy. Maybe it's that we'd just run out of quaaludes and had dispensed with our regular drug day.

Chapter 31

KARU

California, 1982

So, we start again. Back at the drawing board, cups of coffee in hand. Duncan and me in Los Angeles, starting a new thing, turning the page. The Rollers are dormant now. To my mind, we're done. There's no announcement in the press, no final tour or greatest hits album, no one last go around the block. There's no one crying in the streets, no scenes of hysteria and the world doesn't slip off its axis. It's like, one day there's a band called the Rollers, and the next day there isn't. I gather Eric's doing something in management, Derek has decided to cash in his chips and train as a nurse, and Shang (aka Al) is back at the bar in the Dollar Arms. The bloom has fallen from the rose and it's time to move on to something new. That's the plan, at least, but it's like I'm forever in a boardroom.

Aside from enjoying the occasional 'D-Day' in New Jersey, I spent most of 1981 sitting across the table from an accountant, waiting for him to look up as he runs the columns of figures in front of me. In between trying to keep the band afloat in a changing market, this past year has been dominated by the nuts and bolts of the business. When I look at the calendar, it's just months of business meetings with our lawyers and our lawyers' lawyers, with our manager Tam with his lawyer and his lawyer's lawyer, our accountants with their lawyer and their lawyer's lawyer, and on it went.

By the end of the cycle of meetings, nothing is resolved and our heads have turned to mince. It never used to be so complicated. I'd get off the stage somewhere and go on to the next show. Someone would deposit a lump sum into the Bay City Rollers account – songwriting, record sales, live shows – every three months and that would be distributed into each of our individual bank accounts. It was never millions, even in our heyday, but because you had a bank statement showing a couple of grand in the black, it was okay. It wasn't like I was going anywhere. I didn't have a life outside the band and I was fine about that. I was on a tour bus or in a recording studio, or I was in the green room of some TV show in Shitsville, Wisconsin. I didn't need to think about it. I thought I was like royalty. They don't need money, because they never have to go to Sainsbury's. For a couple of years, I was the same – my mistake for not paying close enough attention. Now there are meetings practically every week. Someone explains in minute detail why we're not getting paid, that the money is going from the record label – always sure to take their percentage – through half a dozen shell companies. It's like a giant machine. Someone's putting hundred-dollar bills in one end and we're waiting at the other end, holding up a cup for a few pennies to trickle out into.

I don't know that's it's deliberate, but certainly it's deliberately convoluted. At every stage in the process, someone creams off their few bucks, and by the time it gets to you, it's like, *Was it worth it? All that work, for this?* It's no wonder that Duncan and I get tired of it and want to see if the grass is greener on the other side. We don't leave the Rollers exactly, but once we landed on the idea of branching off, getting back to writing, playing, creating again, it was quite an enticing idea. Starting up a three-piece band in LA, we started to feel some of that old excitement. Our only worries would be finding a drummer and finding a good weed connection. If nothing else, it would be good to take a break from the endless round of business meetings and topping up the coffers of the lawyers, who seemed to be the only people doing okay out of the situation.

Then, a couple of calls come in, asking whether we fancy getting back together. It's a curious feeling because we've not long stopped. Just last year, 1981, we released *Ricochet* – still ploughing that power pop furrow, making very little headway. After getting out of the Arista deal with a contractual obligation special, we're signed to CBS–Epic in the UK. Epic sort of ended up with us whether they wanted us or not. Whatever the case, we feel Epic aren't promoting the record, just running the clock down on the contract so they can show us the door. Diminishing returns, I guess. I don't want to disparage anything, because it's our record, but it's not like before when we were selling millions of records. You know, the Rollers heyday, when everything we touched made someone – usually someone else – a ton of money. Most frustratingly, copies of the record were sent out to radio and TV companies as a mystery album in a brown paper bag to test the waters, and there was a great reaction. When they found out it was by us, musical snobbery kicked in and they all backtracked and made out it was shite. We weren't swept up in the tides of what was commercial. The sound of the band had just developed and we were playing what we wanted to play, but maybe people have moved on from us. We imagined we would grow up with our audience, and together we would stay the course, but the records just don't connect anymore. Still, I take pride in them. It is slightly vexing, though. We get all these Beatlemania comparisons wherever we go, but the Beatles were allowed to grow up, while we're forced to live this life of eternal nostalgia at the age of 24.

So, long story short, we take the call and – full disclosure – because we all need the money, we agree to undertake a week-long tour of Japan, as the Bay City Rollers. I've loved Japan since that first time, so I know it'll be fun to get out there and make a few thousand people happy. I'd be lying, though, if I said I didn't need the money. Soon we're back on the west coast. We have some cash on the hip again and can live our lives a bit, but also it means Duncan and I can get back into the studio again. The Rollers are done, and I'm done too.

Back home in California, Duncan and I are watching the Falklands War unfolding on the telly. I'm fixing a joint, as

Duncan hands me a newspaper from back home and my jaw is on the floor. I'm reading about Tam Paton back in Scotland. He's been jailed for sexually abusing ten boys over a three-year period. That's probably just the tip of the iceberg, I think. Obviously, the press being who they are, the headline says BAY CITY ROLLERS MANAGER . . ., so immediately it's personal, and I hate that our lives are intertwined with Tam's like this. Our paths haven't crossed in a long time. The last I heard from him, my parents and my kid brother had called around to his compound and, while walking around the garden, Tam went heel first into a pile of fresh, steaming dogshit and skidded right through, leaving a streak of shite right up his back. My mum and dad managed to not laugh, but Ronald, well, he's a nipper, so he pure pished himself.

Personally, I haven't spoken to the guy since telling him to get tae fuck in 1979, but even so, I get that feeling of someone walking across my grave whenever I see his name in print. Rosetta Stone, the band he was trying to get off the ground, didn't make the grade, so Tam's been diverting his money, developing a property portfolio around Scotland. He tried it on with everyone, we knew that, but the news makes my blood run cold. Duncan's shaking his head sadly. 'Fuckin' monster,' I say. 'They should throw away the fuckin' key.'

Sometimes I feel homesick, but not so much now. I'm glad to be out of the UK because I don't want to be associated with Tam. I don't want to be associated with the Rollers because we're all tarred with the same brush now and it's just pure shite. Here in Hollywood, I'm insulated against the storm a little. No one in LA is picking up the *Daily Mail* or the *Sun* and pointing a finger at me, so I can get on with my life a bit. It hits the news over here, but it only makes a small splash and the story is gone quite quickly, which is a small mercy. Sorry to be selfish here, I know how lucky I am, really I do, but I've got this brief window of anonymity and I couldn't be happier to be away from all the tartan bullshit a while.

We've a new band, Karu. We came up with the name while we were smoking, Duncan and me. I've no idea if it means anything other than it's a desert in Africa – though spelled differently – but it looks striking on the posters. We're back on the first rung of the ladder, playing small club shows up and down the strip and towards Redondo Beach – cool punk and new wave hangs like Madame Wong's – but usually not much further afield. On the west coast, you're almost a prisoner of geography. Travel east, and you just hit desert, travel west and you'll drown in the Pacific, so it's up and down the coast, south to San Diego and north to Malibu, playing the same shows at the same dozen venues on a kind of six-week cycle.

It's a decent little band, kind of a McCartney-esque take on power pop, but we've nothing behind us. We're living off what we last pocketed from the Rollers, but it's a good life for a couple of years. The record business is in LA and we're attracted to the lifestyle, the sunshine, the beaches and the women, but it's confining. They don't have weather in LA. It's just sunny. All the time. Maybe once a month you might see a cloudburst, and I'll run outside and jump in the puddles like an idiot, just delighted that it's not baking hot for five minutes.

Often, we don't get paid at all. Duncan and I did a vocal harmony session in LA and were paid in lines of coke. I'm immediately thinking I don't want to get caught up in this world, but it was such a blast, I could see why some people got hooked. At the same time, I'm starting to think we're getting nowhere. There are some west coast Bay City Rollers fans who show up, regular as clockwork, but it's clear we're not winning any new fans. It's like wading in treacle, playing the same penny ante shows and not cutting through.

Eventually, we do record an album, basically scrounging studio time off someone on the promise that if the record gets released, they'll get reimbursed. So when the record comes out in Japan, I spend my $5,000 advance repaying the studio bill. There's not much else for us to do but play shows and lick our wounds, so we go through the motions a while until someone has the nerve to say, *That's enough.* Karu are booked to play an end-of-semester ball at the University of Los Angeles. There are two big rooms; we're set up in one, and there's a larger kind of ballroom or gym with all the food and drink laid out on trestle tables. The promoter comes by to check on us after we set up. 'Guys, you might as well start playing,' he says. There's no one here, but I can hear four or five hundred people in the next room, laughing and talking, loading up their paper plates with pork chops and potato salad. It's just the three of us – me, Duncan and George, our drummer – standing up on stage and playing our show. No one even pokes their head around the door to see what we're doing. They're having a great time and so are we. I tell a pal what happened later and they tell me, 'Oh, that's bad', completely missing the point. I'm trying to capture a moment from the past, and the fame is slipping away, not realising that it's not the fame that's important.

Obviously the money is helpful, so you're forever searching for this lost chord or something, the magic ingredients you need to come up with a hit record. I know that's a kind of sweet madness of mine, but if you're not searching for it, you're never going to find it. The fame is just a weird by-product of me wanting to play music with great people. Being famous is a pain in the arse. Just wanting to go to the shops becomes a military operation, so in those terms, life is better now. Even so, I'm uncertain. I think maybe I'm losing faith when we're invited over to South Africa, to play a festival show at the Jabulani stadium in Soweto. It's probably not the biggest crowd I've played, but we're the only three white guys in front of an audience of 12,000 people from the townships and it's beautiful and it restores my faith in music a little. No scratch that. It restores my faith in *people.*

Returning to LA after Soweto is a little like coming back down to Earth. We're back in suburbia – this wee place on Flanders Street, in Granada Hills. In terms of landmarks, we're not far from the Spahn Ranch and all that Manson family madness, but we're in reduced circumstances. It's strange, because everyone I meet clocks that I'm Woody from the Bay City Rollers and assumes I'm a millionaire, but aside from a trickle of songwriting money occasionally coming in, I'm practically living hand-to-mouth. I'd love to tell you it was some massive conspiracy, some clear and obvious theft, but the truth is more opaque. If anything, it would be a neat bow to tie around the story – to say that Tam robbed us blind – but he was just a bad businessman. We had a bad businessman nodding through the deals, but it's a nightmare of our accountants' making. Because of the mess of companies set up in our names, the label manage to use that mess as an excuse to claim they don't know who to pay. As a result, the record royalties are still not being distributed, so I've hardly a dollar to my name. Every time I check my statements, I'm edging closer to zero. We're having to rent out rooms so we can afford the mortgage payments. We picked up our couch from a dumpster at the end of our street and I suddenly realise I'm leading this strange, topsy-turvy life. Where I started out all bright and shiny playing *Top of the Pops*, eight years later I'm slap in the middle of my bohemian hungry years. Still, it's exciting, but only until it isn't.

Despite the world's studied disinterest in what we're doing, we're completely caught up in our little world. We build a make-shift rehearsal studio in the garage, and while the suburban kids are pootling around on dirt bikes and shooting hoops on their front drive, we're plotting our next moves, or smoking a little weed in the house, cooling off with a dip in the wee pool we've got – at least until it starts to get dirty in there and none of us has any idea how to clean the thing. That's us, Monday through to Friday, then off to U-Haul to hire a van for the gigs at the weekend.

Ultimately, though, Karu becomes a grind, as much as I love my life in LA. I've a girlfriend here, and the band, but it's going nowhere fast. I'm thinking that the final straw for me is when I get a knock at the door and there's a bunch of guys standing there in protective suits, looking like beekeepers or something.

'We're from the EPA,' they tell me.

'Oh, aye. What's that then?'

'We're the Environmental Protection Agency, sir. We'd like to take a look out back if that's okay?'

On the way around, the head beekeeper-looking guy is explaining that the neighbourhood has been infested with mosquitoes and there's a malaria alert for the area so they're just checking everyone's pools. Slowly it dawns on me that we're probably the epicentre of the problem. When we moved in, I just assumed the pool water cleaned itself, but, over time, the water got cloudy. Then kind of gloopy. Since then, we've not gone near it, just watched from a safe distance as the water turned to a kind of thick green soup. Occasionally, you'll get this big bubble of air come to the surface and kind of let out these big satisfying burps, but by now, we've given up on the idea of a pool. I'm standing in front of the pool with these guys and they're shaking their heads and calling it in on the walkie-talkies as an environmental catastrophe here in the suburbs. I can hear sirens in the street behind me as an emergency EPA team dash through and pour a vast barrel of oil on the water and suffocate the million mosquitoes we've been cultivating in the hot California sun. I'm peering down into the pool, the toxic water soup, and scrambling about for a metaphor. It's probably time to move on.

Chapter 32

ROLLIN' (REPRISE)

With Los Angeles life looking shaky, history repeats itself again and I get a call from Eric to rejoin the Rollers for a few shows in Japan and Australia. This was after he and Les reconnected and buried the hatchet. I'm sceptical about the truce between them, but I figure I'll take the money; it will cover studio costs for a time in Los Angeles. It's not the classic five, but a variation. Derek and Alan aren't involved, so I persuade George, our drummer from Karu, to come along for the Australian leg. The Japanese fans will have to make do with a drum machine, because George is South African and that means he can't get a visa. The cash I earn for my part in a miserable couple of weeks on the road will keep the wolf from the door here a while, I figure, but it's not anyone's finest hour. On the flight over, I'm necking whiskies, wondering, *Is it too soon for nostalgia? Another reunion?*

Prior to us flying Down Under, we play the Japanese shows and they're fine. Only fine, though. There's still a lot of love there for us, as if the news of our death hasn't travelled to this part of the world just yet. For a minute there, I start to think we can make this work, but the Australian leg is a bloody nightmare. I don't know what it is about the place. In 1976, we played some shows when I was tired and depressed. At one point, I collapsed on stage halfway through a performance. Back at the hotel, as I was sleeping, Tam arranged for a press photographer to take a couple of pics of me while I slept, tucking a teddy bear under the covers with me, for maximum pity points. Now I'm back again and it's worse somehow. Everybody is succumbing to ego or fatigue along the way – Rollers old and new are dropping like flies. From my perspective, it's like watching a marathon, all these guys getting wobbly suddenly, then falling by the wayside, getting wrapped up in Bacofoil a hundred metres from the finish line. The Australian dates are part of what they call a pub tour, a step down from the previous trip, when we played the theatre circuit. That sounds probably underwhelming, a marker of our decline, but these were shows for up to 1,500 people, so it's not small potatoes, just smaller than we're used to. Beggars, as the saying goes, can't be choosers, so even though I know I'll have to grin and bear it working with Les, I really don't think twice. It's an easy five or six grand in each of our pockets.

Financially, we weren't going to be millionaires – that's kind of a recurring theme here – but we have a lot riding on the shows being a success. The promoter's talking about this being just a start, something we can build on, but by now, if there's a way to pluck defeat from the jaws of victory, we'll always find it. We're meant to be promoting this new album, *Breakout '85*. It's a half-arsed affair, if I'm honest. Most of the songs were brought in by Les and Pat, who are thick as thieves now. I spend a couple of days working on the project, but it's not like the Rollers LPs of old. It's just a hook to hang the tour on, a reason for us to show up and play. The resultant album, another in a run of flops, only sees the light of day in Australia and Japan. It's kind of Pat and Les's white-bread take on funk. In fairness, these songs are actually fun to play, but it wasn't what the Rollers were about. Put it this way: no one was coming to the shows to hear tracks from *Breakout '85*.

From the very first note in Australia, you can see the audience drifting away to the bar, or just losing interest, checking their watches and wondering when we're gonna play 'Bye Bye Baby' so they can go home and release the babysitter. That first night Down Under, we lose the tour bus. That's quite an achievement, even by our dysfunctional standards. The reason was I hear that Les and Pat were turning the bus upside down looking for drugs. When they couldn't track any down, they started tossing all the crates of beer out onto the pavement, with Les telling the driver, 'Okay, no drugs, then no beer either.' The driver probably just looked at the broken glass and suds pouring into the storm drain and decided life was too short. By morning, the driver was gone but, as a parting gesture, I guess he must have alerted the police, because we were raided by them at 5 or 6 in the morning. They found nothing! After that, it's fine for a couple of days, but maybe the signs are there for all to see. We have

Foster's lager sponsoring the tour, so it's us travelling around Australia on a bus filled with tins of beer and bitterness, not so much the beer now!

A few days later, the road crew crash the bus. I take it as a sign from above that this wasn't meant to be. The first road crew are battered and bruised, sent home with their arms in slings and legs in splints and we hire a new bunch of guys. We wind up in three separate vans, all going in the same direction, but by now, none of us wants to talk to the other. There's George, Ian and me in one, Les's wee entourage in another and Eric's girlfriend Karen and the support act, a female singer he was managing, in the final van.

Our roadie, a nice guy called Russell, had to walk around without shoes for a couple of days after Les stole them. The reason for the theft? Well, Russell refused to go out and get drugs for Les. By the time of the final shows, everyone's taken off. Eric left a note under my door in the hotel saying, 'Sorry Woods. I've got to go.' Les didn't even bother with a note. According to our promoter, a couple of days before the last show, Les crashed his hire car into a wall and fucked off, presumably taking Pat with him. I find the whole affair utterly depressing, getting all those old feelings coming back, none of them good. So now there's just Ian Mitchell, George Spencer and me. We have to rope in the support act to fill out the band so we wouldn't be in breach of contract and so we – and those who had buggered off – would all get paid. While they were with us, Les and Pat had their own thing going, their own little team of two, but none of us were getting along, so we divided off into our own camps.

Probably the beer didn't help. I know. Quelle surprise. The drugs probably didn't help either, smoking weed before shows, like everyone has given up. I'd like to tell you I didn't, but the truth is, I found myself giving up too. The bad feeling between us all meant the shows were never going to be better than okay. The only reason I don't fly home myself is we had agreed to do these shows, and Ian, George and I were determined to do so in spite of all the fuck-ups. Somehow, the final show at the Coogee Bay Hotel is our best of the tour: a mix of Roller hits and a few covers the support guys played. Despite everything, we go out with a bang. It made up for the previous gigs, but I know it's time to get back to LA to reconvene with Duncan. After the past couple of weeks, I realise it's not such a bad life, hanging out at the Rainbow or Madame Wong's, getting friendly with the locals, a few people in other bands. Then I have to remind myself we're not making any inroads so maybe it would be a backward step? I'm mulling this over in my head, even thinking about going to Scotland to see my folks and to maybe regroup somehow, when George says to me, 'Why don't you and Ian come with me to South Africa? There's a couple of guys I know. Maybe we can put a band together.' I'm living out of a suitcase anyway, so I figure, *What the hell, why not?* A change is as good as a rest, and all that. I know it's a big leap of faith, like when Jim Taylor came and saw me play at the Odeon. Am I going to take a chance? It's another step forward maybe. Or even a sideways step, but it's movement, so I tell George, 'Aye, let's go for it! Maybe it'll be an adventure.'

I scramble together some coins, find a payphone and call my girlfriend in LA to tell her the news. She's none too happy. Not that I won't be coming home to her loving arms, you understand. No. She's pissed that I've left a ton of my gear in the apartment and I just asked her to mind it for me for a while. A month, perhaps. Or maybe five years, but she's not to know that. And nor am I.

Chapter 33

PASSENGERS

I arrive in Johannesburg in the clothes I'm standing in. Aside from a big canvas army bag, my acoustic guitar and a keyboard, I've no other baggage. At least that's what I think. I'm a nomad now. I pass through the terminal, flash my passport at the gate and start my life over. George has organised a caravan for us to stay in on a farm north of Pretoria. Ian in one side, me in the other. The first night, George's musician pals come along for a cookout and a meet-and-greet. They're a mixed bunch, like a United Nations of musical waifs and strays: a Scot, an English guy, a Welshman, an Irishman, a Cypriot and a Lebanese singer. No one mentions the Bay City Rollers once. I'm just another musician and we're scoping each other out on merit, rather than reputation and it's . . . it's lovely. It's the life I probably wanted most for myself. I don't want to sound corny, but it's the music that led me here. Rehearsing, playing. You know, just having a laugh. We smoke some weed under a blanket of stars, cook a few sausages on the braai, talk about music, talk shite about the lions who live nearby, talk about planning our next steps. I'm probably a wee bit jetlagged, certainly a little stoned, and one of the guys leaves the encampment and starts pretending he's a lion, roaring from the undergrowth. In fact, there's no lions here, but I'm just stoned enough to think about it a minute and to chart an escape route from the fire to the caravan. While we've been making these new friends, I realise I've left the caravan light on all night, so we can't see our beds for mosquitoes and freakish-large bugs and beasties. Stoned off our heids, we spend two hours staggering about the caravan, trying to fan out all these bugs, and moths the size of a child's face.

I'm literally and figuratively in the wilderness right now and it's a fine time. We stay here three months, putting the band together, gradually turning the land outside the caravan into a makeshift camp, the caravan and a row of tents set against the African plains. Neil Solomon, our singer, lives in a flat in Pretoria, but the rest of us are in our wee campsite. Greg, the guitarist, lives in one tent, the bass player in another. You're waking up to nature – cows from the farm, the occasional tree snake, bright sun or flash floods. And maybe instead of rehearsing, the band are out on the land digging ditches to divert the flood water. The rest of the time, we're just a band. We decide to call ourselves the Passengers.

We have a ton of bookings right out of the gate – mainly nightclubs, holiday camps and hotels around Cape Town, Pretoria and Johannesburg, usually a two- or three-week residency playing a few times a night, seven nights a week, getting our room and board. We often stay in the hotel, but sometimes, if it's a long stint – something like a couple of months of solid gigging – I'll get a wee flat and stay there for the duration. Wherever the green army bag goes, that's where I go. Most of these places are new, freshly minted, so we're booked to build up the club night. We start out with a couple of dozen pished holidaymakers, but by the end of six weeks, we're a known quantity and the places are jam-packed.

It's a great feeling when we all hit the same vein, when we get locked in together. And these guys are all such good musicians – way better than me and I love it. I remember someone advising me years ago to work with musicians who are better than you because it'll up your game. It's true. After every rehearsal and every show, I feel I'm better than I was before, just by osmosis, just by watching these guys and building a musical understanding. It's a strange feeling because I've been in the heart of this tornado for so many years now and no one has thought to ask me about music once in all that time. That's a weird situation for a musician, right? Here, it's like the world is upside down. No one's asking me what my favourite drink is. No one gives a shit about whether I like the colour blue or red or whatever because I'm just another guy in the band and it's great. I'm looking forward to every show, every rehearsal. Nothing's a chore here. Instead it's about getting up on stage and feeling that vibration between us, feeling that energy from the audience and not taking it for granted. No one's telling us to be anywhere by a certain time because we're adults and we're here because we want to be.

I haven't thought once about how much we're getting paid. It's just 'When are we playing?'

South Africa is a vast country, but in terms of the music business, it's a tiny garrison that scarcely moves the needle of popular culture, so we do try to bring the bandwagon to home shores briefly. It's not exactly a busted flush of a visit, but it's not a huge success either. We're signed to a label in South Africa, a kind of outpost for British music in South Africa, but I'm always optimistic someone back home will pick up on what we're doing and call us over for a bit of promotion. But we wind up doing it off our own backs. I go into it wide-eyed, full of optimism.

I'm a better musician all round. I've so many more strings to my bow than I had back when Tam was shouting at me to wave and fuckin' smile. Back in Scotland, a few of the guys – Ian, Greg and Neil – find digs in a flat in the centre of town, sleeping on the floor, waking up every morning to the cold, finding a guitarist's feet up your nose. George and Chris from the band stay with me at my parent's place. I sign on the dole, so I'll have some money to pay my mum for room and board. That's a curious feeling. I sold millions of records and I'm standing in line at the labour exchange for £30 a week. I probably paid enough tax in the day to not worry about needing to take a few quid back, but it's still weird being back at square one, staying in my old bedroom, wondering what's going to happen next.

There's a feeling we could make inroads, this hot new South African band, live and in person, in the wind and rain of my homeland. South Africa is so beautiful, but because of apartheid, we have an inkling that maybe we need to spread our wings a little. Meantime, George and Chris help my dad with the gardening as a way of paying their keep while I try to pick up club gigs in Scotland, testing the water. It wasn't a terrible plan, but it was poorly executed. I want to start a fresh page, but people here won't let you forget where you came from. I tell the booking agent not to advertise us as the Bay City Rollers, but that goes in one ear and out the other. No one here's heard of the Passengers and so, with an eye on his bottom line, either the agent or the venues bill the shows as Woody from the Rollers. We're playing this jazz-fusion-rock hybrid, a world and a half away from the stuff we played with the Rollers, and the audiences are standing there, completely bemused. Where's the tartan? Where's the fuckin' hits? I'll try and put a positive spin on anything, that's my nature, but even I start to find the whole thing dispiriting.

At one show, we're booked to play an early and a late set. There's a crowd of people watching the first show, screaming for the old Rollers hits and we're heads down, getting serious on stage, dying a death. It wasn't quite Spinal Tap playing 'Jazz Odyssey', getting the thumbs-down from the crowd. It was more like a bunch of musos playing their hearts out and the audience staring at the stage, totally confused. Between sets, the promoter takes me to one side and says, 'Don't take this the wrong way, but don't bother playing the second set.' The guys in the band are super-hot, talented musicians, so it's disappointing, but maybe also it's a relief that we weren't subjected to another hour on stage because we couldn't cut through. People don't want to see a new band, we realise, and at that point, Ian decides he's seen enough and leaves us. It's a 'We've tried this. It's not working.

No hard feelings' kind of thing. We bid him farewell and the rest of us return to South Africa.

We have a couple of records out, a wee flurry of activity on South African radio, hitting the highs on the radio charts, if not the sales charts, so we're well set for building up an audience and then moving on to the next resort. It's an 8pm kick-off every night, play for half an hour, four or five songs to get the mood going, a 20-minute break, grab a beer or a whisky (although you're always behind the crowd who are a few drinks ahead of you), then back on stage a couple of times and off by 1am. This means we've tons of downtime to get up to whatever. We roll into bed at three or four in the morning, wake up, wipe away the sleep and, if we're not booked into the studio, I'll drag my carcass to the cinema and hammer a vast bucket of popcorn for lunch and a gallon of Fanta. Then come the end credits, back to rehearsals, and then start up again the next night.

Maybe we'll have a radio interview but, as I've said, I don't want to even mention the Rollers, so it's almost a breath of fresh air to be able to travel around freely, wearing a cloak of anonymity. The Rollers are yesterday's news and it's still recent enough that it hasn't been tied up in any phony sense of nostalgia, so I'm just a guy in a band now. We're a tight bunch and we get along great, but maybe it's a bit of a disconnected kind of life. There's no time to form any bonds with anyone. Maybe there's an occasional fling, but soon enough you find yourself back on the bus and moving on to the next month-long stint to start the whole weary process again. It's hand-to-mouth sometimes. I'm not sending money home or buying farms or Range Rovers, but

I'm not struggling either. It's kind of a hamster wheel, I guess, but I'm not complaining. Whatever the drawbacks, it's still better than the tour of Australia. My head is clear, finally. I can hear my own thoughts.

I'm not political. This isn't Sun City, a bunch of millionaire rock stars playing to a wealthy whites-only crowd. We play everywhere and to anyone who'll have us. Apartheid is the way here, but we're outsiders and we have black friends and musicians in other bands who'll come up and join us on stage or for a jam session around the braai. Nobody is treated any different by us regardless of the colour of their skin and I expected the same in return. I'm informed that it was the black South Africans from the townships that built the big cities and, returning to their townships, they only had basic utilities after a hard day's work. I mentioned earlier that I once played at a festival with Karu in the heart of Soweto (which stands for the first two letters in **So**uth-**We**st **To**wnship) – it was three white guys playing to 12,000 locals. I wasn't sure how we'd go down, but it was brilliant. A reminder of what it's all about and why we play music; no chips on shoulders, just radiant smiles all around. It made me cringe when I'd see signs on the beaches in Durban saying, 'Whites Only'. Following a club gig one night, I went down to the beach, having my usual couple of whiskies before heading to bed, and I see one sign stating, 'No Blacks Allowed', so I prised it out of the sand and left it there on its side as it is too heavy for me alone to do much more. I told the guys in the morning what I'd done and later that night we headed down and threw it off the pier on North Beach and into the Indian Ocean, never to be seen again.

It's weird, but I'm as happy as ever – maybe even happier than at any point. All the shite with the Rollers is in the past at last, and I feel free, unencumbered. I'm just Woods here. No one knows me from Adam, and I start to feel like a bohemian almost, living this carefree, taxes-be-damned lifestyle – an artist rather than a wee bit of a product. Maybe once in a while, someone will come up and say, 'Oh, you're Woody from the Rollers' or something, perhaps ask for an autograph or want me to tell them an old war story, and I can feel myself go tight, as if they're going to poke around or test the foundations of my happiness, or as if it's a reminder of all the hysteria. Any reminder now is like dredging up some long-lost past life. Usually I'll just laugh, say, 'Ach, not that shit again.' Other than those occasional reminders, I'm thinking I could live here forever. A friend of mine gets my work permit renewed with some government friend whenever I need it, so I'm living the life of a journeyman musician, playing three or four sets a night at dances and clubs, holiday camps in the sun, thinking, *Aye, this is all right for me.*

And for a while there, it really is.

Chapter 34

JOLLY ROGERED

I'm here at the Jolly Roger nightclub, deep in the guts of the downtown Johannesburg Holiday Inn. Geographically and figuratively, I've travelled some way from playing to 15,000 screaming girls at the Budokan. We're the resident band here for a month or so, playing three sets a night, seven days a week, from 8.30pm. Fill up on shrimp if you're so inclined and come down and catch us. *Have you tried the veal?* As it's Friday, I'd recommend getting along early if you want to catch the support act. I know we make a point of getting down in plenty of time, taking extra care and attention over our soundchecks. Did I mention that Friday afternoons at Jolly Roger's is given over to female mud wrestling? We can barely get to the stage to do a line check. There's a hundred South African businessmen, suits and ties, all crowded around this blow-up paddling pool, filled to the brim with mud and bikini-clad women. The place stinks of spilt beer and testosterone, and we're tip-toeing through the carnage in our jeans and T-shirts like we're walking through a minefield.

To be honest, the novelty has started to wear off for me. The first Friday, I was here bright and early, eyes on stalks, but now that I've got to know some of the wrestlers, it seems a bit wrong to be there being all lecherous – especially when the grand finale arrives. Covered in mud, the wrestlers scramble to the sides of the mud bath and attach tassels to themselves – a bit of spit on a rubber suction cup – and set them spinning. Cue scenes of bedlam. Every time, the crowd are the same faces we saw last time, everyone from the CEO down to the photocopy kid, united in a crazed, beer-fuelled frenzy. Their shirts are open to the waist and their ties are wrapped around their head, like they're playing out a scene from Lord of the fuckin' Flies. I'm desensitised to it now, standing on the stage, checking my tuning in front of this end-of-times kind of scene playing out in front of us. The girls bring one of the smart-dressed – but now sweaty and red-faced – men up on stage, coaxing him gently by his necktie, unbuttoning him and slapping the suction cups onto his nipples and having him do a little show for the crowd. I'm thinking, *Better him than me.* Last Friday, while I was waiting in the wings to come on, gazing down at the setlist at my feet, I felt a warm sensation at the back of my head. I looked up and realised the half-naked performer was beckoning me to come up on stage and join her to try the tassel thing. 'Awe fuck! No' me!' But she looked desperate, so, to a decent round of applause from the audience, I allowed her to drag me on stage. It was not my finest hour. Standing on stage, two tassels stuck on me, trying to ape her movements, while this near-naked woman had her tassels spinning like helicopters. I remember I had them going for a minute, both going in opposite directions, and that got the crowd going, at least. Or maybe it was the naked woman. Now I think about it, it was probably the naked woman.

It's only when the band starts to unravel, when the bass player is on the way out, that I start thinking about home again. I could keep going like this a while maybe, but we're like a big fish in a small pond. There's nowhere to go, after years of plugging away in this beautiful, troubled place that's been home for the past few years. I'm not homesick exactly, but I start to feel this calling for me to move on and try on a new life for size, to maybe stop living out of this army kit bag a while. I've not seen my mum and dad for years, my grandparents are knocking on a bit, and I just have an inkling it's time to move on and start the next chapter in my life.

My head is clear finally. If you want to be all new age about it, I didn't even know I needed healing. but healed I am – probably for the first time in years. It's disconcerting that I didn't notice, that I didn't think for a second it needed clearing, but here I am. Really, I thought I arrived here with no baggage, but I was wide of the mark there. I was carrying a lot more than I thought when I arrived five years ago. I couldn't hear myself think. The best way I can describe it is like this. We used to go for a drink in our local in Edinburgh. Just a regular pub, a nice place, but it's stayed in my head. They had a fan behind the bar, which you only knew was on when someone turned it off. We'd be standing around chatting, having a beer or a glass of something, and when the fan went off, everybody said, 'Thank god for that.' I didn't realise it at the time. If I was damaged by what came before – all the hysteria around us, me in the eye of the storm – I feel like someone finally turned the fan off. It was my saving grace.

Chapter 35

JOURNEYMAN

When I return from South Africa at the start of the 1990s, I've a clear head. Certainly, clear enough to see I'm right back at square one. For a year or so, I try to get a band off the ground in Edinburgh. It's fun, but it's slow going. My dad had the foresight to set up a savings account for me back in the day, and that kept the wolf from the door a while, but I'm on my uppers now and in need of something. Then the phone rings and it's Eric. He sounds excited, bursting with plans and schemes. 'Fancy another go around the block, Woods?' he asks. He's got some shows lined up in Australia under the banner the Eric Faulkner Co-Operative or something, like he's this jazz player, playing a bunch of the old hits. I mull it over, while studying the red ink on that morning's stack of bills. I wonder if there's any gas left in the Rollers tank, if anyone would be interested. Eric laughs. He tells me we can make a killing. A modest killing, leastways.

Nostalgia rolls in 20-year cycles, I guess. I know when we first started out, there was a lot of harking back to the 1950s, and we're now 20 years out from our heyday. 'Time to make hay,' Eric suggests, so I tentatively agree to think it over. Meantime, booking agents up and down the country – and farther afield – are looking for 1970s pop acts to play the clubs and festivals, and there's an opportunity for us. I'm checking my savings, realising I'm maybe a month away from not making the mortgage on my flat, so I get on board.

To start out, it's Eric, a few session guys, me and Karen, Eric's girlfriend, on vocals. Kass is great and has a fine voice, but I think she's chiefly there to keep an eye on Eric. Once Tam let go of the reins, it was like we had our freedom finally. No more having to drink milk and live a chaste existence. For Alan and me, we leant into the drink, hanging out every night after the shows, making up for lost time that way. For Eric, it meant that after years of having women throw themselves at his Doc Martens, he could finally do something about it. I remember one night after Tam was given the boot, we're heading down from our hotel rooms to a show and I give a little tap on Eric's door.

'Eric, are you coming?' I hear shuffling behind the door. 'Aye, aye,' he says, his voice is strained. 'I'm coming.' A minute later, the door opens and he's all red-faced, doing up his fly as an embarrassed chambermaid steps out into the corridor. He played with a smile on his face that night.

So, we play some shows in Australia, though now it's being sold as the Bay City Rollers. Two original Rollers is better than none, and the crowds of thirtysomething mums are more than happy to see us. Once the diary starts to fill out, I go and see if Alan's up for it. Eric picked up the Rollers trademark when all the companies went bankrupt, so there's no reason why we can't, and we start booking more shows. The wolf that's at my door starts to recede from view a little.

We're in the local, Alan and me, talking about him coming back into the fold. It's a weird thing about having a close friendship like ours. We can go years without seeing each other, but within a minute, we click and it's like we were hanging out the day before, picking up precisely where we left off the last time. We're unburdened by fame now, getting noticed once in a while, rather than having to walk about the city in disguise or being squirrelled away in the trunk of someone's car. Alan has always been pragmatic. He enjoyed the old days, but that was then.

Occasionally word gets through to us about the money, the years of unpaid royalties on our records. Maybe we'll daydream a while about what we'll do with our hard-won lost fortune. I ask if he misses it and he kind of looks off into the distance. He asks me the same question and I genuinely don't know how to respond. 'I don't miss all the shite,' I say finally, 'but it's nice to be able to walk around again though.' Alan nods in agreement and starts telling me about the last time someone recognised him. He had his plumbing qualifications, so naturally he fell back into fixing pipes and whatnot, and he doesn't seem a bit concerned about his reduced circumstances, taking everything in his stride, the way he usually does. He fell through a ceiling not so long back, working a job at a pal's house. It was one of these old houses and their Victorian floors, riddled with woodworm. The fall ripped shreds out of his backside. At the hospital, he's getting his arse stitched back up and the nurse, staring intently at his bottom, says, 'Are you no Alan fae the Bay City Rollers?' He's lying there in one of those hospital gowns, his arse on full display. 'Aye, that's me,' he says. The nurse doesn't look up, just carries on stitching.

With Alan back in the band, it's not quite like the old days, but close enough. I don't notice at first, but he's drinking more. It's hard to spot when it's your drinking pal, but it dawns on me over time. Get a one-hour flight down to London and he's wanting a couple in departures, and another couple on the flight, to get a light lunchtime buzz going on. I didn't really do the daytime drinking thing while I was in South Africa. Sure, I'd gotten into the habit of settling in for a long stretch after a show, seeing things through 'til dawn, but I would always try to stay focused on what was ahead. Having a few drams after a show was the thing to look forward to, but with Alan, I'm not sure if it's him holding the bottle, or if the bottle has hold of him now. Whatever the case, it's not at the front of my mind. It's more of a nagging sensation, probably because the shows with Alan and Eric are usually great. None of us are making a fortune. There are no holidays, no luxuries to speak of. Alan carries on doing the odd plumbing job, we all have fingers in pies, but I figure if I can earn £1,000 a month playing a couple of club shows as a journeyman musician, that's my mortgage taken care of and maybe a few 'beer vouchers'. Aside from the 1970s-themed weekends at British holiday camps, brushing shoulders with the surviving members of Mud or whatever glam band, or Alvin Stardust or Leo Sayer, we're playing some decent-sized festivals across Europe and Scandinavia. There's no organisation behind us, just us with a bunch of round-the-world tickets, landing in the US to play some theme parks, or in Japan, or wherever, playing a run of shows and getting back on the plane to the next city. The last time any of us got any royalties from Bay City Rollers record sales was in 1978. That's a long time to not pay someone their dues. In the years since our heyday, the world has embraced the compact disc and re-bought all their favourite albums on shiny silver bits of plastic, so we're getting the idea there's a hefty pile of cash accumulating in our names, if we could only persuade someone to write a cheque. You're not thinking about it every day, but the idea there's this nice little nest egg being set aside for you is quite intoxicating. The annual statements we get from the record company are light on detail, so we have no idea how much money might be piling up in our names. Everything is, frankly, as much of a mess as a mess can be, and in some regards, it's a mess of our own making. Or rather, a mess of our accountants' and so-called management's making. In the meantime, the record company could just survey the chaos, throw up their hands and say, 'We'd love to pay you, really we would. We just don't know who to pay.' It's a neat bit of legalistic sleight of hand, intended to run down the clock. We're powerless really. Just sending a legal document every year is the best we can do to keep the case from slipping past the statute of limitations, at which point the record company can just say, 'Well, we tried. We really did.'

We've been awarded the rights to the name Bay City Rollers after a long dispute with Les, following a ruling made by Justice Mervyn Davies in February 1992. Les was in Japan for a long time, married and had a son, but then came back to the UK and started touring under the name Bay City Rollers. We only notice when the promoters start asking us which version of the band ours is, because they're getting approached by another Bay City Rollers. We run through the usual cycle of letters and injunctions, which he bats away, and we're left with a legal bill of over £30,000 and I don't sleep for a full week. At that point, we're having to take shows just to pay the lawyers and, just like that, it stops being fun. Eventually, we see Les in court. He loses, but he's on legal aid, so it's cost him nothing and we're in a deep financial hole, despite winning. The outcome is, he can call himself Les McKeown's Legendary 1970s Something-or-Others, but he can't lay claim to the Rollers name. Obviously, he just carries on.

Meanwhile, Sony, who now own Arista, and the Rollers catalogue, must be loving this. The more divided we are, the easier it is for them to continue down the path of shrugging and not knowing who to pay. Then we're introduced to this English guy, Mark St John. He takes over our modest letter-writing campaign, keeping our claim for the lost money alive. He's a tough guy, a little older than us, doesn't suffer fools, but he's got a real warmth about him too. His first act as our new consiglieri is to sit everybody down in the same room and explain that we all need to stop touring as separate entities. For a minute there, it's like there's a thaw in the cold war between us, some vague talk about a new Rollers album, a concept record called *Pink Satin* or something, featuring a bunch of songs Eric has written, all with names like 'Gossamer's Dream'. Les and I are both pushing to have our own songs featured alongside Eric's more conceptual tracks, and there's some of the old signs, flickers of the old ego problems between us all. I don't know about 'Gossamer's Dream'. None of us buy into the idea – the Rollers are pure pop, after all – and the idea fizzles away to nothing.

Even so, I feel optimistic about our prospects. Like Mark told us, whatever bullshit there is between us, we need to set it to one side and put up a united front. 'It's for the greater good,' Mark tells us, and everyone agrees, although we're all giving Les a sideways glance just to see he hasn't got his fingers crossed behind his back.

You might imagine with all the familiar Rollers politics simmering away in the background, I'd have a full plate, but I begin to realise that maybe there's something missing from my life.

I meet Denise in the early 1990s and we become instant friends. I was just drinking in my local pub one night, and there she was. Formerly a model, now an accomplished artist, she's super-smart and beautiful, and over the course of a few months, we start to realise there might be more to this than just friendship. We come from similar backgrounds, both have had our brushes with celebrity and the problems that can create. She's always 100 per cent straight with me, doesn't put up with any prima donna behaviour from me and she understands the madness that sometimes accompanies my life as a Roller. She isn't fazed by it and isn't in the least bit interested in basking in the reflected limelight. It's like water off a duck's back when she sees it happening around me. I think we both realise at the same time that we're a perfect fit for each other.

When I meet her family and start getting along famously with her dad, it's like the die is cast and we both know we're in this for the long haul. I had girlfriends in the past, but this was different from the get-go. If I'm away with the band, she's in my mind the whole time and I'm desperate to speak to her when we arrive somewhere for a show, wanting to hear her tell me all about her day. You'll know yourself if you were lucky enough to find your soulmate and that's what we are. We get married a few short years after our first meeting, on 8 March, 1997 – a registry office affair on Victoria Street in Edinburgh with just close family. Alan is my best man, shuffling along on his walking stick following his recent stroke and delivering the shortest wedding toast in history – 'All the best. And the buffet is now open!' – as the Hale–Bopp comet passes across the skies above, kind of an honorary guest. It's such a fine warm evening as Denise and I walk hand in hand together down the cobblestones to the Balmoral Hotel afterwards then on to the Assembly Rooms for a party with all our friends and family. It's just the greatest feeling I can ever recall.

While I settle into a life of domestic bliss, the happiest and most settled period of my life, I still have to keep the wolf from the door, so usually I'm working on something in the Music Kitchen, this record company of ours.

The Music Kitchen started one day in the late 1990s. I was walking through my village and this guy ran up to me and introduced himself as Gordon Campbell. Gordon wrote a few hits for Shakin' Stevens, worked with Elton John, and was a college lecturer who created and ran the first music business course in UK higher education. I was impressed. Funnily, every time I saw him, I avoided him, thinking he was a bit of a bam, but he was quite the opposite. Denise encouraged me to meet him as she thought I needed to push myself. At the time, I was writing and producing my own songs in my wee attic studio. Denise felt Gordon would be the guy to take things up a level, so she pressed me to give Gordon a tape. Eventually I took her advice, and he and I had a very positive meeting. Within a couple of weeks, he had an idea to run by me. Could I do moody acoustic guitar versions of classic Scottish songs? I told him I'd give it a go and, just like that, we set to work on an album.

Through Gordon, I started working as a visiting lecturer in music production. When he touted the idea, given my personal history with education, I laughed in his face, but he twisted my arm and it's been a real blast. I needed the money at the time. Because of all the legal stuff bubbling away in the background in the 1990s, it seemed wise to not be touring under the Rollers banner, so having a guaranteed income seemed like a good idea. I've accumulated hundreds of awards and have cupboards full of tartan memorabilia at home, but I don't think I was ever so proud as when I achieved a HNC and reached the 2nd stage in TQFE (Teacher Qualification in Further Education). I was at Stow College in Glasgow, lecturing on sound production and showing a bunch of students around a mixing desk. They were mostly too young to know who I was, or who the Rollers were, but usually by the end of their first term, word would get out that teacher was once a pop star. You'll be talking the class through something, and someone will pipe up, 'My mum loves you.' You're just grateful they didn't say their grandmother. I get a real kick out of mentoring these students. I'm showing them how a recording studio works, how to connect amps, guitars, etc., just like Jake showed me 30 years ago. It's like the circle of life.

Meanwhile, *Scottish Moods*, the record we came up with, becomes a big success. It just keeps on selling, not just in Scotland, but everywhere there's someone with a bit of Scots blood. So Gordon and I strike up a partnership and work together making these Celtic albums. They are going brilliant, so I move out of my home studio and we wind up in an office together in the early 2000s, Gordon and me and another guy, Neil Ross, all directors of a new company called the Music Kitchen. My role is to oversee the recordings and the engineering side of the business, the nuts and bolts of making a record. Gordon deals with the business side, as well as the music, and Neil provides the space and infrastructure. If you were reading closely earlier about me sitting in a boardroom not paying attention, or having half an eye out of the classroom window, the idea of me becoming a company director will probably make you smile. But it happened and I loved it. And not just the playing, either – brainstorming ideas with other musicians and singers and seeing if we can make a good record, just like I'd been doing since starting out with the Rollers. I don't think of myself as a master songwriter or anything, but I'm still completely in love with the mechanics of putting songs together. Taking a bit of this and that and coming out with something joyous, like it's some mad mathematical equation I figured out.

Then, twice a year, it's time to do our artists' royalties. Time for the Excel spreadsheets where we sort out all the downloads and streams from around the world and work out what each of our artists has coming to them. I know what it's like to not get paid for work you have done and, unlike the Rollers, and all the shenanigans around our finances, we make sure everyone gets paid on time.

We achieved great success with the Music Kitchen. A few of the albums went platinum and I received several awards as a result. Keeping the Roller name out of things probably helped us in not being judged by the music snobs. I am hugely proud of what Gordon and I achieved through the Music Kitchen because once again it was all about the music.

Chapter 36

DEPOSITION

After years of frustrating back-and-forth, Mark St John's plan for the Rollers' united front – the classic five of Les, Eric, Derek, Alan and Yours Truly – is finally yielding results, although progress is slow. In 2007, practically ten years after we were persuaded to pack in the infighting, our case is brought to the Southern District of New York federal court and begins its stuttering journey through the US judicial system. Mark, now the Rollers manager, and I fly into JFK. For the most part, the uneasy truce between the Rollers has held somewhat true – at least Eric, Alan and I haven't toured under the Rollers banner, unlike Les – and so, after years of letters and Mark's petitioning, the record company attorneys and their armies of associates have been required to fetch the ball back from the long grass and to grant us an audience.

Arriving on the east coast, there's no waiting limo, no banners being held up, no weeping girls screaming my name. Just security checks every hundred yards, because we're in this post 9/11 world and New York City and the US are twitchy as fuck these days. I'm nervous as hell too, to be fair. Picking up my carry-on, and waiting at the baggage carousel, my brain is swimming as we walk through the concourse. I look around me. Everything's coloured green, covered in four-leaf clovers and spilt Guinness for St Paddy's Day tomorrow. Eventually, we shuffle through immigration checks and stand in line for a yellow cab to take us into the city. We're travelling incognito, passing as weekend tourists, fully blended with the day trippers, those families heading into Times Square to take in a show later and grab a drink at the Russian Tea Room. Personally, I'd rather we just strolled into an Edinburgh law office and got this done there, but because our original deal was signed in New York in 1976, it's subject to New York state rules and laws, so we're being good soldiers and flying out, going to play this whole thing out on their turf.

It really couldn't be more of a David and Goliath story if I was carrying a slingshot through customs. I try not to think about it, but I've got this weight of expectation on me. Practically the past 30 years of my life has been people asking me when I'm getting my money, and suddenly it's all too real. Everything comes down to this three-day trip to the US.

We're booked into the Hilton in Midtown and I can't sleep for trying. I'm alone in my room, looking out my window, watching a party unfold on one of the rooftops across the way. I hear the hubbub below, the sirens wailing, and think back to us signing with Clive Davis across town – how we had the world at our feet – and wondering how it came to this. That day, Clive sent us out into the city in an open-topped limo, up through Harlem, past all these kids who were either waving or flipping us the bird, then back down to Manhattan, us getting swept from fancy restaurant to restaurant, gladhanding New York's elites, forgetting everyone's name the minute you heard it. That night, we were treated to a ride along with New York's finest, getting taken through the rough neighbourhoods, past the junkies and hookers, and shown the murder hotspots, but 20-plus years later, I'm here alone.

Mark's a good guy. He's got a bit of presence about him. You know when he's in the room. He's not bluffing, the way you find with some music business types. He knows his brief. He's got a handle on publishing and catalogue, and seems to understand every trick that's going to be played before the other guy tied his Windsor knot that morning. The main reason we've taken to him, though, is that he's got a track record for getting musicians their fair dues. It happened regularly in the before times – unscrupulous managers, shackling eager young kids to eternal contracts that paid them next to nothing. Our case is entirely different, though. It's more complex. Because of the acrimony between Les and the rest of the band, it was always going to be more difficult to work out. Unpicking an untidy tangle of unnecessary companies became harder with every passing year we were fighting each other.

Was there anything underhand going on? I mean, there was always something happening; another document would be shoved under your nose and you just signed away without thinking about it. Money was getting syphoned in one direction or another, without us knowing. Back in the day, we used this same limo service so often that we were persuaded to just buy the company because nobody could foresee a day ever dawning when we wouldn't need a limo. The company was run out of an old caravan in London somewhere and we owned a fleet of limos and employed a bunch of drivers. Then our accountant pointed out something was amiss with the company books. When he went along to scrutinise the accounts more closely, he arrived to find the caravan ablaze, like he'd been caught up in an episode of *The Sweeney*. Once the London Fire Brigade put out the fire, the accounts were just a pile of ashes, tied up in a ribbon.

To be fair, Eric and Derek were both quite watchful when it came to the business side of the Rollers, but I was so green that I didn't notice and I kick myself for that. Still, when your accountant tells you they're setting up dozens of expensive life insurance policies in your names and numerous companies for the individual members, you tend to believe they're on the level and they're working in your interests. As well as the numerous Rollers companies, it only became apparent there was something rotten going on when we discovered the same money men were auditing all those accounts quarterly and billing us for the pleasure. We started an expensive and lengthy legal action on that front, and eventually settled out of court, but by then the damage was done. All the companies they set up gave the record company an opportunity to tell us they didn't know who to pay. It's still almost impossible to believe they maintained that position for practically 40 years, but I've always suspected that this case was never about the rights and wrongs. It was about who had the best legal team.

What I'm trying to say here is that the waters around us became so muddy that we needed someone to come in and make sense of our situation. And Mark is focused on the fine details like that. He's been prepping us all for months, telling us to play nice, even when there's obvious friction between the parties. He tells us to just speak the truth, to only answer the question asked. Don't elaborate. They don't need your life story, kind of shtick. I'm held up in this ante room, kicking my heels, staring into space. There's so much riding on this. We're under the impression we could be due millions. Even Mark figures we could be looking at a big payout. I mean, he's a good guy and has our best interests at heart, but he's not doing this for the good of his health. I'm not even going to try to ballpark the figure I think I'm owed because I just want this to be over. The main thought in my head is, *How did we get here?* I'm thinking I just want my life back, to get home to Denise and curl up beside her, and then finally I'm called in. Mark gives me a final pep talk, telling me 'You've got this', like he's a football dad and I'm coming in off the subs' bench to score a winning goal.

We're ushered into a large conference room, which stinks of coffee and company stationery. I sit beside our US attorney on one side of a long streak of mahogany, facing a team of lawyers for Sony on the other side, and a camera pointing directly at me, red-light blinking, like the mad computer in *2001: A Space Odyssey*. Mark gives me a final squeeze of the shoulder for good luck. I feel my throat go dry, take a sip of water and that's me for the next ten hours, answering questions from people who don't want to pay me for the work I did almost 30 years ago and asking them, pretty please, to reconsider maybe, and perhaps throw a few crumbs down from this endless fuckin' table.

The questions come thick and fast. I'm okay. Our attorney does okay. He's not the guy Mark recommended, nowhere near as cutthroat as the team he wanted, but Les was adamant. He had his own supposed superstar legal team in mind and dug his heels in, as is usually the way with Les. For the sake of harmony, we go along with his choice. The questioning starts out friendly, but you can feel them ratcheting up the tension. 'How much exactly do you think you're owed?' one of the Sony suits asks me. He's smiling a thin smile. It feels like a trap, so I don't give him anything. I say, 'How long is a piece of string?' and I can see a bunch of attorneys and paralegals frowning, shuffling through rafts of notes. I remember to stop short, not to give up too much, just the facts ma'am, like in the old TV show *Dragnet*.

When I get bogged down, facing a few bewildering questions about companies set up in our name, I try the old trick of imagining the people on the other side of the table being naked. If I'm honest with you, that's not a big help, so I scrap that plan out of hand. Then I remember it's their job to stop me from getting what I'm due. It's easy to forget that. It's not just the lawyers thinking that way, either. It's a cultural malaise now, this idea that everything should be free, but that only seems to count for art. You spend all these years learning your craft and there's a raft of people quite happy to see you not get paid for it.

I don't know if it's a false equivalency, but you'd not call a plumber out, someone who spent years out on the tools learning a trade, have them fix your knackered pipes or leaky faucet and send them on their way with a pat on the head. No. You would pay the plumber. By the same token, you're obliged to pay me for the work I did, for all the millions of dollars you earned off my back. But, in the meantime, I'll jump through these fuckin' hoops for you because the game is rigged against me, and in favour of you. As if to underscore that point, with probably all of us down to our last brass farthing, Les battling dependency demons and Alan's health deteriorating at a rate of knots since his stroke, the proceedings collapse in 2010 on a technicality and the whole sorry process has to be started up again. The ball is hoofed back to the long grass. About now, I'm starting to think this case is never going to end.

Chapter 37

REUNION BLUES

It's 2016 and I'm standing on stage with the Bay City Rollers again, if you can believe that. For the sake of clarity, this isn't a dream. It's more like a waking nightmare. We walk on stage to the sound of a piper playing and a kilted Les, carrying a bit more timber these days, runs centre stage, seizing the limelight, the place he was born to be. We launch into 'Summerlove Sensation'.

This crowd is not just a few hundred mums and daughters. It's a well-oiled, bona fide festival crowd and they're completely beside themselves. It's boundless joy out there, like we've never been away. Seventy thousand souls, camped out in a makeshift temporary city here at Strathallan Castle, for T in the Park, Scotland's premier music festival. I'm looking out at a sea of happy, smiling faces, but they've no idea what a shitshow this all is. I've just got it filed in my head as 'usual shite, different decade'. I'm clapping and playing along, smiling, just like Tam always told me, but my heart isn't in it. I've witnessed first-hand the results of giving in to someone's narcissism – giving the pushy kid all the sweets and all the toys, not telling him when it's his bedtime because it's easier that way. Everyone's beginning to understand that if you give that kind of person everything, they're still not satisfied because they never can be satisfied. They're surrounded by crumbs and wrappers, face smeared in chocolate, looking across the table at your plate of biscuits and wondering why you've still got a custard fuckin' cream left. But I'm getting ahead of myself here. Let me catch you up.

This all starts a year back, in 2015, when I hear there's a new Bay City Rollers record coming out. It's a Christmas single apparently and it's news to me. The weird thing is, I'm 100 per cent sure I'd remember recording it. The sleigh bells would have stood out in my memory. For everything that's gone down over the years, one thing I do know is I never once left the Rollers. Sure, they left me a couple of times, disintegrated around me occasionally, but I never once said, 'Right, that's me done. Fuck all of youse.' But now there's this new Rollers single and I'm questioning my memory for a second or two, wondering if I need to get checked by a doctor.

The first I hear about our miraculous comeback was from my wee brother Ronnie. He's out and about in Edinburgh and sees it advertised on one those big electronic hoardings. When we get down there to see it in person, I look at Denise and she looks at me. We both shrug, completely clueless. Someone's using the band's name again and I probably don't need to think too hard about who it is. If this were an episode of *Taggart*, it wouldn't be a classic. He'd be rocking up at the door of the culprit in the first five minutes with an arrest warrant for Leslie Richard McKeown. Standing there under the advertising hoarding, my brain immediately switches from carefree to exhausted. I don't know that I've the energy for another round of legal action with anyone, least of all Les. I've a pretty good life. Denise and I are happy, two halves of the same coin. She's become my rock – or, as I like to joke, my rock . . . and roll. Still, part of my brain is wondering how this could be happening again.

The trademark for the Rollers has been in my hands since 2003. It was a pragmatic kind of deal, I thought, trying to salvage the last remnants of the band's legacy. Also, I was still carrying this hope that, someday, the stars might align and the so-called classic five – Eric, Alan, Derek, Les and Yours Truly – might one day bury the hatchet and we'd play together again. I tried on several occasions and, every time, either Les or Eric was there with a spanner for the works. In the run-up to 2003, Eric had gone AWOL and I got word the company – Bay City Rollers Ltd – was set to slide into liquidation because no one was minding the shop. It was the kind of stuff you love to hear as a musician, up there with tax returns not getting done or men in suits knocking at the door. We could probably just not answer the door, but it meant we'd lose the trademark to our band. As I saw it, we'd been through a lot to retain those rights. In the absence of a resolution of our case with Sony, it was the only thing of value we still had, so I didn't want the rights falling into the hands of Her Majesty's Exchequer.

After mulling it for a while, I stepped in and formed a new company. I thought this would be a good opportunity to make the classic five equal shareholders. To save any infighting, I made Derek, Eric and Les non-voting shareholders, but only my pal Al and I could make decisions. In truth, Al wasn't really interested in the day-to-day running of things, so he left everything to me. Personally speaking, I invested a lot of time and money setting up and running the company. But now this Christmas record is coming out and it's like the law of the land doesn't matter. I don't need the aggravation of more litigation, but I write a letter to the management of the advertising company stating Les has no right to use the name as per the court ruling back in 1992. Les bats that away with a letter to us saying, 'I am the Bay City Rollers. You're not using the name, so I'm taking it.' Never mind the fact we'd all agreed to not trade under the name the Bay City Rollers to allow the court case against the record company to go through. Les is built differently, though. It's like he just thrives on conflict or something because now there's a deluge of cease-and-desist letters coming through my door every day. Just the idea of sitting in another courtroom, having someone else decide my fate, fills me with despond.

Thankfully, though, I get a call from this guy, John McLaughlin, who wants to meet up to try to sort something. The upshot is, to avoid a protracted round of litigation and handing over fistfuls of my hard-earned to a bunch of faceless attorneys, that the idea of a reunion is floated, with John stepping into the breach as the band's new manager. We're caught up in a blizzard of legal letters from Les's lawyers, telling us we're interfering with his business, so a reunion will bring an end to all that shite. Maybe it sounds spineless, but getting the band back together feels like the path of least resistance, like I can turn a loss into a small win somehow. It means I can sleep again for the first time in months, that I'm no longer tracking the progress of the postman coming down the path and wondering what nightmare is going to unfold when the letters land on our doormat today. In the meantime, as a show of goodwill, Les is allowed to finish his upcoming solo dates, billed as Bay City Rollers starring Les McKeown, which proves to be a daft decision on our parts, because we're essentially giving him an inch, in full knowledge that he's going to take a mile.

Ultimately, for the sake of my mental health, I decide to just keep my gob shut with the Les thing. I've established his credentials as a frontman, I hope, but the intervening years hadn't done much to smooth the sharp edges of his personality. He's on record saying a lot of things about his experiences with Tam. Just terrible things, about him getting drugged and abused, and I'm sure they cast a shadow over his life because that stuff cast a shadow over all our lives. There's no accounting for personal tragedy, obviously, because we all have different ways of coping. When it comes to Tam Paton, we were all survivors, but with Les it felt like it hit him harder. It's not like I locked all those experiences away, stuffed down the bad memories, pretending they didn't happen. I just choose to not let them shape my life. But, with Les, the abuse got tangled up with the business stuff, the death spiral of the band, the fact he couldn't cut it as a solo star, probably because the world had moved on from Rollermania, and he let it eat away at him. That's the main issue, in terms of my diagnosis. The man's addicted to fame, devastated that it's over, that the world has moved on from him. From my perspective, he was always a difficult person, but Tam and the music business in general didn't help him. Over time, Les's bitterness morphed into sheer hatred and he became this different character. He had a wife and a son, and it's sad he couldn't heal the wounds, or find a way to move on in the way some of us managed, because he had the basis of a happy life just staring him in the face. It was frustrating because sometimes you caught these glimpses of him the way he used to be. Sometimes he was genuinely funny to be around, like he could throw a switch somewhere in his head, and I'd be rolling on the floor laughing. A second later, though, he was back to being a sociopathic narcissist.

Whatever the ins and outs, though, the reunion was on and my mind turned (again) to getting the classic line-up together. It was a non-runner of an idea as it turned out. We tried to persuade Eric, but he'd had encephalitis, which fair took the wind out of his sails, and his arm couldn't be twisted. The Derek situation was entirely different, way more depressing. In 2000, he was found to have illegal pornography on his computer and was arrested. He claimed to have been set up, but pled guilty to avoid a media circus. We'd been close throughout the Rollers' heyday, but hadn't seen one another in years after he stepped back from performing. He trained as a nurse once the band came apart at the seams and our paths rarely crossed again. When the idea of a reunion was floated, Derek didn't want to be involved. If I'm honest, we were all relieved. Nobody wanted the band to be tainted by association, but thanks to Tam and Derek, this is exactly what has happened. With Eric and Derek out – although I made sure they got a cut from the future shows – the reunion eventually consists of Les, Alan and me, and the nucleus of Les's touring band. It was always going to be hard to get up on stage with people that had been using our name, so we agreed Les's backing band would be replaced over time. The replacement musicians never materialised, of course, because it was never going to happen. Al isn't bothered. He's just happy to be up on stage.

Obviously, there's a ton of press hoopla around the reunion. Major shows sell out in seconds flat and we're back in the limelight. You'd think everyone would be happy, but Les is constantly manoeuvring behind the scenes. We play a bunch of shows at Christmas 2015, these incredible outpourings of emotion from tens of thousands of diehard fans – the biggest shows we've played since we were at our peak. John had a two-year plan that we all agreed to, starting with these 2015 Christmas shows, followed by tours here, there and everywhere, but Les had other ideas. These should be great memories, especially the sold-out nights at Barrowlands, but mostly I remember Alan and I getting sidelined, way out on the far edges of the stage, usually with no lighting, or maybe only minimal lighting on us, like we're there as an afterthought. I can get over the fact that Les hates anyone getting the spotlight, even removing Alan's party-piece and fan favourite song 'Rock & Roll Honeymoon' after the first few shows. Or every time I play a guitar solo, seeing Les beckoning his guys to mob around me, just so I'm not centre of attention for 30 seconds. It's such a grim time and I fall sick with pleurisy. The girl from our support act, a Blondie tribute band, has a day job as a doctor and, when I become seriously unwell, she gets me antibiotics. I'm there all bleary-eyed, thinking I'm at death's door and somehow Debbie Harry's tending to me as I pass beyond the veil.

Still, despite the mind games and the hard emotional toil of dealing with Les, it feels good seeing the joy on people's faces. With the legal guardrails off now, Les spends much of 2016 touring without the band, which was not what we agreed, but still under the Rollers banner – as Les McKeown's Bay City Rollers. It's not like he's being particularly crafty about it, because we all know. I'm getting inundated with calls and emails from fans turning up for these shows and wondering where we are. He couldn't even do cloak and fuckin' dagger properly. Alan and I are bemused, but not surprised. Then Alan starts to drift away from me. Following a second stroke in the last few years, he's not in great health and there's people in his ear, with one foot in Les's camp, chucking poison in the waters around us. Alan doesn't have an entourage exactly, but for reasons I'll never fully understand, there's people around him positioning themselves between me and my friend of the past 40-plus years.

Consequently, over the course of Les's enforced reunion, mine and Alan's friendship starts to break down. Before long, Alan's occasionally playing with Les's band, but his presence is entirely ornamental. He's on stage, looking dreadful, like he's no idea what's going on. After his second stroke, he can't play properly anymore, so he's not even plugged in.* From my perspective, it's obvious Les is trying to control Alan. Not out of friendship, or because of their shared history, but as a business strategy. If he has a director and voting shareholder on board, he can paint on an innocent face whenever he's challenged over his use of the trademark. Credit where it's due, whatever chaos surrounds us, Les always keeps his eye on the prize: ownership of the band's brand and legacy. He understands if he can cause a falling-out between Alan and me – the only voting directors of the company – it will be to his advantage and that's precisely how things play out. Like a chess grandmaster, Les asks Alan and his wife to join him on a tour of Japan. The next time Alan and I speak, I urge caution, knowing exactly what Les is up to here. Al reassures me it's fine. 'Les is an arsehole,' he says. 'I don't trust him at all.'

The next thing I hear, Al has signed on for the tour with Les, billed as the Bay City Rollers. Now I think about it, it's not a huge plot twist, but things between Al and me spiral quickly after that. I reach out to my friend several times, but there's folk in Alan's orbit with both feet in the McKeown camp who don't like Alan and me speaking at all. Al being Al, of course, just wants a peaceful life, wants to go with the flow, so after a time, I decide to stop hassling my pal. Right or wrong, he's an adult, he can make

* This was something that Denise had stated on social media in a bid to stop Alan and I being used to help boost sales for an album we didn't play on. For the record, she had said, 'Alan "wasn't plugged in" at the reunion shows so how could he play on an album?' Somehow this got twisted into 'Alan's guitar playing is shit', which she never said.

his own decisions, and I don't want to cause any friction for him. When I email him now about Rollers business – there's always a lot that needs to be addressed, particularly with all this Les business swirling around us – whenever I get a reply, it's obvious he hasn't written a word. He's been my closest pal for 40 years, so I know how he speaks, all his wee turns of phrase, and it's as clear as day he's no longer in control of his own destiny. If it was just a phantom emailer I had to deal with, it would be okay, but there's all kinds of manoeuvring going on in the background. At one point, I discover that Les has managed to persuade the rest of the band – Eric and Derek included – to boot me out the company I set up to save the copyright from lapsing. It's a short-lived situation, but another headache for me to deal with. In the midst of all this pain, we get word that the case with Sony is done. After years of delay tactics, with the case finally looming, we're informed that, through a technical issue, the case is over and so a settlement is agreed. Depending on what you've read, the Rollers' sold north of 300 million records. Consequently, everyone's expecting millions, because that's the story: The Bay City Rollers' Missing Millions, right? Well, it's nothing like that, not even the same ballpark. I sign a legal document saying I won't reveal how much I do get paid, so I can't tell you here, but you know the figure you heard? Well, that's how much we got. It's an unsatisfactory outcome in some respects, but at least it's over. I'm not opening my emails with a grimace on my face, wondering, *What is it now?* It's done. I can move on, finally. I can't speak for the others, whether they're happy or not, but no one is buying any castles soon, unless they're made of Lego.

This is all in the air when we play T in the Park, swilling around us like a disappointing broth. I'm wearing a T-shirt with the Star Wars logo emblazoned on the front. I've no idea just how apt that is. Backstage, where there should be cheer, there's nothing but enmity. Moments before our stage time, we're milling around the green room, essentially a big tent, with a few chairs and trestle tables. Les has his camp and, over here, it's just me and Denise. I should have seen it coming. All the signs were there when I signed on the dotted line. Right now, there's a lot of bullshit to negotiate. Les is doing his best to stir the pot. Stories are getting out to the fans and battle lines are drawn between the different camps, but they don't know the half of it. All the while, Les has been getting cosy with Alan's nearest and dearest, getting them riled up about me and Denise, saying we're badmouthing Alan behind his back, which is pure bullshit. I can handle that okay, but suddenly the atmosphere changes from grim to violent. I look up and see a woman from Les's wee entourage making a bee line for Denise, screaming in her face and grabbing at her. I've been aware that Les has been manipulating the people around Alan but, still, I can't believe what I'm seeing. Alan, Denise and I had always gotten along famously, but in a very short space of time, since Alan's health problems escalated, Les has persuaded his closest associates that we're the enemy somehow. Les, as only Les can, has been slowly drip-drip-dripping misinformation in earthier ears, and somehow turned our friendship sour. It's such a depressing moment for me, for Denise. But maybe not for everyone, because as this woman launches herself at my wife, I can see Les across the tent, smirking, like he's enjoying the show he instigated. Meanwhile, everyone in the tent freezes, with other performers, crew and staff all watching this scene play out. A minute before, there was hustle, bustle and loud backstage conversation, but now everything's fallen still. There are half-eaten sandwiches frozen in time between hand and mouth, and all eyes are on this woman as she starts on her rampage. What should have been a real triumph for us has descended into farce before we even set foot on stage. I'm devastated. Denise is absolutely fuming as we notice one of the woman's false nails in the mud at her feet. It got dislodged during the set-to. In a funny way – not *funny ha ha*, you understand – that nail is kind of the final nail in the Bay City Rollers' coffin.

As we take to the stage, Les is still smirking. I'm absolutely raging, of course. I've got a thick skin and can handle the endless mind games he's playing. I've had plenty of years to get used to them. But now he's gone too far. As far as I'm concerned, Les just made it personal, so I announce this will be my last performance with him and his band. You probably wouldn't know it to see us on stage, but this is one of the real low points for me. Of course, the fans are amazing and it's a great show but, come curtain call, I can't even find it in myself to stand with Les and his guys to take a final bow. Meanwhile, Denise is so stunned by the events backstage – she's got bruises up and down her arms from where this woman physically (wo)manhandled her – she files a police complaint, but later retracts it to avoid a press circus. If only everyone else was as keen to avoid circuses.

That would possibly make an apt end to the story – a dramatic one, anyway – but my departure isn't permanent. Les digs in, says some shitty, unforgivable things about me and mine on social media, stuff I won't repeat here, but the fact remains that I can say I'm leaving all I want, but I've made a commitment and it's a mess to try and untangle myself. Meantime, Denise gets sick. She's held in isolation for a week – blood transfusions, the lot – so ultimately I have to recalibrate. My dad is in the same hospital, two wards down from Denise. It's like everything that can go wrong goes wrong in the space of a couple of weeks. Our dog gets sick, I'm still getting over the bout of pleurisy and it's just a dreadful time. Meantime, many of the band's fans have been divided and conquered by Les's blizzard of bullshit in interviews and on social media. I'm built of stern stuff and can handle the Les sideshow well enough, but it's clear the well has been poisoned when Denise starts receiving hate mail from a bunch of fans in the Les camp. I appreciate it only stems from a vocal minority – we have the best fans – but, even so, it's brutal and it's toxic. It's 100 per cent not what the Bay City Rollers were meant to be about. Whatever the case, whatever your perspective, in my eyes, once Denise is dragged into it, Les's actions switch from narcissistic to unforgivable.

I speak to John McLaughlin, our new manager. I think it's about now that John's realising how much of this reunion was built on a foundation of Les's lies, but between us we come to an arrangement. He's on the line personally if the shows don't happen and stands to lose a lot of money, so for his sake, and that of the fans, I stay true to my word. The shows at the end of 2016 will be my last with Les and they can't come soon enough. It's a depressing time, all told. This is truly sad, because while Les was running this powerplay of his, I was holding the fort with the company – hanging on to the Rollers trademark, reaching out to Derek and Eric, still harbouring this idea that we might come together again. Now, though, my friendship with Al is hanging by a thread and, as a result of Les's attempted takeover of the band, after umpteen attempts to contact Derek, and me speaking with Eric only via his PA, my aspirations for a true Rollers reunion are in tatters.

In the run-up to the Rollers Christmas tour, I've a TV interview to do with Alan and Les to promote the upcoming show at Glasgow's SECC. We're booked to appear on STV's *Live at Five* and it's a complete horror show. We're in the green room and there's no warmth at all. We're like strangers, really, but we have a job to do, so I do my best to make nice. While we're waiting for our slot, there's a knock on the door: a delivery for Les. He makes a big show of wondering what it could be, tearing open this box of CD copies of his new solo album. I look at Alan and he just shrugs. He's not the Alan of old. He's lost a step or two since his stroke. He always hated conflict and I can tell he just wants to take the easy road, to let Les have the win here, but I'm not having that. The moment I realise he's planning to steer the interview away from the Rollers shows and on to his solo career, I tell him that's not happening.

'We're not sitting down the end of a TV sofa like fuckin' ornaments while you promote your solo record,' I tell him. True to form, Les tells me to fuck off and I can see the researchers bristling, a few interns with clipboards running around in a panic. Les has his heels dug into the carpet now, walking onto the set with a copy of the CD. I try to snatch it out of his hand and it's just like we're back in 1978 all over again, Les steamrolling everyone around him, that 'I *am* the Bay City Rollers' mentality he's got tangled up in his DNA somehow.

The papers report it as a scuffle, but it's more like handbags – me getting angry and Les sneering like he's already won, because, in a way, he has. The producer steps in and assures us it's a Rollers interview and there'll be no Les solo sideshow, but he still has the CD in his hand. As the hosts look on, I ask Les one last time to please put the CD away, but no. He can't help himself. To save myself losing my temper on TV, I walk back to the green room, leaving Les and Alan to face the cameras without me. Les is his usual arrogant self and Alan's just sitting at his side meekly, smiling, not saying much. Obviously once the red light goes on, Les manages to plug his solo record because he was always going to plug his solo record, regardless of what he was told. It's a pattern we've seen a hundred times; every time he was asked to stop using our brand for his own ends, he just went and did it anyway. It's kind of sad really. We were all screwed over in one way or another, but we didn't actively screw each other the way Les did. While all the legal nonsense between the band was going on, I told Les we were all happy to take a back seat and for him, as the lead singer and perceived frontman, to take the limelight, whether that was in interviews or in a live situation. It was as if we were giving him everything he'd ever wanted and he still wasn't satisfied.

Chapter 38

S-A-T-U-R-D-A-Y NIGHT

Someone said to me the other day that I must have PTSD, but I don't know about that. It seems a bit hyperbolic. Despite what you've seen in all that grainy footage – fans passing out, getting dragged limp from the front of the stage and waved awake by the St John's Ambulance – it really didn't seem so mad at the time. It happened so gradually, but people don't believe you when you say we just kind of shrugged, then plugged in and played. Probably it's perspective, but I didn't wake up one morning to hysteria. I was like the frog in a pan of water. Don't try this at home, obviously, as I'm speaking proverbially, but throw a frog into a boiling pan and it leaps out straight away. However, place a frog in a cold pan, heat the water gradually on the stove and the frog stays put, dying a slow death as the water starts to bubble around it. Well, we were the same. Someone had the heat turned up, just a wee bit at a time, and we didn't notice. We just kept simmering away. It happened over the course of a year, and by then we were acclimatised to it.

It could have gone wrong a thousand different ways, but I've a fine life now and I'm grateful for that. Just me and my wife Denise, the two of us against the world. We were best friends before we were married. Genuinely, I can't believe my good luck. She is a wonderful cook – not just mince and tatties, mind – and her flair for design has made our home the most amazing place to wake up to every morning. As much as I love to play shows and tour, I also long for our cosy nights in, just the two of us.

We're 28 years married now and I wouldn't change a thing. We have wonderful friends and have arrived together at a happy time in our lives. Whatever you've read about the Rollers and what might have been, we don't have millions, but we have everything we could ever need. A good life, great friends and Elvis, our dog. It's the opposite of how things were. You'll allow me that, I hope. It's controlled contentment, relaxed and happy, a nice headspace to find yourself in. There's no one tapping the face of a watch, getting antsy in the downstairs hallway, wondering why I'm late getting into the van or limo. I don't set the alarm. I don't need to. Regardless of the weather – cold, windy or sheeting down with rain – Elvis will tell me when it's time for breakfast or for his walk. We're close to the sea and it's very calming, except for the dog chasing the gulls and barking at the tides. Like me, he's well behaved. Most of the time.

You know that pub I mentioned, with the fan switched off and being able to hear yourself think? It's like that now. I tell Alexa to put on some jazz while we make our breakfast, Elvis pawing at my trousers. The background noise, all that screaming – I only hear it when I dream now. Or if I see an old clip of the insanity on the television – fans wrapped in tartan, weeping in the streets of Carlisle, Dundee, Toronto, wherever. Denise and I look across at each other. *What was that all about?* It's a lifetime ago and it's as if it all happened to some other kid. Not me, anyway.

So today, I'm still rollin', obviously. Since Les's attempted takeover and the bad blood that generated, I've had no contact with Eric or Derek. I kept the door open for them but, eventually, it became clear they weren't coming through. Obviously, Eric has had his health issues and Derek wanted nothing to do with the Rollers. Following the reunion, all direct communication with Eric dried up. I can only contact him via his PA, so who knows if he even gets my messages? It's a sad end to our relationship, but who knows? He may read this and get in touch. As for Al, he tragically passed away in 2018. That was a real wrench. After all our years of friendship, I couldn't even attend his funeral. The situation with Alan, the fall-out from the backstage incident and all the bullshit stirred up in its wake meant I had to say my own personal goodbyes to my best friend.

Meanwhile, Les was Les. We weren't talking anymore. He caused so much grief. Any chance he got, he would go out under the Bay City Rollers banner, start a war, drawing battle lines when I was simply trying to protect the legacy for all of us, him included. No one put more time into getting the classic five back together than me, I can assure you. Whatever he thought about himself *being* the Rollers, I knew all along it was a group, not one guy. But I guess we were always like oil and water in that regard: never going to mix.

Still, I'll say it again, he was a remarkable frontman, and though there weren't many, we had some fine times together. When I think about him now, I try to remember those occasions, us laughing and jumping on a Circle Line train together, that first time in London. Or the time we were driving around California in an open-top Jeep, right at the height of Rollermania in the States. We pulled up alongside a vast cornfield, him looking at me with mischief in his eyes – should we? – before steering into the corn, driving wildly through the field and leaving a swirling trail of chaos in our wake. I choose to think about that stuff rather than the shitty, self-centred bastard he could be most of the time.

The sad irony is, Les spent his last 25 years telling everyone who would listen that he'd been ripped off by Tam, by the record company, by anyone he met basically. From my perspective, you don't want to carry that bitterness around on your shoulders the rest of your life. I appreciate not everyone is so lucky, but it's always been my view that you can't let someone else define your life. Sadly, Les allowed the narrative of the Rollers' missing millions to define him. In that respect, I consider him to be another victim of the music industry, another in a very long line. The same as Kurt Cobain, the same as Amy Winehouse, the same as Liam Payne – the ones who aren't built to take the pressure. It's so hard for some people, and it's tragic and inevitable at the same time. And beyond the regular pressures of fame we had to contend with, there was still the abusive dynamic we had to withstand from Tam Paton, one of the true monsters of pop culture.

My take is that to have a healthy mind, you have to let some things go, as much as it might pain you to do so. So, when Tam's squalid little life came to an end in 2009, I stopped thinking about him. He was a terrible fuckin' human being, but the way I see it, he doesn't get to define me. Tam fuckin' Paton doesn't get to win. Les wasn't as fortunate in that regard. He carried that bitterness with him for the remainder of his days. Following the pain of the 2016 reunion debacle, it was still going on. He was twisted out of shape and that should be seen as a real tragedy, because he was never the same.

After the pandemic, Les (inevitably) instructed his lawyers to sue me – and Denise – over the band's name yet again. It was a dreadful, anxious time for us both. Denise was sick of Les's bullying, knowing he'd been that way since the first day I met him. And that's what this was: more bullying. But by now, we'd had enough and were both prepared to stand up to him, even if it meant losing our home. We had plenty of evidence of his hate towards us. We were reading through our lawyer's advice on what he could be charged with and there was plenty, so I knew we had a strong case. Still, it was going to get messy. I don't think Les even remembered half the things he'd done to us. Then, out of the blue, a couple of weeks later, on 20 April 2021, Les suffered a heart attack and died. The coroner concluded his death was due to a combination of cardiovascular disease and hypertension, at least partially caused by years of drug and alcohol abuse. It was sad that he was gone, but at the same time, I had mixed feelings. His most recent lawsuit and attempt to hijack the band had left a bitter taste. My stomach was up in my throat for weeks with worry. If it had gone ahead, there was a chance we might have had to sell our house to pay for the lawyers, so in a way, after the initial sadness, I was just overcome with relief. That's a sad state of affairs, right? You've got all that history together and this shared past – some good, some bad. In any other situation, we should have been brothers in arms. But instead of celebrating our achievements, letting bygones be bygones, he was so caught up in his own story, he couldn't even pick up the phone to talk through our issues without threatening legal action.

I don't want to burst any bubbles here, but there are plenty of bands out there who don't get along together. Being best pals is not a prerequisite for success, but if you can find a way to work past your disagreements, you can make it work. Probably no one is 100 per cent satisfied but, by the same token, no one's 100 per cent dissatisfied either. The same as everyone in the world. Whether you're working in a hospital or an office, or you were in a band that was famous for a few years in the 1970s, very few of us get to work with our best friends every day. For some reason, though, Les was railing so hard against everything and everyone else that, in his mind, he was always blameless.

Now, when people talk about us, if they're not talking about Rollermania, it's the other stuff and that's sad. The brand has been tainted by those things. It's become about the money and the shite with Tam's vile wickedness and Derek's (for the sake of argument, let's call it) stupidity. Maybe it makes me foolish, but I decided a few years back that I'm here to reclaim the Rollers' good name because, for a few years there, we had actual magic up on stage. It was natural, never manufactured, and I'd like us to be remembered that way instead. Aside from all the bickering and bullshit over the shillings and pounds, while all that was going on, no one was looking after the band's catalogue. It's a sadness that we're not able to take a little more control over our own history. Sure, you get the latest greatest hits released every five years or so, but there's no box set, no reissues. No one's taking care of that stuff, so I take care of what I can, when I can. The Rollers baton has wound up with me and I've had to adapt to survive. And I'm making a decent fist of things, I think.

Once again, I don't know where I'll be from day to day, although it's usually a safe bet that, if it's a Saturday, the Rollers are playing somewhere. I'm working my tail off, not knowing if I'm coming or going. In between shows and promo, I'll take myself off to a quiet room, work on a new song or fiddle about with an arrangement or a harmony. Finally, I feel like I can steward the band's legacy. It was never Tam's band. It belonged to us, and it belonged to the fans who followed us so loyally. I know I was never cut out to be a solo artist and I never tried. At heart, I'm a collaborator, someone who needs people around him. So, what I have now is still the Rollers, just not the classic five.

Playing with the new Rollers, I feel like I'm fifteen again, as if I'm walking to the chippy on our dinner break, talking about our plans for Freezin' Heet. Our new line-up is a handpicked bunch and they know the importance of our legacy. I've no plans to stop anytime soon and these are good folk for me to pass the torch to someday. You know, the Glenn Miller Orchestra are still out there playing and I see the Rollers following a similar path, rollin' on forever.

The best thing is, we all get on. We identify with each other. You look forward to rehearsals, spending time in each other's company. Nice, talented, good-hearted people. We get our van nicked in the Midlands and lose all our gear, but these guys have this same 'Ach, it'll be fine' attitude as me, a desire to keep on keeping on. We have a great manager – and band member – in John McLaughlin, who brought us together with Les in 2015. He's a lovely, and – crucially, after everything we went through before – trustworthy guy. Then there's Ian Thomson who came on board as a singer after the 2016 reunion came apart at the seams, when he and I put together a wee acoustic group, the Roller-Coasters. A Japanese promoter reached out and asked me over to play some shows, so Ian was roped in and has been with me ever since. He doesn't sound like Les, he doesn't sound like Nobby, but when he sings, he stamps his personality on the track and he sounds like the singer in the Bay City Rollers, if that makes sense. By 2018, we were having so much fun that we put together a five-piece electric band, with John joining us on keys, and our drummer, Jamie McGrory. Jamie and Ian grew up together and have been in a bunch of bands, and he's just a great guy. Mikey Smith, our bass player, has been with us a year now – a shit-hot musician and, in his early thirties, the kid of the band. He doesn't touch a drop, so he's the band's designated driver. Whether we're in the studio or on stage, we're all on the same wavelength. This is, and always has been a BAND, not a boyband, as we've frequently been labelled. Boybands were a '90s phenomenon, but we were always a proper group. We played our own instruments before the all-singing, all-dancing boyband thing started. It's like saying the Beatles or the Stones were boybands when they started out, simply because they were young guys in a band.

When I look in the diary now, there are gigs lined up everywhere. No one's telling us to smile anymore because we are smiling regardless. I don't know if you'd call it nerves but the best part is getting that wee tickle in your belly just before we get up on stage. It's a money-can't-buy sensation even today. I think that if I didn't get that feeling – the feeling I've had since we played the old folks' home in Edinburgh with the battered acoustic guitar and the drum without a bass drum pedal – then I'd quit now.

I owe it to the people who paid for a ticket because it's thanks to them that I'm still here and the band's still going. I know it's pure nostalgia, but don't knock it. Nostalgia is a real emotion, a shared connection between me and them. None of us are getting any younger, but looking out, seeing everyone's faces, they're all 16 again. It's a beautiful thing, as if music is a time machine taking us back to a moment in history. I don't know how many thousands of times I've played 'Shang-A-Lang'. I've lost count. I went right off the song in the 1990s, but I've gone full circle now and I always play that first chord as if I'm playing it the first time. It gives me chills every time. It's helped me realise that you don't feel any different to how you felt hearing a song when you were 16, so why would I feel any different playing it? And I don't. It's so heartening to do something that's just 100 per cent joyous.

No bullshit and no politics, because there's more than enough of both in this world. Just putting smiles on a few faces. That's the essence of the band. That's what I always felt we represented.

Meantime, we're working on a new record. The music industry landscape has shifted – and will probably move again between me writing these words and you reading them – but it's the same game as ever, and I know full well how it works. Unless you're Taylor Swift, it's likely you're not going to make money from records anymore – although you could argue we sold a ton of records at the height of the industry and, even then, we didn't make the money we should have – so you have to be creative. You can have a million streams online, but barely make a penny.

A new charity version of 'Shang-A-Lang' – recorded to mark the 50th anniversary of the original, and the Scotland men's football team's (brief) appearance at the Euro 2024 tournament – recently busted into the official chart top 20 and resulted in a few ripples of media frenzy. It's madness, but it's contained madness, if you like. The other guys talk about like it's a whirlwind – TV appearances, getting calls from the press and radio, just 24/7 activity – but if we're at the eye of a storm, it's a little more manageable than what occurred around us 50 years ago. Still, when you have all these strands – TV, radio, newspapers and social media – all connecting at the same time, it's pretty sweet to see such positivity. No one's fainting in the streets and getting loaded onto the back of an ambulance. They're coming over and grabbing a selfie or telling you about that show you played or the first time they went to Woolworths and handed over their pocket money for the latest Rollers LP or 45. And that's brilliant.

There are still the calls: 'Be at the airport in an hour' or 'The car's coming now' and I'm always prepped and ready. It just maybe takes me a little longer to get into gear. Sometimes the journeys can be quite arduous, and I'm not sixteen anymore, but fuck me, when you arrive and take to the stage, it's completely worth it. There's no record company laying down the law for us and maybe that's me thinking once bitten, twice shy on that front. It means we don't have promotional support, but we get to decide what we do, to forge our own path. It's a smaller pie, but the slices are bigger maybe, certainly tastier. You pay for everything out of your own pocket, of course, but you know you're not going to rip yourself off.

So this new record is how we want it: some old songs, some new, hopefully building a bridge from the golden era of the Rollers to the present day. I've no idea how it will turn out, but the truth is, we do it for ourselves and the fans. The old fans bring their kids and their grandkids to the shows and it's like the flame is still burning bright. Whenever we can, we stay a while after, chat and pose for selfies and sign albums and listen to the old stories from back in the day. We didn't get to hear them during Rollermania because we were getting swept out the back door, past a hundred girls getting treated by the paramedics, mascara-streaked, out for the count. Maybe they'd summon one last scream before passing out again, as we bundled past and into a waiting van or car, then whisked away with a police escort. After a time, we didn't even bother to play an encore because it wasn't safe for us or for the audience. More than once, we were stuffed two at a time into a car boot. You just heard the tap of someone's hand on the car and we were driven away in darkness amid the muffled screams and footsteps of the chasing pack.

It's emotional, sometimes. There's a lot of pent-up love in the room and we're always careful to be mindful of the journeys people have been on. There's a real weight of responsibility. You can feel it in the room. For me, it's the millionth time and it's normalised, but I always try to bear in mind for them it's the first time and there might be a lot hanging on it. We're tangled up in their lives and memories so much, so you want to ensure you treat everyone with the same respect. That means I'm listening more than I'm talking, taking in their stories, hearing them for the first time. But I'm a good listener, I think. It's curious because I'm just a regular person, but I was once this other thing, this pop person and, as unreal as that was, it's real to them and it was real to me. The Rollers were their first love – mine too – and your first love is the one that stays with you. It holds the strongest memories, and you carry them with you all your life.

ACKNOWLEDGEMENTS

I would like to thank ALL the Rollers past and present through the good, the bad and sometimes the very ugly . . . though I prefer to remember the good times.

I want to thank the fans for their continuing support all these years. I know the band helped many through some of their darker times and I'm glad we were able to help in some way.

I also want to thank my family for keeping me grounded and giving me a loving home to return to during the craziest of times.

My wife Denise, who has often been a victim of the hate that goes along with being married to a Roller, thank goodness, she's been here for me, and not forgetting my wee dog Elvis who also keeps me grounded these days.

The Rollers are and were always about entertaining people and making them happy, that should be the legacy of the band and not all the other crap!

To all the victims of this ruthless industry and the survivors that carry on.

I agree with the old saying 'everyone has a book in them', although it is not so easy to write it! A big thanks to Peter Stoneman for putting all the 'jigsaw pieces' together and also to James Lilford and the rest of the Bonnier team for the finishing touches.

Keep on Rolling (KOR).

With love,

Woody x